More Long-Life Chinese Cooking from Madame Wong

S.T. Ting Wong and Sylvia Schulman

Contemporary Books, Inc.
Chicago

Library of Congress Cataloging in Publication Data

Wong, S. T. Ting.
  More long-life Chinese cooking from Madame Wong.

  Includes index.
  1. Cookery, Chinese.   I. Schulman, Sylvia, 1920–
II. Title.
TX724.5.C5W66   1982   641.5951   81-69612
ISBN 0-8092-5766-1   AACR2

Illustrations: Jeannie Winston-Davis

Food in Chinese Culture, a book edited by K. C. Chang and published by Yale University Press, has been helpful to us in so many ways in understanding how important food has been to the Chinese through the ages.

Published by Contemporary Books, Inc.
180 North Michigan Avenue, Chicago, Illinois 60601
Manufactured in the United States of America
Library of Congress Catalog Card Number: 81-69612
International Standard Book Number: 0-8092-5766-1

Published simultaneously in Canada by
Beaverbooks, Ltd.
150 Lesmill Road
Don Mills, Ontario M3B 2T5
Canada

*This book is dedicated
to our grandchildren
Angelina,
Sean, and Michael*

Contents

Foreword

China was the world's most sophisticated, artistic, scientific, cultural center 2,500 years ago. Europe wasn't yet in its infancy when Chinese art, literature, architecture, beauty, and emphasis on learning were highly developed. The Chinese invented paper and block printing. China's poetry, bronzework, painting, and calligraphy became part of its pageantry and tradition.

Some 2,500 years ago China was already cultivating rice, and the Shih ching (said to have been compiled by Confucius himself), told tales of feasting. In 2000 B.C., I Yin wrote:

> In making a mixture you must judge what is sweet, sour, bitter, sharp and salt . . . enunciating the importance of the Five Flavors; lamb was aromatically seasoned with garlic before being cooked on a bed of fragrant southernwood.
>> High we load the stands,
>> The stands of wood and earthenware
>> As soon as the smell rises
>> God on high is very pleased
>> What smell is this, so strong and good?

One's food was not meant for survival. It must be ritually correct. One must not eat anything that is discolored or that smells ugly. One must not eat that which is overcooked, nor what is undercooked, nor what has been crookedly cut. Nor any dish that lacks its proper seasoning. In the Li-ch (B.C. 202) there is the articulating of the Eight Delicacies. The language is rich with the love and importance of food: jadelike wine, chicken braised in honey, rice like snowy beauty, ribs of the fatted ox cooked tender and succulent, sour and bitter blended in the soup of Wu . . . a bed of herbs creating scented steam.

Today the place of Chinese cookery in the hierarchy of fine food is well established.

Sylvia Schulman, herself a beautiful lady, a cultured, sophisticated connoisseur, has again joined with lovely and lively Madame Wong, the embodiment of her heritage, to create this second of their Chinese cookbooks. The old and unusual recipes make the collection unique. They will delight you—your palate, your eye, and your sense of accomplishment—as they delighted us.

Irving and Jean Stone

Preface

Since the publication of our first book, Madame Wong and I traveled to China together. We thought you might enjoy reading about some of our trip highlights. Hopefully, they will give you a little insight into the Chinese people and their culture to go along with the recipes that follow. China, a civilization more than 5,000 years old, has an endless supply of recipes plus ideas on which to base original ones.

We visited Hong Kong, Canton, Hangchow, Shanghai, and Peking. Our experiences were varied and exciting, even though we were instructed to exercise caution in many ways. We were told not to ask embarrassing questions. We were to avoid political discussions. We were to dress in monotones and know the names of the cities we planned to visit.

Our first stop was on the fabled island of Hong Kong. Although English is the official language in this British crown colony, the majority of the residents are Chinese and hardly speak English at all. Hong Kong is a free port, so one can still make purchases at fairly low prices. We found shops galore on the famous Nathan Road and proceeded to bargain all morning.

One lasting impression of our first steps into China was of the crowds. We seemed surrounded by throngs of people, both tourists and native Chinese, carrying bundles and packages.

Another memorable event was our wonderful train ride to Canton. The train itself was reminiscent of those we used to take from New York to Atlantic City—the old ones with swivel seats, wide aisles, and lace doilies on top of each seat. From this charming vantage point we had our first glimpse of the Chinese countryside. The approach to Canton (Kwangchow) is beautiful farmland. The earth is a fertile brick red. The peasants, as the rural workers are called in China, work the rice paddies in the ancient, traditional way. Rainwater is stored in ponds and ditches, and when they are ready to plant they use an old hand plow pulled by a water buffalo. The only other machine the peasants use is one that plows the mud to loosen it for planting. The rice is planted in rectangular flats. When it has grown to a certain height it is transplanted to a larger paddy, where it matures. Rice is the staff of life to the Chinese. It is served for breakfast, lunch, and dinner.

Canton is a very old city dating back to the 9th century B.C. Today it is characterized by abject poverty and squalor, and the workers live in primitive hovels. Like its more prosperous counterparts, however, Canton is a bustling city; it is also the home of the world trade fair, which takes place every April and October. The mode of transportation is bicycling, and we were surprised to learn that the bicycles are made right in Canton.

Craig Claiborne, restaurant editor for the *New York Times,* wrote an article about his favorite restaurants in China. We tried following some of his suggestions and spent our first Craig Claiborne evening at the famous Pan Hsi in Canton. It is situated on a lagoon and has many rooms on different levels. On the first level we saw workers, who were all dressed alike in their Mao jackets, smoking, and quite noisy. The second level served a different class of people. The level for tourists was the best. The dinner we had included a variety of dishes. One was a cold plate, consisting of thinly sliced chicken, thinly sliced duck, thinly sliced beef, shrimp, egg slices, carrots, mushroom slices, and cucumber. The various pieces of food in the beautiful cold plate specialty were presented in the form of a phoenix, symbolic of the female to the dragon or the King. The menu also offered suckling pig, crispy chicken, fried shrimp balls, fried pigeon, steamed fish, Buddha's delight, Cantonese fried rice, sweet oranges, and tea.

As we drove along the countryside between Canton and Hangchow we noticed that every bit of land is used for growing vegetables and rice.

Hangchow (Hangzhou) is a beautiful city surrounded by West Lake. Rich in culinary tradition, this city is the home of dishes like West Lake fish, West Lake duck, and beggar's chicken. One of the best restaurants, situated in the exquisite botanical gardens, is the Zhi Wei Guan. Here we had West Lake carp taken from the lake just a few minutes before. We also had an unfamiliar vegetable called Shuen tsai, which is served in soups. It comes from the bottom of West Lake. In addition, we tried

small shrimp, stir-fried with young, tender tea leaves (lung jing).
At every restaurant we were met at the door by the staff, who
were eager and excited to please us. The tables were always
covered with immaculate white cloths.

We had dinner at another restaurant recommended by Craig
Claiborne, the Hangchow. We especially enjoyed the steamed
fish from a menu that included six small cold plates, West Lake
fish, dragon tea with shrimp, beggar's chicken, rice, honey ham,
chicken with Shuen tsai soup, scallops with bamboo shoots,
shrimp with bean curd, Buddha's delight, fried gizzard with
liver, toffee taro, fruit, and tea.

The next morning a young hotel employee entered our room.
(There is no necessity for keys in China; the Chinese are
scrupulously honest people.) He brought the repast that was
provided for us each morning in Hangchow: a thermos of
boiling water, a cup with tea leaves, and an apple. This is the
Chinese version of room service. A regular Chinese breakfast,
served in the dining room, featured a rich congee, which is a
thick porridge and quite bland. It is usually made with rice and
cooks for many hours. Also included were Chinese pickles,
salted eggs, fluffy shredded pork, spicy bean curd, and meat-
filled dumplings.

While still in this area, we visited the Lin Ying Temple, which
is 1,300 years old and contains the largest Buddha in Hangchow.
Our next stop was the Jade Spring Park, so called because of
the variety of shades of green. There were carp of many colors
and sizes in exquisite, huge porcelain bowls. The Chinese believe
that fish are a sign of health and good luck. The movement of
the head and tail represents the continuity of life. At a dinner or
banquet the head points toward the guest of honor.

Next on our tour of China was Shanghai. Looking out of our
hotel windows there, we were able to see the working people
doing tai chi, exercises that stress the individual's harmony with
nature. Doing them before going to work in the early morning is
a national routine. It is quite a sight to behold.

Shanghai is the most heavily populated city in China and is
quite cosmopolitan. The streets teem with bicycles and people.
There are a few more taxis and buses here than in Canton and

Hangchow, but it is the bicycles that make it difficult to get from one side of the street to the other.

On our final evening in Shanghai we ate at the Yangchow Restaurant. Dinner there was quite good. It began with a cold plate with four miniature accompanying plates and continued with cherry shrimp, chicken pagoda, braised wild duck, pomfeit with tomato sauce, fan-shaped braised shark's fin, almond beef soup, steamed chiao tsze, steamed volcanos, rice, and three-flavored lo mein (noodles). The meal concluded refreshingly with fruit, ice cream bars, and tea.

The last city we visited was Peking, and there we dined at the Fu Shan Restaurant. This was the finest meal we had in China—expensive but well worth it. A meal for one cost about $15. Our menu included pressed duck, bamboo shoots with oyster sauce, frog legs with bean sauce, rice, twice-cooked pork, clear fish ball soup, lychee nuts, and tea. The service was elegant, and the owner gave each of us a pair of red lacquered chopsticks as a gift.

While we were in Peking our guides took us to an herb store. There are many of these all over China. The Chinese believe in herbs as preventative medicine. We purchased ginseng and some herbs to prevent colds and influenza. The experience of shopping and looking around at the tremendous variety of herbs was great fun.

On our last night in this country we went to a Mongolian hot pot restaurant. To eat a Mongolian hot pot, you dip raw foods into a broth and cook them yourself. Then you dip them into various sauces. Our hot pot offered plates of sliced lamb and round sesame seed buns. The wide range of sauces included cilantro sauce, scallion sauce, hot pepper sauce, sesame seed paste sauce, mustard sauce, peanut sauce, soy sauce with vinegar, Szechwan hot pepper oil, ginger sauce, and garlic sauce.

When we first made our plans for this journey, we thought this would be a very serious trip. We planned to study the food, the country, and the people. The surprise element was the fun and laughter we encountered along the way. The Chinese are a wonderful, warm, and industrious people. They welcome tourists and foreigners, even though this influx of strangers is comparatively new to them.

As for the food, the restaurants in Hong Kong reign over those in China. There is greater variety and better quality in food. The service is good in both places, but in Hong Kong it is much more polished. As for the food overall in China, the vegetables were always fresh and most of the time crisp. The chicken stock was weak and watery. We never had the dried Oriental mushrooms that we use here in so many dishes. The mushrooms used were canned. The quality of poultry was good, and the meat was fair, though we did have Mongolian hot pot in Beijing that was excellent. We had a few interesting dishes made with brisket instead of flank steak. These dishes had a stewlike taste.

Many Americans think Cantonese when they think of Chinese food. The Cantonese pay a great deal of attention to appealing arrangements and colorful dishes. They use little soy so they can retain the natural color of foods. The Szechwan foods served in the North are spicier in flavor. Garlic, peppers, and leeks are used in much greater quantities. In Shanghai one can sample many unusual gravies, varied noodle recipes, and a wide range of seafood dishes. In the South rice is the staple; in the North it is wheat.

We prefer our recipes to those in China mostly because we have better ingredients here. The food in China today is like carved jade framed in gold on the surface. Inside, however, it is like a bundle of straw.

When we wrote this sequel to our first cookbook we gleaned what we believe to be the most exotic and challenging recipes. They are all from Madame Wong's family. She lived in China before many of the great chefs left during the Revolution. We have also included more of Madame Wong's philosophical sayings. They are indigenous to her teaching and everybody loves them. They will give you insight into this consummate teacher. Chinese cooking is fun. The more you do it, the better feel you will have for the preparation and the timing. The recipes vary from very easy to difficult. Please don't be afraid; try everything. You will feel creative and satisfied. You will be an artist in your own kitchen.

Acknowledgments

We wish to acknowledge with gratitude the invaluable assistance given to us by our dear student, Linda Ninomiya, who typed our manuscript, and our talented illustrator, Jeannie Winston-Davis. Thanks also to Madame T. Z. Chiao for her help with the Chinese calligraphy and to Mr. Ling Chiao for his helpful ideas.

A special thanks to Samuel Schulman for his continued encouragement.

About the Authors

Madame S. T. Ting Wong

America's number-one teacher of Chinese cuisine is a dark-eyed, witty woman 76 years old. Born into a family of physicians who for generations had practiced in Shanghai, she carries her five-foot two-inch presence with that elegant charisma that marks a special person.

Presently Madame Wong teaches Chinese cooking at UCLA. She received a Western education at a missionary school in China. After her marriage she accompanied her husband to New York; she completed her culinary studies at Columbia University. She returned to Shanghai after the death of her husband in 1936 and founded the Shanghai Home Economics School. Soon Madame Wong had become internationally famous. The wives of English, American, German, and Japanese consuls were among her thousands of students.

After the fall of Nationalist China, Madame Wong was permitted to leave Shanghai to visit her ailing mother in Hong Kong. In 1956 she left Shanghai and opened a cooking school in Hong Kong that was an instant success.

In 1961 Madame Wong returned to New York, where she conducted a series of special classes for chefs from famous restaurants, home economy experts, and writers of household magazines. Among her students were Albert Stockley, director-chef of the Four Seasons restaurant, and Elizabeth Gordon, food editor of *House Beautiful*. No wonder Madame Wong is called the teacher's teacher. In all, Madame Wong has taught more than 10,000 students, including many celebrities.

She has been teaching at UCLA since 1967. Her students love her and mother her. She is dignified, charming—a person who has overcome adversity and still maintains a great love of life, love for people, and love of teaching.

As you approach this book and learn the recipes, you, too, will feel the buoyancy and excitement that Madame Wong's students have experienced from this ebullient woman.

Sylvia Schulman

Sylvia Schulman was born in New York City in 1920. She has been married to Samuel Schulman for 40 years. They have two daughters and two grandsons. She attended Goucher College and New York University, majoring in drama. She graduated from Antioch University in 1979.

She is a braille transcriber certified by the Library of Congress, a vice-president of the International Student Center at UCLA, and has just completed a three-year appointment by the governor of California to the 11th district Medical Quality Review Board of Los Angeles County. She has become a cooking teacher in her own right. She has taught at UCLA, the Ma Cuisine Cooking School, and privately. This is her second collaboration with Madame Wong.

Her hobbies are painting, tennis, and needlework.

Introduction

Madame Wong As I See Her

Sylvia Schulman

Madame Wong is the most memorable person I have ever met. She brought new dimension to my life with the rare gift of her friendship which I treasure so deeply. Like many of my fellow Americans, I, too, have always found it convenient to believe the myth that East could be only East, and West only West, that neither could fully embrace the other. Now, I fully embrace her as one of the dearest and most vital human beings I have ever met. She has taught me so simply that there need be no wall or ocean to separate us, that East and West can fully share and share alike in this world.

She has taught me so much of living—how to face the most severe adversity with head held high and how to smile bravely through all of it. How I admire her! How lucky I feel to have her friendship, and to share in such rewarding projects as this, our second book together.

Sylvia Schulman As I See Her

S. T. Ting Wong

I can never forget the moment I first saw her. It was surely 100 degrees or more of Los Angeles smog and humidity, and there she was, looking the cool and serene person she is, exuding enthusiasm while shopping in Chinatown.

Since then, I've come to love her as my own daughter. If I am discriminating with food, I am even more so with friends, and my friendship with her is perfect proof of that, for she is the finest woman I know—kindhearted, a sweet mixture of gentility and ambition, eager and fully able to meet whatever challenge she undertakes.

This book gives me pleasure, most of all because it means yet another working partnership with her, my most cherished friend, Sylvia Schulman.

xix

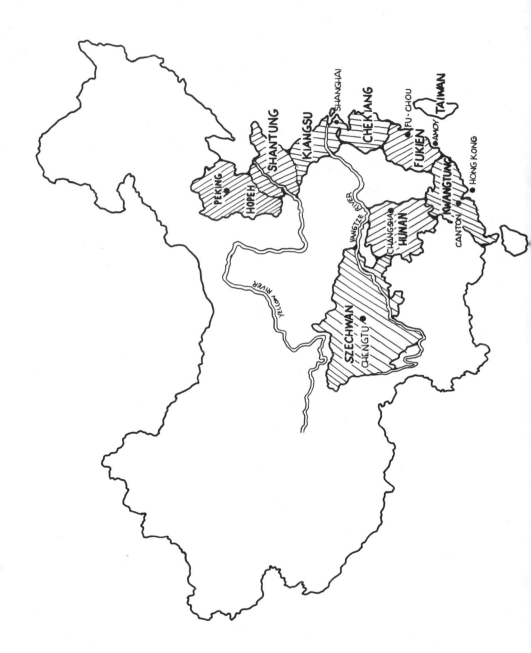

SHANTUNG

SHANGHAI

KIANGSU

CHEKIANG

FU-CHOU

TAIWAN

AMOY

PEKING

HOFEH

FUKIEN

HONG KONG

KWANGTUNG

VANGTZE RIVER

CHANGSHA

HUNAN

CANTON

YELLOW RIVER

SZECHWAN

CHENGTU

1

The Beginning

Food Characteristics of the Culinary Regions of China

SHANGHAI

1. More soy sauce and sugar than other provinces.
2. Unusual gravy dishes.
3. Wide range of seafood recipes.
4. Many varied noodle recipes.

PEKING

1. Wheat flour is staple food.
2. Many famous dishes served with pancakes and buns, such as Peking Duck and Moo Shu Pork.

CANTON

1. Colorful dishes: attention paid to appealing arrangements on serving platters.
2. Less soy sauce to retain natural color of foods.
3. Many fish and lobster recipes.

SZECHWAN

1. Hot, spicy recipes.
2. Salted meat and fish.
3. Generous use of garlic, red pepper, and leeks.

1

HUNAN

1. Hot, spicy recipes.
2. Many sweet and sour fish dishes.
3. Clear soups.
4. Many mushroom dishes.

FUKIEN

1. Best soy sauce in China produced here.
2. Many stewed dishes.
3. Clear and light soups.
4. Seafood often cooked with fermented red wine.

Equipment

A Chinese kitchen does not require many utensils. These are the few necessary ones:

1. Wok. The all-purpose cooking pan. You can improvise with a deep-sided frying pan, but a wok is more fun and cooks food more evenly and quickly. Before using, season your wok with a little oil and then place it on high heat. Do this several times. Each time scour off excess oil that has burned. (Be patient.) This seals the pores and prevents food from sticking. You will know the wok is ready when the scoured bottom remains black. It is not necessary to use a strong detergent to clean your wok; a mild soap and brush will do the job.

2. Steamer. There are two kinds of steamers: one of bamboo that can be set right over the wok and one of aluminum that is complete in itself. Both are used to steam or warm up food.

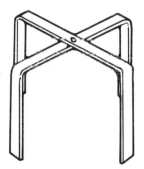

3. Rack. A rack should be placed under bowls or plates if you are using an ordinary pot for steaming. A tin can may be substituted if a rack is not available.

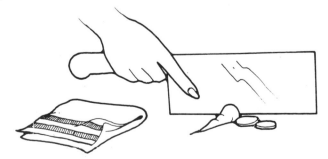

4. Cleaver. This broad, rectangular-shaped blade is used for cutting, chopping, shredding, slicing, mincing, and transferring foods into bowls or pots.

5. Metal Spatula. Used for stir-frying.

6. Metal Ladle. Food is scooped from the wok with a metal ladle.

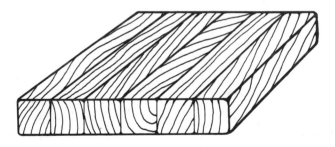

7. Cutting Board. Used for chopping and slicing.

8. Small Bowls. After ingredients have been chopped, they are placed in small bowls. By having all ingredients ready, last-minute cooking is facilitated. Ordinary bowls can be used.

9. Chopsticks. Used for eating and also for stirring ingredients, beating eggs, folding dough—even for spinning sugar. They are sometimes made of plastic. Be sure to use wooden ones for cooking.

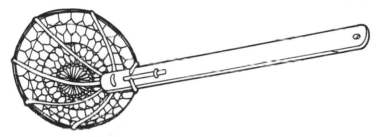

10. Large Strainer with a Bamboo Handle. Used to remove excess oil from food when it is taken out of the wok after deep-frying.

11. Oil Strainer. A small strainer used to remove residue from oil.

12. Earthenware Pot. A heavy pot used for casseroles. Foods can be served directly from it.

13. Yunnan Pot. This pot has an opening for steam. It is placed right in the aluminum steamer for preparing Yunnan steamed dishes.

Methods of Cooking

1. Deep-Frying. Heat two to four cups of oil to about 400 degrees. Place a small piece of scallion top in oil. When it turns brown, oil is ready. Drop food gently into the oil to avoid splashing. Food will change color when finished.

2. Stir-Frying. Use a small amount of oil and stir vigorously and quickly on high heat the entire cooking time, usually a few minutes at the most.

3. Blanching. Immerse vegetables (sometimes meat) in boiling water one or two minutes until color is heightened. Quickly rinse with cold water. This process keeps green vegetables green.

4. Sauteing. Cut food into small pieces and transfer to an open pan. Keep heat constant until food is tender.

5. Braising. Place food in small amount of liquid, cover pot tightly and cook at low temperature in oven or on direct heat.

6. Steaming. Cook food covered on a rack over boiling water or in a Chinese steamer. Water level should be one-half to three-quarters full.

7. Simmering. Cook at low temperature (135–160 degrees) on top of stove. Bubbles appear and barely break.

8. Stewing. Cook in liquid deep enough to cover ingredients; liquid then can be used for sauce.

9. Red Cooking. Food is covered and cooked slowly. It turns dark brown depending on amount of dark soy sauce used. It is called "red cooking" because red denotes happiness.

Cutting Techniques

The most important procedure in Chinese cooking is the way ingredients are cut and prepared. Therefore, you must provide yourself with a very, very sharp knife. A French cutting knife is perfect.

The Chinese are adept at using the cleaver, but this is a skill developed over the years. Any beginner is better advised to depend on his or her own trusty special knife.

In almost every recipe all the ingredients are cut to the same size and shape. There are three reasons for this symmetry: your food looks appealing, it is easier to cook if it is uniform, and simpler to pick up with your chopsticks. (As you know, the Chinese do not use knives and forks.)

1. Straight Cutting. The knife is held straight up and down and the item is cut to desired thickness, from paper-thin to ½-inch. Straight cutting is used for vegetables as well as meat.

2. Diagonal Cutting. The knife is held at an angle of 45 degrees for cutting. This method is used for any vegetable.

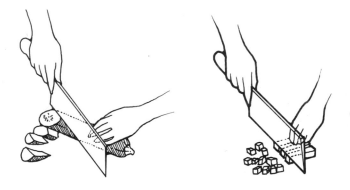

3. Rolled or Oblique Cut. The knife is held at an angle to the item while the opposite hand rolls the item, changing the angle while the knife cuts diagonally. Used primarily on carrots, eggplant, and zucchini.

4. Cubing. Ingredients are cut into small chunks about ½-inch square.

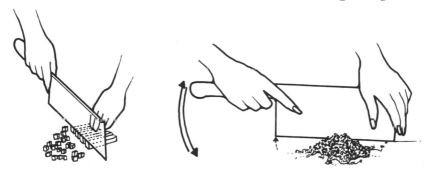

5. Dicing. Ingredients are cut into slices, then into strips, then into very small pieces about ¼- to ½-inch square.

6. Mincing. Ingredients are chopped into rice-size pieces—so fine that they almost become a paste.

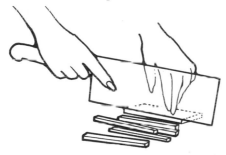

7. Shredding. Ingredients are sliced and then cut into thin strips.

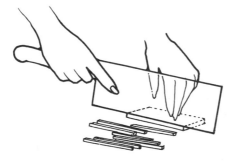

8. Julienne. Ingredients are sliced and then cut into very thin strips that resemble matchsticks.

The Use of Oil in Chinese Cooking

One other secret of Chinese cooking is the use of oil. Any vegetable oil can be used; however, we prefer the polyunsaturated. To prepare the oil for deep-frying, heat the specified amount, add a slice of ginger and a sprig of scallion, and cook for about 2 minutes, until the ginger and scallion are almost burned to a crisp. Then discard them—they take away the raw smell of the oil.

This oil may be used over and over again for cooking meat, poultry, or vegetables, provided that ginger and scallion are heated with the oil every time to eliminate the smell of previous cooking. Pour oil through your fine strainer to remove any residue. Refrigerate used oil in coffee cans. Label cans fish, chicken, or meat for future use.

For cooking sweet dishes or desserts, we always suggest that fresh oil be used.

Sesame Seed Oil is generally used as a seasoning. It is obtainable in Chinatown or in many American markets or health food stores. Be sure to buy the Oriental brand.

Szechwan Pepper Oil is a very important part of seasoning in Szechwan food. It may be purchased in Chinese food stores, and a recipe is included in the sauce section.

Helpful Hints

You will be more successful in your cooking endeavors if you read these hints carefully before you proceed.

1. Read entire recipe through before you begin to prepare the dish.

2. Most recipes are flexible. They serve from four to six persons. How much you will want to prepare depends on how many dishes you are serving—you must use your own judgment. If you find that you need more of any dish, double the entire recipe. Never add more chicken, meat, or fish to the seasonings; you will throw the recipe off balance and change the taste.

3. It is important to cut ingredients in uniform sizes for each recipe, as specified.

4. All recipes using stock can be made with canned, clear, chicken soup, any basic stock recipe, or chicken bouillon cubes, unless otherwise specified.

5. If you pound garlic with a cleaver, the skin will be easy to remove.

6. It is easier to cut meat when it is partially frozen.

7. To prevent lumping, always mix cornstarch in water with one finger.

8. To cook Virginia ham, place in a bowl on rack in pot or in steamer. Steam over boiling water 20 to 30 minutes, depending on the quantity. Always use precooked ham in these recipes. Use regular ham, if not available.

9. Chop your ingredients in advance and have everything ready to use in separate bowls.

10. Shrimp must be very fresh and purchased raw.

11. For the very best flavor, cook foods just before serving.

12. Salt is optional in most recipes.

13. You may stir-fry in chicken stock if you don't wish to use oil.

14. It is best to add salt, egg white, and cornstarch to the meat, poultry or seafood at least 20 minutes before cooking.

15. Red peppers are not always in season. They may be frozen by cutting them in half and removing the seeds. Wrap tightly in aluminum foil.

16. To cut sodium content in half, use Kikkoman Milder Soy Sauce (sold in health food stores) or dilute regular soy sauce with water.

17. If you do not like the deep-fry method, you may stir-fry. They are interchangeable.

18. Never use monosodium glutamate. We consider this unhealthy.

19. Have dissolved cornstarch handy in order to thicken sauces when necessary.

20. Wash Szechwan preserved vegetable (cabbage) before using, to remove the salt.

21. If seasonings such as curry powder or chili paste are too strong for you, lessen the amount and if not strong enough, add a little more to suit your taste.

22. Commercially prepared chili oil can be substituted for Szechwan pepper oil in recipes.

23. A slice of ginger should be about ⅛ inch thick.

24. Four tablespoons and ¼ cup are the same amount. When other ingredients are measured by the tablespoon it is easier to continue measuring this way.

2

Dim Sum and Appetizers

Dim Sum

Eating in China is both a social and a business event. Special restaurants serve only dim sum or bite-size snacks and tea. Here men conduct their transactions at certain times of the day.

We Westerners have taken these finger foods and turned them into hors d'oeuvres. The sweet ones are used as desserts.

Baked Barbecued Pork Buns   CANTON

A very special dim sum dish. Take these on a picnic. Everybody will rave.

Dough:
4 tablespoons evaporated milk
¾ cup lukewarm water
1 package dried yeast or 1 cake fresh yeast
4½ to 5 cups flour
4 tablespoons sugar
4 tablespoons butter or margarine
½ cup boiling water
2 eggs, beaten

Filling:
2 tablespoons oil
1 scallion, chopped fine
1 small onion, cut into small cubes
½ pound barbecued pork cubes or raw chicken cubes
2 tablespoons light soy sauce
2 tablespoons oyster sauce
1 tablespoon sugar
1 tablespoon cornstarch, dissolved in 2 tablespoons water

To brush top of buns:
1 egg white
1 teaspoon water
½ teaspoon sugar
2 tablespoons butter or margarine, melted

1. Mix milk with water. Dissolve yeast in this liquid. Add 1 cup flour. Mix thoroughly. Cover with cloth. Let rise 1 hour until bubbles appear.
2. Dissolve sugar and butter in boiling water. Stir well. Cool until lukewarm. Pour this into the yeast mixture. Add beaten eggs and remaining flour.
3. Knead dough on floured board until smooth. Put into large, greased bowl in a warm place. Cover with damp cloth. Let rise until double in bulk, about 2 hours.
4. Heat oil in wok. Stir-fry scallion and onion 30 seconds. Add pork or chicken. Stir-fry 1 minute. Add soy sauce, oyster sauce, and sugar.
5. Pour in dissolved cornstarch. Stir-fry quickly until pork is glazed. Remove to bowl. Allow to cool.
6. Divide the dough in half. Knead first portion 2 minutes. Repeat with second. Roll each into sausage roll, 12 inches long and 2 inches wide. Cut into 12 pieces each (24 pieces).

7. Flatten each piece of dough with palm of hand. Roll out into 3-inch circles.
8. Place 2 tablespoons filling in center of each round. Gather dough around the filling and twist dough to seal.
9. Place buns, sealed side down, on a greased baking sheet 2 inches apart and let rise 1 hour.
10. Brush with a mixture of beaten egg white, water, and sugar.
11. Bake in preheated 350-degree oven 25 minutes or until golden brown. Brush with melted butter or margarine.

May be prepared in advance. May be frozen.

24 Buns

Barbecued Pork II   CANTON

1 pound pork tenderloin or shoulder
2 tablespoons honey
3 tablespoons light soy sauce
2 tablespoons hoisin sauce
2 tablespoons tomato catsup
1 teaspoon dark soy sauce
1 tablespoon sherry
1 clove garlic, mashed
1 large slice ginger, shredded
1 tablespoon sugar
½ teaspoon red food coloring (optional)

1. Trim meat. Cut into strips about 2 inches wide and 6 inches long.
2. Combine remaining ingredients except for red food coloring in a bowl.
3. Marinate pork in this mixture 2 hours or longer. One-half hour before roasting, add red food coloring.
4. Put hooks through tops of pork strips.* Hang strips from top rack of oven over shallow roasting pan containing a few inches of water.
5. Preheat oven to 425 degrees for 10 minutes. Roast pork 20 minutes. With baster, coat with drippings every 5 minutes. Reduce heat to 325 degrees and roast 5 minutes more.
6. Slice each strip diagonally against the grain into ¼-inch-thick pieces. Serve cold.

---

*Top of wire hanger may be bent into "S" shape for use as hook.

May be prepared in advance. May be frozen. To freeze, wrap in foil; reheat in 250-degree oven for 20 minutes in foil.

Serves 4 to 6

Gift-Wrapped Beef   ALL REGIONS

The Chinese sip their wine and eat their little packages and they are in heaven.

½ pound flank steak
16 squares wax paper or
    aluminum foil, 6 inches by
    6 inches
1 tablespoon sesame seed oil
1 bunch cilantro (Chinese
    parsley)
16 slices cooked carrot
2 tablespoons onion,
    chopped
2 to 4 cups oil for deep-frying
Lettuce leaves

Marinade:
1 tablespoon sherry
3 tablespoons light soy sauce
1 teaspoon sugar
1 tablespoon sesame seed oil

1. Slice beef into 16 slices, 1½ inches wide, 1½ inches long, and ⅛ inch thick, and pound.
2. Combine marinade ingredients in a bowl. Marinate beef 15 minutes. Set aside.
3. Brush each square of paper or foil with sesame seed oil. Arrange a sprig of cilantro, 1 slice cooked carrot, a little onion, and 1 slice beef on each square. Wrap and fold like an envelope. Tuck in the ends.
4. Heat oil in wok to 300 degrees. Deep-fry wrapped beef 1 minute. Do several pieces at a time. Turn occasionally with chopsticks.
5. Remove to platter. Use lettuce for garnish.

May be prepared in advance through Step 3. May be frozen after Step 3.

16 Packages

Meatballs with Spinach Filling   HUNAN

These meatballs may be made with beef, pork, or chicken. They are crunchy on the outside with a surprise on the inside. Served with Fruity Fruity Sauce they are an excellent appetizer.

½ pound spinach or 1
   package frozen spinach
1 pound lean pork, beef, or
   chicken, ground
1 scallion, chopped fine
1½ tablespoons dark soy
   sauce
½ teaspoon salt

½ teaspoon black pepper
½ teaspoon sugar
1 tablespoon sherry
1 tablespoon sesame seed oil
1 egg, well beaten
1 tablespoon flour
1 tablespoon cornstarch
2 to 4 cups oil for deep-frying

1. Blanch spinach in boiling water 30 seconds. Drain. Squeeze dry. Finely chop. If using frozen spinach, thaw and squeeze dry. Put spinach in bowl. Set aside.
2. Put meat in another bowl. Add scallion, dark soy sauce, salt, pepper, sugar, sherry, sesame seed oil, and beaten egg. Mix well with hand. Mix in flour and cornstarch until thoroughly smooth.
3. Roll meat into a cylinder. Divide into 20 portions. Roll into balls with palm of hand.
4. Divide spinach into 20 portions. Roll into balls.
5. Grease palm. Take one meatball. Flatten it into a small round. Put one ball of spinach in center. Fold meat around spinach and roll into a ball. Repeat until all balls are made.
6. Heat oil to 375 degrees. Deep-fry balls 2 minutes. Lower heat and deep-fry another 2 minutes until brown.
7. Serve with Fruity Fruity Sauce (see Index).

May be prepared in advance and reheated in the oven or refried. May be frozen.

20 Meatballs

Sate (Satay) Beef   THAILAND

An original appetizer; the sauce is appealing and the skewers make it attractive for serving.

1 pound flank steak or fillet,
     sliced thin for skewering
Bamboo skewers
Oil

Marinade:
1 onion, minced
1 clove garlic, minced
½ teaspoon salt
1 teaspoon lemon juice or
     vinegar
1 tablespoon light soy sauce

Sate sauce:
½ cup peanut butter
½ teaspoon chili powder
2 tablespoons sate sauce
2 tablespoons oil
1½ tablespoons light soy
     sauce
1 tablespoon onion, minced
¼ cup coconut milk or
     evaporated milk
2 tablespoons chicken stock

1. Combine sauce ingredients.
2. Combine marinade ingredients in a bowl. Marinate beef ½ hour or more. Thread beef strips onto skewers lengthwise. Brush with oil.
3. Broil beef 3 to 4 minutes on each side. Keep turning and brushing with oil. Arrange on a platter.
4. Cook sauce until heated. Pour sauce over beef. Serve with spinach or stir-fried broccoli as a garnish.

May be prepared in advance through Step 2. May not be frozen.

Serves 4 to 6

Steamed Spareribs CANTON

This is a popular snack in Dim Sum restaurants. The Chinese love it. Black bean and garlic creates a very pronounced taste.

1 **pound baby back spareribs**
2 **tablespoons fermented**
   black beans
1 **clove garlic**
1 **tablespoon dark soy sauce**
½ **teaspoon sugar**
1 **tablespoon sherry**
1 **teaspoon cornstarch**

1. Cut ribs into 1-inch pieces.
2. Pound fermented black beans and garlic into a paste with back of knife.
3. Combine soy sauce, sugar, sherry, cornstarch, and the black bean mixture.
4. Pour the above mixture on ribs. Mix well with chopsticks or wooden spoon.
5. Put on plate. Steam over boiling water 30 minutes.

May be prepared in advance. May be frozen.

Serves 4 to 6

Beef Jerky   ALL REGIONS

This sounds like an American dish. However, the Chinese were the originators.

**1 pound flank steak,
    partially frozen, sliced thin**

Marinade:
**4 tablespoons light soy sauce
2 tablespoons honey
2 tablespoons sherry
2 tablespoons sugar
½ teaspoon salt
1 tablespoon hoisin sauce
1 tablespoon oyster sauce**

1. Thoroughly combine marinade ingredients in a bowl. Add beef and cover. Marinate beef in refrigerator overnight.
2. Drain marinade. Bake beef in single layer 45 minutes at 250 degrees. Turn beef twice during baking time. Let cool.
3. Put beef in tightly covered jars or bottles. Refrigerate.
4. Serve cold.

May be prepared in advance. May be frozen.

Serves 4 to 6

Broccoli Stalks with Sesame Seed Oil   ALL REGIONS

Guests always request this easy recipe.

1 pound broccoli stalks

Marinade:
**2 tablespoons sesame seed
   oil**
3 tablespoons light soy sauce
2 cloves garlic, minced

1. Remove leaves and woody part from broccoli.
2. Cut broccoli into long, thin pieces.
3. Thoroughly combine marinade ingredients in a bowl. Add
   broccoli. Marinate at least 30 minutes. Serve cold with
   marinade.

May be prepared in advance. May not be frozen.

Serves 4 to 6

**Don't make things complicated as if the heavens
were falling down.**

Bean Sprout Rolls with Hot Sauce   SZECHWAN

The bean curd sheets become crunchy when deep-fried. An interesting appetizer, serve it with this superb sauce. Everyone loves it.

1 teaspoon salt
10 cups boiling water
3 cups bean sprouts
3 pieces dried bean curd
    sheet, each about 5 inches
    wide and 8 inches long*
2 to 4 cups oil for deep-frying

Sauce:
2 tablespoons sesame seed
    paste or peanut butter
4 tablespoons light soy sauce
½ tablespoon sugar
1 tablespoon sesame seed oil
2 teaspoons red wine vinegar
2 scallions, chopped
1 teaspoon Szechwan
    peppercorn salt (see Index)
½ tablespoon pepper oil (see
    Index)

1. Add salt to boiling water. Blanch bean sprouts 10 seconds. Drain. Rinse in cold water. Squeeze dry.
2. Place bean curd sheet on a flat surface and moisten with hot water 10 minutes. Place 1 sheet on dry towel. Scoop 1 cup bean sprouts onto sheet along 8-inch edge. Roll tightly like a jelly roll. Tuck ends in. Repeat the procedure with remaining bean curd sheets and bean sprouts.
3. Mix sesame seed paste with soy sauce. Mix with remaining sauce ingredients. Set aside.
4. Heat oil. Deep-fry rolls over low heat. Remove and cut into 1-inch pieces.
5. Pour sauce over rolls or use as a dip.

---

*If bean curd sheets are not available, use egg roll wrappers and fry in hot oil.

May be prepared in advance through Step 3. Refry when ready to serve. May not be frozen.

Serves 4 to 6

Pork Turnover   CANTON

A Chinese housewife would be in disgrace if she didn't know how to make these turnovers.

2 to 4 cups oil for deep-frying
1 scallion, chopped fine
¾ pound pork, minced
1 tablespoon sherry
1 tablespoon light soy sauce
1 teaspoon sugar
4 dried black mushrooms,
   soaked 20 minutes in
   boiling water, cooked 20
   minutes, stems removed,
   chopped
6 water chestnuts, chopped
   fine
1 teaspoon salt
Sesame seeds for coating
2 to 4 cups oil for deep-frying

Dough:
2 cups glutinous rice flour
4 tablespoons wheat starch
½ teaspoon sugar
½ teaspoon salt
1⅓ cups boiling water

1. Heat 2 tablespoons oil in wok. Stir-fry scallion and pork until color of pork changes. Add sherry, soy sauce, and sugar. Stir-fry 1 minute.
2. Add mushrooms, water chestnuts, and salt. Stir-fry thoroughly. Remove. Set aside to cool.
3. Mix first four dough ingredients in a bowl. Pour boiling water over. Mix well.
4. Pour on floured board. Knead 4 minutes. Divide dough in half.
5. Roll each portion into sausage roll. Cut each roll into 12 even pieces. Roll with palm into balls. Flatten and roll out into rounds 3 inches in diameter.
6. Place 1 tablespoon of filling in center of each round. Bring top down to make a crescent. Place sesame seeds in a large flat dish. Press the turnover into sesame seeds.
7. Heat oil. Deep-fry turnovers 4 minutes or until golden brown.

May be prepared in advance. May be frozen after Step 6.

24 Turnovers

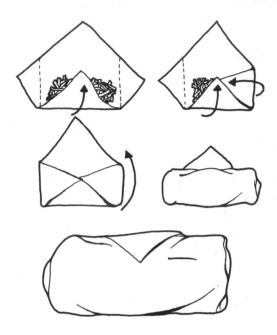

Chicken Egg Roll   SHANGHAI

In China this is called Spring Roll. It is served at the New Year to guests who come to bring greetings. The filling may be made with different meats and vegetables.

1 pound chicken breast, boned, skinned, shredded
1 teaspoon salt
1 egg white
1 tablespoon cornstarch
5 tablespoons oil
1 slice ginger, shredded fine
1 scallion, cut into small pieces
3 tablespoons light soy sauce
1 pound celery cabbage, shredded
¼ cup bamboo shoots, shredded
6 dried black mushrooms, soaked in boiling water 20 minutes, cooked 20 minutes, stems removed
½ pound bean sprouts
24 egg roll wrappers
1 tablespoon cornstarch, dissolved in 2 tablespoons water
2 to 4 cups oil for deep-frying

1. Mix chicken with ½ teaspoon salt, egg white, and cornstarch. Mix well with hand.
2. Heat 2 tablespoons oil in wok. Stir-fry ginger and scallion 30 seconds. Add chicken. Stir-fry 2 minutes. Add 1 tablespoon soy sauce. Stir-fry 30 seconds more. Remove.
3. Heat 2 tablespoons oil in wok. Stir-fry cabbage, bamboo shoots, and mushrooms. Add remaining salt. Stir-fry 2 minutes. Remove.
4. Heat 1 tablespoon oil in wok. Stir-fry bean sprouts 30 seconds. Remove.
5. Combine chicken, vegetables, and bean sprouts in wok. Add remaining soy sauce. Stir-fry until thoroughly heated. Remove to colander. Drain liquid. Cool mixture in refrigerator at least 1 hour.
6. Put 2 heaping tablespoons of the mixture on each wrapper. Roll lengthwise into envelope about 4 inches long and 1 inch wide. Seal with dissolved cornstarch.
7. Heat oil to 375 degrees in wok. Deep-fry 3 to 4 minutes until golden brown. Serve with red wine vinegar or Fruity Fruity Sauce.

May be prepared in advance through Step 7 (deep-fry only 2 minutes). May be frozen after Step 7. Refry before serving.

24 Egg Rolls

Treasures are hidden in the darkest places.

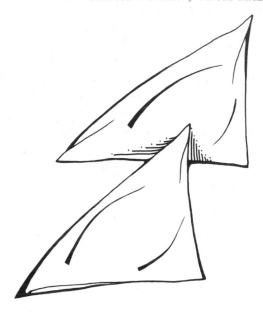

Crab Rangoon   CANTON

We are really excited about this dish. The students give it rave reviews.

½ pound fresh crab meat
½ pound cream cheese
⅛ teaspoon Tabasco
¼ teaspoon Worcestershire
   sauce

1 clove garlic, minced
Pinch white pepper
1 egg white
32 won ton wrappers
2 to 4 cups oil for deep-frying

1. Put the first six ingredients in a food processor. Mix well. If not using food processor, mix with spoon or chopsticks.
2. Wet the edge of each won ton wrapper with egg white. Put ½ tablespoon of the mixture in the center. Bring edges together to form a triangle.
3. Heat oil in wok to 375 degrees. Deep-fry triangles for 2 minutes. Serve with Mustard Sauce (see Index).

May be prepared in advance through Step 2. May be frozen.

Serves 8

Curry Turnover   CANTON

The Cantonese were the first to import foreign ingredients.

3 tablespoons oil
1 pound ground pork, beef,
   or chicken
1 tablespoon light soy sauce
1 teaspoon salt
1 teaspoon sugar
1 onion, chopped fine
1 tablespoon curry powder
   or paste
1 egg, beaten

Dough:
2 cups flour
⅔ cup margarine
1 cup ice water

1. Heat 2 tablespoons oil in wok. Stir-fry pork until color changes. Add soy sauce, salt, and sugar. Stir-fry 1 minute. Remove.
2. Heat remaining oil in wok. Stir-fry onion until wilted. Add curry powder. Cook 1 minute. Add meat and stir-fry 1 minute more. Remove. Cool.
3. Put flour in bowl. Cut margarine into flour with a knife until it is crumbly.
4. Pour ice water into dough. Mix and divide into 2 balls.
5. Roll out the dough until it is very thin. Cut into circles 3 inches in diameter (use inverted glass or cookie cutter).
6. Put 1 tablespoon filling in center of each circle. Fold into half-moons. Crimp edges tightly with fork.
7. Brush tops of turnovers with beaten egg.
8. Bake at 400 degrees 10 minutes. Lower heat to 350 degrees. Bake another 10 minutes.

May be prepared in advance. May be frozen.

About 32 Turnovers

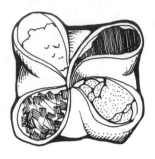

Four-Colored Dumplings   YANGCHOW

Very colorful—red, green, black, and white. Good for a buffet.

Wrapper:*
2 cups flour
½ cup boiling water
1 egg

Filling:
10 ounces pork, chopped fine
2 ounces shrimp, shelled,
   deveined, chopped fine
4 water chestnuts, chopped
   fine
½ tablespoon light soy sauce
1 teaspoon salt
1 tablespoon sesame seed oil
Pinch of black pepper
2 teaspoons cornstarch

Garnish:
2 tablespoons cooked
   Virginia ham, chopped fine
   (red)
2 leaves bok choy or
   spinach, cooked, chopped
   fine (green)
4 dried black mushrooms,
   soaked in boiling water 20
   minutes, stems removed,
   chopped fine (black)
4 water chestnuts, chopped
   fine (white)

1. Put flour in a bowl. Add boiling water. Mix with chopsticks.
   Add egg. Knead in two batches until smooth.
2. Mix pork and shrimp with water chestnuts, soy sauce, salt,
   sesame seed oil, pepper, and cornstarch. Set aside.
3. Remove dough to lightly floured board. Knead and roll into
   two sausage-like rolls. Divide each roll into 16 pieces. (Keep
   dough covered with a damp towel when not using.) Roll each

*Shao mai wrappers may be used.

piece into a circle 3 inches in diameter. Place 1 tablespoon filling in the center of each circle. Pinch top and bottom together. Bring sides in to meet at the center. Be sure there are two holes on each side, as shown in illustration. Put a small amount of a different colored garnish in each hole.

4. Place a wet cloth over holes of the steamer section. Place dumplings on the cloth. Bring water to boil in bottom section. Put section with dumplings over boiling water. Cover, and steam 15 minutes on high heat.
5. Serve with Dumpling Sauce (see Index).

May be prepared in advance through Step 3. May be frozen after Step 3 without the garnish.

32 Dumplings

**Where there is joy, there is fulfillment,
and where there is fulfillment, there is joy.**

Fun Gor   CANTON

The dough of Har Gow and Fun Gor are the same. They are well-known Cantonese snacks. The cooked dough is transparent and has a delicate texture. The technique of making these is rather tricky. Add the boiling water slowly. These are favorites among the Chinese.

Filling:
½ pound pork, minced
1 teaspoon cornstarch
½ teaspoon sugar
1 tablespoon light soy sauce
1 tablespoon cilantro
  (Chinese parsley), chopped
  fine
1 scallion, chopped fine
2 tablespoons oil
4 water chestnuts, chopped
  fine
2 dried black mushrooms,
  soaked in boiling water 20
  minutes, cooked 20
  minutes, stems removed,
  chopped
½ teaspoon salt
Pinch of white pepper
1 tablespoon cornstarch,
  dissolved in 2 tablespoons
  water

Dough:
¼ cup tapioca flour
¾ cup wheat starch
10½ tablespoons boiling
  water
1 scant tablespoon oil

Dip:
3 tablespoons light soy sauce
1 tablespoon sesame seed oil
½ teaspoon chili oil

1. Combine dip ingredients. Set aside. Mix pork with next five ingredients.
2. Heat 1 tablespoon oil in wok. Stir-fry the pork mixture until color changes. Remove.
3. Heat remaining oil. Pour in water chestnuts and mushrooms. Stir-fry 1 minute. Add cooked pork, salt, and pepper. Cook 1 minute more.

4. Add dissolved cornstarch. Stir until the mixture is glazed. Cool.
5. Sift flour and starch together. Gradually add boiling water. Add oil and cool.
6. Knead dough until smooth. Divide dough in half. Shape each half into a sausage. Divide each sausage into twelve pieces. When not working with dough, cover with damp cloth.
7. Oil a cleaver and the working surface lightly. Press a piece of dough with oiled cleaver into a flat round circle.
8. Place 1 teaspoon of filling in center. Bring opposite sides together and pinch to seal. Forms a crescent shape.
9. Place crescents on a greased plate. Place plate on rack. Steam over boiling water 10 minutes. If using Chinese steamer, put damp cloth on rack and place dumplings directly on cloth.
10. Serve with dip.

May be prepared in advance through Step 8. May not be frozen.

24 Dumplings

Har Gow (Shrimp Dumplings)   CANTON

When you make these, you will really feel creative.

Filling:
½ pound shrimp, shelled, deveined, chopped into pieces
1 scallion, chopped fine
4 water chestnuts, chopped fine
1 egg white
1 teaspoon cornstarch
1 teaspoon salt
Pinch of black pepper
1 tablespoon light soy sauce
1 tablespoon oil

Dough:
¼ cup tapioca flour
¾ cup wheat starch
10½ tablespoons boiling water
1 scant tablespoon oil

Dip:
3 tablespoons light soy sauce
1 tablespoon sesame seed oil
½ teaspoon chili oil

1. Mix filling ingredients together. Stir in one direction, mixing thoroughly. Refrigerate 1 hour. Combine dip ingredients. Set aside.
2. Sift flour and starch together. Gradually add boiling water. Add oil and let dough cool.
3. Knead dough until smooth. Divide dough in half. Shape each half into a sausage. Divide each sausage into twelve pieces. When not working with dough, cover with damp towel.
4. Oil a cleaver and the working surface lightly. Press a piece of dough with the oiled cleaver into a flat round circle.
5. To shape each dumpling: Make 3 deep pleats in top half of circle to form a little crescent cap. Fill with 1 teaspoon of the shrimp mixture. Press edges together. Place dumplings on lightly oiled plate or a damp cloth over holes on first level of steamer.

6. Bring water to boil in bottom part of steamer. Place steamer section with dumplings over boiling water. Cover and steam 5 minutes.
7. Serve with dip.

May be prepared in advance through Step 5. (Keep covered with damp cloth.) May be frozen before steaming.

24 Dumplings

Vegetable Chow-Tse (Vegetable Dumplings)   PEKING

For vegetarians this is a must.

1 **package round won ton wrappers***	½ teaspoon salt
4 **pieces baked bean curd**	1 tablespoon light soy sauce
½ **bunch bok choy or 1 bunch spinach**	2 tablespoons sesame seed oil

1. Cut bean curd into ¼-inch cubes.
2. Cook bok choy or spinach in boiling water 1 minute. Rinse in cold water. Squeeze dry and chop fine.
3. Combine bean curd with bok choy or spinach. Add salt, soy sauce, and sesame seed oil. Fill center of wrappers with this filling. Fold over to form crescent shape. Seal ends with water.
4. Put damp cloth on steamer rack. Steam dumplings 10 minutes over boiling water. Serve with Vegetable Dip (see Index).

---

*Also called shao mai wrappers.

May be prepared in advance through Step 3. Cover with a damp cloth until ready to steam. May be frozen after Step 3.

About 50 Dumplings

Szechwan Dumplings SZECHWAN

The spicy sauce adds a distinctive flavor to these light and fluffy dumplings.

½ pound chicken breast, boned, skinned, minced
1 teaspoon salt
2 egg whites
1 teaspoon cornstarch
1 tablespoon sherry
3 tablespoons chicken stock
1 tablespoon sesame seed oil
1 bunch spinach, blanched, chopped fine, all water removed
1 package shao mai wrappers
3 tablespoons cilantro, chopped (Chinese parsley)

Sauce:
4 tablespoons light soy sauce
2 cloves garlic, minced
1 tablespoon pepper oil (see Index) or chili oil
2 tablespoons Szechwan preserved vegetable, chopped fine
1 scallion, chopped fine
1 teaspoon sugar
4 tablespoons red wine vinegar

1. Combine sauce ingredients.
2. Combine first eight ingredients in a bowl. Mix well. (You may mix these ingredients together in a blender or food processor.)
3. Put 1 tablespoon of the filling in the center of each dumpling wrapper. Fold and seal the edges with water, forming a half-circle or crescent. Continue making dumplings until all the filling is used.
4. Cook the dumplings in a large pot in a large quantity of boiling water. Boil until they float to the surface. Add ¼ cup cold water. Bring to boil again. Remove.
5. Drain the dumplings and place on platter. Sprinkle with chopped cilantro. Serve with sauce as dip.

May be prepared in advance through Step 3. May be frozen after Step 3. Freeze on lightly floured wax paper.

About 50 Dumplings

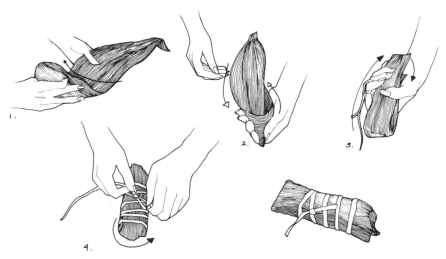

Tsoong Tse Rice Dumplings   SHANGHAI

This snack is usually served on the fifth day of the fifth moon of the Dragon Float Festival, a national holiday, in memory of a loyal knight.

1 pound sweet glutinous rice	1 scallion, chopped fine
6 tablespoons light soy sauce	1 slice ginger, chopped fine
1 pound chicken,* boned, skinned, cut into 2-inch pieces	Bamboo leaves for wrapping

1. Wash rice. Cover with water and let stand overnight. Drain. Mix with 3 tablespoons soy sauce.
2. Mix chicken pieces with remaining soy sauce. Add scallion and ginger. Let stand 1 hour.
3. Hold two leaves together in both hands. Bring bottoms up and over to left side to form pocket. Place a large spoonful of rice and one spoonful of chicken in the pocket. Bring sides in and then fold top down. Add another leaf if necessary. Tie securely with string.
4. Bring water to boil. Cover and simmer dumplings 4 hours.

———————
*Pork may be substituted for chicken.

May be prepared in advance through Step 3. May not be frozen.

Serves 10

Shrimp Banana Fritters   PEKING

Shrimp and bananas combined are extraordinary, especially so with Fruity Fruity Sauce.

2 ounces shrimp, shelled,
   deveined
½ teaspoon salt
½ teaspoon sesame seed oil
1 teaspoon sherry
Pepper to taste
2½ tablespoons cornstarch
2 bananas
2 to 4 cups oil for deep-frying

Batter:
½ cup flour
6 tablespoons water
¼ teaspoon salt
½ tablespoon baking powder

1. Finely chop shrimp. Mix with salt, sesame seed oil, sherry, pepper, and ½ tablespoon cornstarch.
2. Slice bananas in half lengthwise. Coat each slice with remaining cornstarch.
3. Mix flour with water, salt, and baking powder. Stir thoroughly.
4. Spoon half of the shrimp mixture on half of a banana. Cover with other half to make a sandwich. Repeat with second banana. Cut each banana sandwich into 6 pieces crosswise.
5. Dip each banana sandwich into batter. Heat oil. Deep-fry a few at a time until golden brown. Serve with Fruity Fruity Sauce (see Index).

May be prepared in advance. Refry before serving. May not be frozen.

Serves 4 to 6

Shrimp Fragrant Tingling Bells ALL REGIONS

Bean curd sheet is made with soy beans and is paper-thin. Your guests will be amazed with this unusual, crispy wrapping. An hors d'oeuvre supreme.

1 **pound shrimp, shelled, deveined**	1 **teaspoon sherry**
1 **teaspoon salt**	1 **egg yolk**
¼ **teaspoon white pepper**	1 **teaspoon cornstarch or flour**
1 **scallion, minced**	4 **bean curd sheets**
4 **water chestnuts, chopped fine**	2 to 4 **cups oil for deep-frying**

1. Mince shrimp. Sprinkle with salt, pepper, and scallion. Add water chestnuts and sherry.
2. Mix egg yolk and cornstarch or flour into a watery paste.
3. Place a bean curd sheet on a flat surface and moisten with hot water. Let stand 20 minutes. Pick sheet up and place on dry towel. Scoop one quarter of the shrimp mixture onto long edge of sheet. Roll like a jelly roll to within 2 to 3 inches of the end. Moisten end of sheet with the egg yolk mixture. Roll sheet to the end. If bean curd tears, use extra pieces and patch with dissolved cornstarch. Repeat process with 3 remaining sheets.
4. Cut each roll into 1-inch pieces. Dip each end into dry cornstarch to seal.
5. Heat oil. Deep-fry until crisp. Serve with Fruity Fruity Sauce, Sweet Sour Sauce, or Peppercorn Salt (see Index).

May be prepared in advance through Step 4 or frozen after Step 5. Refry before serving.

Serves 4 to 6

Shrimp Toast II   ALL REGIONS

Another version of the recipe from our first book.

9 slices extra-thin white
   bread (day old preferable)
1 pound fresh shrimp,
   shelled, deveined, chopped
4 water chestnuts, chopped
   fine
½ medium onion, chopped
   fine

1 scallion, chopped fine
1 slice ginger, chopped fine
1 teaspoon salt
1 teaspoon sherry
1 tablespoon cornstarch
1 egg, slightly beaten
Pepper to taste
2 to 4 cups oil for deep-frying

1. Trim crusts from bread. Cut each slice into 4 squares (36 squares).
2. Soak 4 of the squares in water 1 second. Squeeze out liquid. Set aside.
3. In a bowl combine shrimp, water chestnuts, onion, scallion, ginger, salt, sherry, cornstarch, egg, pepper, and soaked bread squares. Mix well.*
4. Place 1 teaspoon of the shrimp mixture on each of remaining bread squares, slightly mounded.
5. Heat oil to 375 degrees in wok. Slide bread pieces into oil, a few at a time, with shrimp side down.
6. Deep-fry about 1 minute. Turn and fry other side until golden brown.
7. Drain on paper towels.

---

*All ingredients may be chopped in food processor. Chop onion first, then add remaining ingredients.

May be prepared in advance through Step 4. May be frozen after Step 6. Refry before serving.

32 Shrimp Toasts

Walnut and Shrimp Eggs   YANGCHOW

In China this was a banquet dish. Quail eggs were used. An hors d'oeuvre for a special dinner party or a main dish served with spinach!

6 small eggs*	2 ounces walnut halves
½ pound shrimp, shelled, deveined	2 to 4 cups oil for deep-frying
1½ teaspoons salt	2 tablespoons flour
½ egg white	1 pound spinach, washed, stems removed
2 teaspoons cornstarch	

1. Boil eggs 10 minutes. Shell and cut into halves.
2. Chop shrimp. Add ½ teaspoon salt, egg white, and cornstarch.
3. Sprinkle a little cornstarch on top of eggs so that the shrimp mixture will stick. Cover each half of egg with the shrimp mixture.
4. Place a walnut half on shrimp-topped egg half.
5. Gently roll egg in flour. Deep-fry 2 minutes at 375 degrees. Drain. Remove.
6. Heat 2 tablespoons oil in wok until smoking hot. Stir-fry spinach 1 minute. Add remaining salt.
7. Arrange eggs on plate. Garnish with spinach.

---

*Quail eggs can be purchased in cans in Chinatown. (They are already cooked.) Or use small chicken eggs.

May be prepared in advance through Step 4. May not be frozen.

12 Egg Halves

Sesame Seed Cake (Shao Ping)   PEKING

This is a national cake. The Chinese serve this with soy bean milk and eat it for breakfast.

Yeast dough:
½ package dried yeast
1 cup lukewarm water
2 teaspoons sugar
2 cups flour

Oil-flour mixture:
⅓ cup oil
½ cup flour
1 teaspoon salt
1 tablespoon white corn syrup, diluted with 2 tablespoons water
Sesame seeds

1. *Yeast dough:* Dissolve yeast in lukewarm water. Add sugar and flour. Knead until smooth.
2. Cover with damp cloth. Let rise in warm place about 1 hour.
3. *Oil-flour mixture:* Heat oil in frying pan. Add flour. Stir-fry over low heat 5 minutes or until the mixture turns a golden brown. Set aside to cool.
4. Knead the yeast dough 5 minutes. Roll with rolling pin into a large rectangular sheet, about ¼ inch thick, 20 inches long, and 8 inches wide.
5. Sprinkle with salt. Brush the cooled oil-flour mixture evenly on the yeast dough. Roll up on the long side to make a cylinder.
6. Cut the dough into 20 1-inch-wide pieces. Roll each piece into rectangles 4 inches long and 2 inches wide. Fold into thirds.
7. Roll each rectangle out with rolling pin until it is 4 inches long and 2 inches wide again.
8. Brush diluted corn syrup on top of each rectangle.
9. Place sesame seeds in a large flat dish. Dip brushed side of dough into sesame seeds. Lightly press dough into sesame seeds with hand. Place on a cookie sheet. Cover and let rise 20 minutes.
10. Preheat oven to 350 degrees. Bake cakes 20 to 25 minutes.

May be prepared in advance and reheated in 350-degree oven 10 minutes. May be frozen.

20 Pieces

Cocktail Peanuts   ALL REGIONS

*We guarantee you will not be able to stop until you have eaten
every single one.*

1 **pound unsalted peanuts,**
   skin on
1 **can Mai Ling pickled**
   cabbage
Boiling water
2 **star anise seeds**
1 **tablespoon salt**

1. Put peanuts in boiling water to cover. Add remaining ingredients. Bring to boil again. Cover and simmer 45 minutes.
2. Drain. Remove cabbage and star anise seeds. Put in bowl.

*May be prepared in advance. (Cool and store in jars in refrigera-
tor.) May not be frozen.*

Serves 4 to 6

3

Soups

The uniqueness of a Chinese meal is that one may serve clear soup at any time during the meal, just as we serve water or wine. This is used to refresh and make you serene. Hearty soups consist of a good stock with meat and vegetables. This can be a one-dish meal. There is no end to the variety of soups in Chinese cuisine. The Dowager Empress ate White Fungus Soup daily to keep her young and healthy.

Basic Chicken Stock   ALL REGIONS

Although canned chicken stock can be used in recipes, a good homemade stock is always richer and more wholesome. You can bottle it and it will keep in the refrigerator about five days. If you wish to keep it longer, reheat it, cool it again, and replace in the refrigerator. You can also freeze stock indefinitely. Use this recipe wherever stock is indicated unless otherwise specified.

12 cups water
1 whole chicken, about 3 to
    4 pounds*
1 scallion
2 slices ginger
1 tablespoon sherry

1. Bring water to boil in pot. Add chicken, scallion, ginger, and sherry. As soon as it comes to a boil, turn off the heat and skim off foam.
2. Bring to boil again. Simmer 4 hours.
3. When stock is cool, strain and discard chicken.
4. Refrigerate in bottles. Skim off fat from jellied stock and discard.

---

*Bones and carcass may be used in place of whole chicken.

May be prepared in advance. May be refrigerated about one week. May be frozen.

Approximately 10 Cups Basic Stock

Crab Meat with Cream of Corn Soup   ALL REGIONS

An incomparable soup.

2 tablespoons oil
4 slices ginger, minced
2 scallions, chopped fine
½ pound crab meat
1 tablespoon sherry
½ teaspoon salt
6 cups chicken stock
1 17-ounce can creamed corn
2 tablespoons light soy sauce

2 tablespoons cornstarch, dissolved in 4 tablespoons water
2 eggs, beaten slightly
2 tablespoons parsley, chopped
4 tablespoons cooked ham, chopped fine
Black pepper
White vinegar (optional)

1. Heat oil in wok. Stir-fry ginger and scallion 30 seconds. Add crab meat. Stir-fry 1 minute. Add sherry and salt. Set aside.
2. Pour stock into a large pot. Bring to boil. Add creamed corn and light soy sauce. Thicken with dissolved cornstarch, if necessary. (The soup should not be too thick.) Add the crab meat mixture.
3. Pour eggs in slowly. Stir gently with a circular motion until they form thin shreds.
4. Pour soup into a serving bowl. Garnish with parsley and ham. Sprinkle with black pepper.
5. Add vinegar to taste.

May be prepared in advance. May be frozen.

Serves 4 to 6

Green Jade and Red Ruby Soup   ALL REGIONS

A few simple ingredients and the Chinese sense of beauty, as well as taste, is found in this soup. Cucumber is the symbol of jade and the red flavorful ham is symbolic of the ruby.

2 **cucumbers, peeled**
5 **cups chicken stock**
½ **teaspoon salt**
2 **tablespoons cooked**
   Virginia ham, chopped
   coarsely

1. Cut cucumber in half lengthwise. Scoop out seeds. Slice crosswise into ¼-inch pieces.
2. Bring stock to boil. Add salt and cucumber. Cook 5 minutes.
3. Pour in tureen. Sprinkle ham over. Serve hot.

May be prepared in advance. May be frozen.

Serves 4 to 6

Life is like a play. Each one must play a part.
Play well and play your very best.

Fish Ball Soup   YANGCHOW

This is quite a sophisticated soup. The fish balls are similar to the French quenelles. It is served on festival days and especially at the New Year celebration.

1 thick slice ginger
1 scallion, cut into thirds
8 tablespoons water
½ pound fish fillet*
1 tablespoon sherry
1 egg white
1 tablespoon cornstarch
1 teaspoon salt
8 cups water

6 cups chicken stock
½ cup boiled bamboo shoots, shredded
½ cup thin chicken slices
¼ cup cooked Virginia ham slices
¼ cup pea pods, strings removed

1. Pound ginger and scallion with cleaver. Soak ginger and scallion in 4 tablespoons water. Set aside at least 30 minutes. Strain the liquid. Reserve.
2. Dry fish. Cut into cubes. Put into blender or food processor. Finely chop fish. Add remaining 4 tablespoons water slowly. Add sherry and egg white. Blend until smooth.
3. Combine the ginger-scallion liquid with cornstarch and salt. Mix well. Slowly add this liquid to fish. Mix 1 minute more.
4. Put 8 cups water in wok on low heat. Have a tablespoon ready to dip into a bowl of cold water.
5. Wet left hand. Put a small amount of fish paste into palm. Scoop out with wet spoon to form 28 balls. Drop fish balls into wok. When balls float to surface and turn white, they are ready to remove (about 10 minutes).
6. Bring stock to boil. Add bamboo shoots, chicken, ham, and pea pods. Bring to boil again. Ladle the fish balls into the soup.
7. Let the soup come to a boil slowly. Serve immediately.

---

*Sea bass, flounder, or sole.

May be prepared in advance through Step 5. Put fish balls in cold water in refrigerator. Will last for 3 days. May not be frozen.

Serves 4 to 6

Hot and Sour Soup with Fish   SHANGHAI

This dish is very refreshing. Another version of hot and sour soup—low in calories and a meal in itself.

1   pound fish fillet,* cut into
    2-inch-square pieces
1½ teaspoons salt
1   tablespoon sherry
1   slice ginger, shredded
7   cups chicken stock
1   teaspoon black pepper
4   tablespoons red wine
    vinegar
4   water chestnuts, sliced thin

8   snow peas, cut into
    quarters
1   jar (2½ ounces) button
    mushrooms
3   tablespoons cornstarch,
    dissolved in ¼ cup water
1   tablespoon cilantro
    (Chinese parsley), chopped
3   egg whites, slightly beaten

1. Rub fish with 1 teaspoon salt. Put in a bowl, pour sherry over it. Add ginger.
2. Bring stock to boil. Add ½ teaspoon salt, pepper, and vinegar. Add vegetables.
3. Thicken with dissolved cornstarch.
4. Add fish and cilantro. Cook 30 seconds.
5. Add beaten egg whites, stirring quickly. Bring to boil. Serve immediately.

——————
*Sea bass, red snapper, or flounder.

May be prepared in advance through Step 3. Do not freeze.

Serves 4 to 6

Pork and Cucumber Soup   SZECHWAN

This is a famous Szechwan soup. It is clear and refreshing.

½ pound pork, shredded
1 tablespoon light soy sauce
1 teaspoon cornstarch
2 teaspoons oil
1 cucumber, skin removed
2 cups water

5 cups chicken stock
1 teaspoon sherry
1 teaspoon salt
2 tablespoons cilantro
   (Chinese parsley), chopped
1 tablespoon sesame seed oil

1. Mix pork with soy sauce, cornstarch, and oil.
2. Cut cucumber in half lengthwise. Scoop out seeds. Slice crosswise into ¼-inch pieces.
3. Bring water to boil. Pour in pork. Cook 1 minute. Drain.
4. Bring stock to boil. Add pork and sherry. Cook 2 minutes.
5. Add cucumber. Cover. Cook 2 minutes more. Add salt to taste.
6. Add cilantro and sesame seed oil.

May be prepared in advance. May be frozen.

Serves 4 to 6

Seafood Bean Curd Soup   CANTON

We found this to be a specialty at the Mon Kee Restaurant in Los Angeles. Very delicious and has an excellent seafood flavor.

5 cups chicken stock
· 2 ounces shrimp, shelled, deveined, cut into small pieces
½ cup scallops, cubed
2 ounces crab meat
2 pieces bean curd (to-fu, 4 pieces in a box), shredded
1 scallion, chopped fine

1 slice ginger, chopped fine
1 teaspoon salt
2½ tablespoons cornstarch, dissolved in 5 tablespoons water
Red wine vinegar (optional)
Chili oil (optional)
½ teaspoon pepper

1. Bring stock to boil. Add shrimp, scallops, crab meat, and bean curd.
2. Add scallion, ginger, and salt. Bring to boil. Thicken with dissolved cornstarch. If more spice is preferred, add a little red wine vinegar or chili oil. Sprinkle with pepper.

May not be prepared in advance. May not be frozen.

Serves 4 to 6

Soup with Vermicelli and Vegetables   THAILAND

We are taking the liberty of borrowing a few delicious recipes from Thailand.

2 ounces vermicelli
   (cellophane noodles)
4 cloves garlic, minced
2 tablespoons cilantro
   (Chinese parsley), chopped
½ teaspoon black pepper
2 tablespoons oil
1 large onion, sliced thin
¼ pound pork, shredded

½ pound medium shrimp,
   shelled, deveined, cut in half
8 cups chicken stock
5 scallions, cut into 1-inch
   pieces
3 tablespoons fish sauce*
1 tablespoon sugar
1 tablespoon light soy sauce
2 eggs, slightly beaten

1. Soak vermicelli in hot water at least 20 minutes. Drain. Cut into thirds with scissors. Set aside.
2. Mash garlic, 1 tablespoon cilantro, and black pepper to a smooth paste.
3. Heat 1 tablespoon oil in wok. Stir-fry onion 5 minutes on moderate heat until transparent. Stir in the garlic mixture. Remove.
4. Heat remaining oil in wok. Stir-fry pork and shrimp. Remove.
5. Bring stock to boil in a large pot. Add scallions, fish sauce, sugar, and soy sauce. Add shrimp, pork, the onion-garlic mixture, and vermicelli. Slowly pour in the beaten egg.
6. Garnish with 1 tablespoon chopped cilantro.

---

*Sold in bottles in Chinatown.

May be prepared in advance. May not be frozen.

Serves 4 to 6

Sour Shrimp Soup   THAILAND

This is a much requested recipe.

1 stalk lemon grass, washed, outer layer peeled off, cut into 1-inch pieces*
1½ cups water
4 cups chicken stock
2 tablespoons fish sauce
2 tablespoons lemon juice
12 medium shrimp, deveined, shelled, tail on

1 cup fresh mushrooms, cut into quarters
½ teaspoon chili powder
8 sprigs cilantro (Chinese parsley), chopped (reserve 2 sprigs for garnish)
1 scallion, cut into 1-inch pieces

1. Boil lemon grass in water, uncovered, about 10 minutes. Add 1 cup strained lemon grass water to chicken stock. Add a few pieces of stalk to stock. Bring to boil.
2. Reduce heat. Stir in fish sauce and lemon juice. Boil 5 minutes. Add shrimp and mushrooms. Boil 3 minutes more.
3. Add chili powder, cilantro, and scallion. Remove from heat. Garnish with cilantro sprigs. Serve immediately.

---

*Two pieces lemon peel and 2 tablespoons lemon juice may be substituted.

May be prepared in advance through Step 2. May not be frozen.

Serves 4 to 6

Chicken and Watercress Soup CANTON

Watercress, according to the Chinese, clarifies the system.

½ pound chicken breast, boned, skinned, shredded
1 teaspoon salt
1 egg white
2 teaspoons cornstarch
2 cups water

1 bunch watercress, leaves only
5 cups chicken stock
¼ cup cooked Virginia ham, shredded
1 tablespoon sherry

1. Mix chicken with ½ teaspoon salt, egg white, and cornstarch. Set aside 30 minutes.
2. Bring water to boil. Pour in chicken. Stir gently to separate the pieces. Drain. Remove.
3. Bring water to boil again. Drop in watercress. Drain. Remove.
4. Scatter watercress on bottom of tureen or individual bowls.
5. Bring stock to boil. Add chicken, ham, and remaining salt. Bring to boil again. Pour over watercress. Add sherry. Serve immediately.

May be prepared in advance through Step 3. May not be frozen.

Serves 4 to 6

Spinach and Bean Curd Soup (Gun)   ALL REGIONS

Gun in Chinese means thick. Spinach and bean curd—two healthy ingredients combined into a thick and beautiful soup.

½ pound spinach, cleaned, stems removed

¼ pound chicken breast, skinned, boned

6 cups chicken stock

⅓ cup bamboo shoots, cut into ¼-inch cubes

4 dried black mushrooms, soaked 20 minutes in boiling water, stems removed, cut into ¼-inch cubes

3 pieces bean curd (¾ box of to-fu), cut into ¼-inch cubes

4 tablespoons cornstarch, dissolved in 4 tablespoons water

1 teaspoon salt

¼ teaspoon black pepper

2 tablespoons cooked Virginia ham, minced

2 tablespoons cilantro (Chinese parsley), chopped (optional)

1. Blanch spinach in boiling water 1 minute. Rinse in cold water. Squeeze dry. Chop fine.
2. Cook chicken in boiling water to cover 5 minutes. Cool. Cut into ¼-inch cubes.
3. Bring stock to boil. Add chicken, bamboo shoots, mushrooms, and bean curd. Thicken with dissolved cornstarch.
4. Add spinach. Bring to boil. Add salt and pepper. Stir until well blended.
5. Sprinkle ham on top. Garnish with chopped cilantro, if desired.

May be prepared in advance through Step 3. May be frozen.

Serves 4 to 6

Szechwan Cabbage and Pork Soup   SZECHWAN

This is a favorite soup for the Westerner, as well as for the Chinese.

½ pound pork, shredded
1 teaspoon cornstarch
1 tablespoon light soy sauce
1 tablespoon oil
¼ cup bamboo shoots,
   shredded

6 cups chicken stock
½ cup Szechwan preserved
   vegetable,* shredded
1 tablespoon sherry

1. Mix pork with cornstarch and soy sauce.
2. Heat oil in wok. Add pork. Stir-fry 2 minutes. Add bamboo shoots. Stir 1 minute more.
3. Heat stock. Add bamboo shoots, pork, and Szechwan preserved vegetable. Add sherry. Bring to boil. Cook 1 minute.

---

*Also called Szechwan preserved cabbage.

May be prepared in advance. May be frozen.

Serves 4 to 6

A great man is never one-sided.

Steamed Chicken in Yunnan Pot*   YUNNAN

To make it is to believe that this is chicken soup at its height. This is a special, unique pot from Yunnan. Chicken steamed in it has a superb flavor.

1 chicken, about 3 pounds	1 scallion, cut in half
2 ounces cooked Virginia ham	1 slice ginger
	1 tablespoon sherry
1 cup water	1 teaspoon salt

1. Chop chicken into 1½-inch pieces. Cut ham into ½-inch pieces.
2. Place chicken in the pot. Place a layer of ham over chicken. Place all other ingredients in pot.
3. Cover pot tightly. Steam over boiling water for 1½ hours.
4. Serve immediately from Yunnan Pot.

---

*Pyrex casserole may be used.

May be prepared in advance. May be frozen.

Serves 4 to 6

White Fungus Soup ALL REGIONS

We had this soup in Peking. Fungus has always been considered a food for health and increased potency in China. Now it has truly arrived here in our country.

½ cup dried white fungus
4 ounces chicken breast, boned, skinned, cut into 1-inch-thick slices
1 teaspoon salt
1 egg white

1 teaspoon cornstarch
1 cup water
5 cups chicken stock
8 fresh mushrooms, sliced thin, stems removed

1. Soak dried fungus in cold water overnight. Remove hard part.
2. Mix chicken with ½ teaspoon salt, egg white, and cornstarch. Set aside 10 minutes.
3. Bring water to boil. Pour in chicken. Stir gently 1 minute to separate the pieces. Drain. Remove.
4. Bring stock to boil. Add fungus. Simmer covered 30 minutes.
5. Add chicken and mushrooms. Cook 3 minutes.
6. Season with remaining salt. Serve hot.

May be prepared in advance. May be frozen.

Serves 4 to 6

Yin and Yang Soup   PEKING

To have a proper balance of foods in the body, the Chinese follow the Yin Yang principle. This soup has ingredients that possess both qualities.

½ pound chicken breast, skinned, boned
1 teaspoon salt
1 tablespoon sherry
4 cups chicken stock
2 egg whites

1 bunch spinach
2 tablespoons cornstarch, dissolved in 4 tablespoons water
2 tablespoons cooked Virginia ham, minced

1. Chop chicken fine. Mix with ½ teaspoon salt and sherry. Add ½ cup cold chicken stock. Blend well.
2. Beat egg whites until stiff. Fold in chicken until the mixture is soft and fluffy.
3. Bring water to boil. Boil spinach for 30 seconds. Drain and rinse in cold water. Finely chop or puree in food processor. Slowly add remaining salt and ½ cup chicken stock.
4. Bring 1½ cups of stock to boil. Add the chicken mixture. Thicken with half the dissolved cornstarch.
5. Bring the remaining 1½ cups of stock to boil in another pot. Add spinach. Thicken with dissolved cornstarch.
6. Pour the chicken soup and the spinach soup into a serving bowl. Hold a pot in each hand and pour from opposite directions.
7. Garnish with minced ham.

May be prepared in advance through Step 3. May be frozen.

Serves 4 to 6

4

Chicken

In old China a chicken was not killed unless an honored guest came to dinner. Chicken was considered a specialty. Confucius said, "If there is nothing important, don't kill the chicken." There are countless ways of cooking it. Every part of the chicken is used. Nothing is wasted. A gourmet meal can result from preparing chicken wings and mixing them with other ingredients or boning and stuffing them. The breast is used as a delicacy in a variety of ways. We have included our favorite chicken dishes.

Chicken Wings with Onion   SHANGHAI

*Students are always asking for more recipes using chicken wings.
They are tasty, easy to prepare, and economical.*

10 chicken wings, cut in half,
   tips removed
4 tablespoons dark soy sauce
4 tablespoons oil
2 large onions, sliced
1 tablespoon sherry

1 cup chicken stock
1 tablespoon sugar
1 tablespoon cornstarch,
   dissolved in 1 tablespoon
   water

1. Mix wings with 1 tablespoon soy sauce. Let stand at least 20 minutes.
2. Heat 2 tablespoons oil in wok. Stir-fry wings until golden brown. Remove.
3. Heat 2 tablespoons oil in wok. Stir-fry onion until quite wilted. Add wings. Add sherry, remaining soy sauce, and stock. Cover and simmer 30 minutes.
4. Bring to boil. Add sugar. Thicken with dissolved cornstarch. Baste wings with sauce until glazed.

May be prepared in advance. May be frozen.

Serves 4 to 6

Every extra thing you own is a burden to yourself.

Chicken Wings with Leek   SHANGHAI

This is a family dish, economical and tasty, wonderful as an hors d'oeuvre or entree.

10 chicken wings, cut in half, tips removed	1 tablespoon sherry
4 tablespoons dark soy sauce	1 cup chicken stock
4 tablespoons oil	1 tablespoon sugar
1 pound leek, cleaned, cut into 1½-inch pieces	1 tablespoon cornstarch, dissolved in 1 tablespoon water

1. Mix wings with 1 tablespoon soy sauce. Let stand 20 minutes or more.
2. Heat 2 tablespoons oil in wok. Stir-fry wings until golden brown. Remove.
3. Heat 2 tablespoons oil. Stir-fry leek until wilted. Add wings, sherry, 3 tablespoons soy sauce, and stock. Cover and simmer 25 minutes.
4. Bring to boil. Add sugar. Thicken with dissolved cornstarch. Continue basting until wings are glazed.

May be prepared in advance. May be frozen.

Serves 4 to 6

Chicken Wings with Curry   SHANGHAI

Curry is used frequently in Chinese cooking, even though the condiment comes from India.

10 chicken wings, cut in half, tips removed	**5 cloves garlic, minced**
1 teaspoon salt	**1 tablespoon Indian curry paste***
½ teaspoon pepper	**1 tablespoon Indian curry powder***
2 tablespoons flour	**1 cup chicken stock**
4 tablespoons oil	**1 tablespoon dark soy sauce**
1 large onion, sliced	

1. Sprinkle salt, pepper, and flour evenly on wings.
2. Heat 1 tablespoon oil in wok. Fry onion and 3 cloves garlic until slightly browned. Remove.
3. Heat 3 tablespoons oil in wok. Brown chicken wings.
4. Add curry paste, curry powder, the onion-garlic mixture, and stock to wings. Cover and simmer 25 minutes.
5. Uncover. Bring to boil. Add soy sauce. Add remaining garlic. Stir-fry thoroughly until sauce is glazed.

---

*If you prefer less spice, use ½ tablespoon of each.

May be prepared in advance. May be frozen.

Serves 4 to 6

Spicy Chicken Wings   YANGCHOW

This is a simple family dish. Easy to prepare. We suggest doubling the recipe because it goes so quickly.

12 chicken wings, cut in half, tips removed
2 tablespoons light soy sauce
1 slice ginger
2 teaspoons sugar
½ teaspoon salt
1 scallion, cut into 4 pieces
1 tablespoon cornstarch

2 to 4 cups oil for deep-frying
1 cup chicken stock
Pinch of five-spice powder
1 teaspoon pepper oil (see Index) or chili paste with garlic
1 tablespoon dark soy sauce

1. Mix light soy sauce, ginger, 1 teaspoon sugar, salt, and scallion together. Pour over chicken wings. Let stand at least 10 minutes. Mix well with hand.
2. Mix cornstarch with chicken wings before frying. Heat oil for deep-frying until smoking hot. Fry chicken wings until light brown and crispy. Drain. Remove.
3. Return 1 teaspoon oil to wok. Pour in wings. Stir-fry 1 minute. Add stock. Bring to boil. Sprinkle wings with five-spice powder and 1 teaspoon sugar. Reduce heat. Cover and simmer 25 minutes.
4. Uncover. Bring to boil. Add pepper oil and dark soy sauce. Stir constantly until wings are glazed. Serve immediately.

May be prepared in advance. May be frozen.

Serves 4 to 6

Thousand-Year-Sauce Chicken Wings   PEKING

Keep this sauce in the refrigerator and use it over and over again. This will be one of your easiest dishes.

10 chicken wings, cut in half,
  tips removed
½ cup dark soy sauce
¼ cup sesame seed oil

¼ cup sherry
2 pieces star anise
2 cups water

1. Put soy sauce, sesame seed oil, sherry, star anise, and water in wok. Bring to boil. Add chicken wings.
2. Cover and simmer 25 minutes.
3. Remove wings from liquid and reserve liquid for future use.
4. Serve wings hot or cold.

May be prepared in advance. May be frozen.

Serves 4 to 6

Stir-Fried Frog Legs   SHANGHAI

Fresh frog legs are very popular in China. Chicken wings with the tips removed, separated at the joint, can be substituted. Serve with snow peas.

1 pound frog legs
1 teaspoon salt
1 egg white
1 tablespoon cornstarch
2 to 4 cups oil for deep-frying
1 red pepper, diced
1 green pepper, diced

2 tablespoons bean sauce
2 tablespoons sugar
4 tablespoons chicken stock
2 tablespoons sherry
1 bamboo shoot, cooked in
  boiling water 2 minutes,
  diced

1. Wash, trim, and clean frog legs. Wipe them dry and place in bowl.
2. Mix frog legs well with salt, egg white, and cornstarch. Use hand to mix.
3. Heat oil for deep-frying. Fry legs 1 minute. Drain.

4. Return 2 tablespoons oil to wok. Stir-fry green and red peppers 1 minute. Remove.
5. Heat 2 tablespoons oil. Stir-fry bean sauce 1 minute. Add sugar and stock. Bring to boil.
6. Pour in frog legs and continue to stir 3 to 4 minutes. Add sherry, peppers, and bamboo shoots. Stir thoroughly until sauce coats the frog legs.

May be prepared in advance through Step 4. Do not freeze.

Serves 4 to 6

Chicken Legs with Scallion ALL REGIONS

Here is a delicious dish using the legs of the chicken.

4 tablespoons dark soy sauce	½ cup cornstarch
1 tablespoon sherry	2 to 4 cups oil for deep-frying
¼ teaspoon pepper	½ cup scallions, chopped
12 chicken legs	coarsely

1. Combine soy sauce, sherry, and pepper. Marinate chicken legs 30 minutes. Drain.
2. Coat chicken legs with cornstarch.
3. Heat oil in wok. Deep-fry legs about 4 minutes at 375 degrees or until golden brown. Drain. Remove.
4. Clean wok. Reheat 2 tablespoons oil. Add scallion and chicken. Stir-fry 1 minute. Remove to platter.

May be prepared in advance through Step 2. May not be frozen.

Serves 4 to 6

Chicken Thighs with Black Mushrooms   SHANGHAI

This is Chinese stewing, which we call "red cooking." This dish is delicious hot or cold.

10 chicken thighs
4 tablespoons dark soy sauce
2 tablespoons oil
1 slice ginger, pounded
1 scallion, cut into quarters
1 tablespoon sherry
1 cup water

12 small dried black
   mushrooms, soaked in
   boiling water 20 minutes,
   cooked 20 minutes, stems
   removed
1 tablespoon sugar
1 teaspoon cornstarch,
   dissolved in 1 teaspoon
   water

1. Marinate chicken in soy sauce 1 hour. Reserve soy sauce.
2. Heat oil. Stir-fry ginger and scallion until there is an aroma.
3. Add chicken thighs. Fry until golden brown. Add sherry, reserved soy sauce, and water. Bring to boil.
4. Cover and cook over low heat 30 minutes.
5. Add mushrooms and sugar. Simmer 10 minutes covered. Uncover. Bring to high heat. Stir-fry 5 minutes. Thicken with dissolved cornstarch.

May be prepared in advance. May be frozen.

Serves 4 to 6

You cannot quarrel with a quarreler.

Au Chicken PEKING

This sauce can be used with meat or poultry. In China each restaurant has its own special sauce. The more aged the sauce is, the better the flavor. This chicken is good as an appetizer or as a cold plate. Au is the Chinese word for marinate.

1 cup sesame seed oil	1 cinnamon stick
¼ cup dark soy sauce	3 star anise seeds
½ cup sherry	1 tablespoon Szechwan
1 scallion, cut into 2-inch	peppercorns
pieces	1 chicken, about 2½ pounds
1 slice ginger	1 tablespoon sugar

1. Pour sesame seed oil, soy sauce, and sherry into a large pot. Add scallion and ginger.
2. Place cinnamon stick, star anise seeds, and peppercorns in a cheesecloth bag. Put the bag into the sauce mixture.
3. Bring the sauce mixture to boil. Put the chicken in. Bring to boil again. Cover. Simmer on low heat about 35 to 40 minutes.
4. Add sugar. Bring to boil 5 seconds.
5. Cool the chicken. Cut into bite-size pieces for serving. Serve cold.
6. When the sauce is cold, bottle and refrigerate for future use.

May be prepared in advance. May be frozen (without sauce).

Serves 4 to 6

Boneless Jade Chicken   CANTON

The Chinese usually serve this chicken dish with the bones, but Westerners seem to like the boneless version. The grapes add exquisite color.

½ pound Ribier grapes
2 chicken breasts, boned, skinned, cut into 2-inch pieces
1 teaspoon salt
1 egg white
1 tablespoon cornstarch
2 to 4 cups oil for deep-frying
4 cloves garlic, minced
2 tablespoons fermented black beans, soaked in 2 tablespoons water and drained

1 tablespoon water
1 cup onions, diced
1 tablespoon sherry
1 cup chicken stock
1 tablespoon light soy sauce
1 teaspoon sugar
2 tablespoons cornstarch, dissolved in 2 tablespoons water
1 small red pepper, cut into 1-inch squares

1. Remove skin from grapes. Set aside.
2. Mix chicken with salt, egg white, and cornstarch.
3. Heat oil to 375 degrees. Deep-fry chicken until color changes. Drain. Remove.
4. Pound garlic and black beans together to a paste. Add water. Mix well. Set aside.
5. Reheat 2 tablespoons oil in wok. Stir-fry onions. Add black bean paste over low heat. Stir-fry 1 minute. Raise heat. Add chicken. Add sherry, stock, soy sauce, sugar, and dissolved cornstarch. Bring sauce to boil. Add red pepper. Boil 1 minute. Add grapes and boil 1 minute more. Remove to a serving platter.

May be prepared in advance through Step 4. May not be frozen.

Serves 4 to 6

Chicken with Asparagus   ALL REGIONS

One of the easy recipes with gourmet results.

1 pound chicken breast,
  boned, skinned, cut into
  thin slices 1½ inches long
1 teaspoon salt
1 egg white
1 tablespoon cornstarch
2 to 4 cups oil for deep-frying
1 slice ginger, minced
1 scallion, shredded
1 clove garlic, minced
1 pound asparagus,* cut
  diagonally into 1-inch
  pieces

Sauce:
4 tablespoons oyster sauce
6 tablespoons chicken stock
1 tablespoon sherry
1 tablespoon light soy sauce
1 tablespoon sugar
1½ teaspoons cornstarch

1. Combine sauce ingredients. Set aside.
2. Combine chicken, salt, egg white, and cornstarch. Mix well with hand.
3. Heat oil to 350 degrees in wok. Deep-fry chicken until color changes. Drain. Remove.
4. Reheat 2 tablespoons oil on low heat. Stir-fry ginger, scallion, and garlic 30 seconds.
5. Add asparagus. Stir-fry on high heat 1 minute.
6. Pour in the sauce mixture. Bring to boil. Add chicken. Stir-fry briskly. Serve at once.

---

*If asparagus is not in season, use broccoli.

May be prepared in advance through Step 3. May not be frozen.

Serves 4 to 6

Chicken with Garlic Sauce   SZECHWAN

Elegant and light—don't worry, the garlic is not overwhelming.

1 pound chicken breast,
   boned, skinned, cut into
   small cubes
1 teaspoon salt
1 egg white
1 tablespoon cornstarch
2 to 4 cups oil for deep-frying
4 large cloves garlic, minced
4 slices ginger, chopped
½ cup dried black
   mushrooms, soaked in
   boiling water 20 minutes,
   stems removed, cut into
   quarters
4 water chestnuts, sliced thin
1 cup snow peas, strings
   removed

2 scallions, chopped fine
1 teaspoon chili paste with
   garlic (optional)

Sauce:
¼ cup plus 2 tablespoons
   chicken stock
2 teaspoons cornstarch
2 tablespoons light soy sauce
1 tablespoon sherry
1 tablespoon pepper oil (see
   Index)
1 teaspoon red wine vinegar
1 teaspoon sugar
2 cloves garlic, chopped

1. Combine chicken with salt, egg white, and cornstarch. Mix
   well with hand. Combine sauce ingredients in a bowl. Set
   aside.
2. Heat oil in wok to 375 degrees. Deep-fry chicken. Drain.
   Remove.
3. Return 1 tablespoon oil to wok. Stir-fry garlic over low heat.
   Turn heat up. Add ginger, mushrooms, water chestnuts, snow
   peas, and scallions. Stir-fry 1 minute.
4. Pour in the sauce mixture. Bring to boil. Add chicken. Add
   chili paste. Serve hot.

May be prepared in advance through Step 2. May be frozen.

Serves 4 to 6

Chicken with Double Mushrooms   ALL REGIONS

The combination of fresh and dried mushrooms gives this dish a dual personality.

1 pound chicken breast, boned, skinned, cut into cubes
½ teaspoon salt
1 egg white
1 tablespoon cornstarch
2 to 4 cups oil for deep-frying
½ pound fresh mushrooms, sliced, stems removed
6 dried black mushrooms, soaked in boiling water 20 minutes, cooked 20 minutes, stems removed, cut into quarters
4 water chestnuts, sliced thin

Sauce:
2 tablespoons light soy sauce
1 teaspoon sugar
1 tablespoon sherry
4 tablespoons chicken stock
1 teaspoon cornstarch

1. Mix chicken with salt, egg white, and cornstarch. Use hands to mix. Set aside 10 minutes.
2. Combine sauce ingredients in a bowl. Set aside.
3. Heat oil in wok. Deep-fry chicken 1 minute. Drain. Remove.
4. Return 2 tablespoons oil to wok. Stir-fry fresh mushrooms 30 seconds. Add black mushrooms and water chestnuts. Stir-fry 30 seconds more.
5. Pour in the sauce mixture. Bring to boil.
6. Pour in chicken. Stir-fry until thoroughly heated.

May be prepared in advance through Step 3. May not be frozen.

Serves 4 to 6

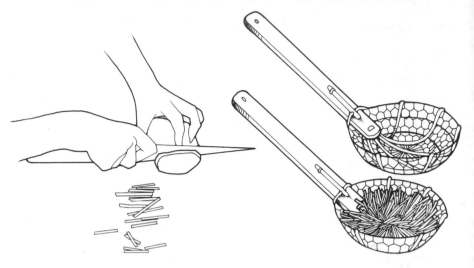

Chicken in Taro Root Basket   ALL REGIONS

Taro root belongs to the potato family. You can obtain it in Chinatown. The basket looks elegant and the chicken is delicious enough to feature at your next party. Potato or noodles may be used as a substitute for the taro root.

Taro Root Basket

1½ cups taro root, peeled and
   shredded like matchsticks
1½ tablespoons flour
1 teaspoon salt

Pinch of white pepper
1 tablespoon water
2 to 4 cups oil for deep-frying

1. Put taro shreds in a bowl. Mix with flour, salt, pepper, and water.
2. Heat oil for deep-frying. Dip large strainer in oil to heat (about 2 minutes). Drain.
3. Arrange taro shreds evenly in the strainer. Place second smaller strainer on top of the taro to hold its shape.
4. Fry basket on high heat, spooning oil onto basket. Fry until golden brown about 5 minutes.
5. Remove top strainer. With knife carefully remove basket.

May be prepared in advance (keep warm in oven). May not be frozen.

Chicken Filling

1 pound chicken, boned,
  skinned, cut into ½-inch
  cubes
1 teaspoon salt
1 egg white
1 tablespoon cornstarch
2 to 4 cups oil for deep-frying
1 cup cashew nuts
1 slice ginger, minced
1 scallion, chopped fine
1 clove garlic, minced
½ red pepper, cut into ½-inch
  cubes
½ green pepper, cut into ½-
  inch cubes

Sauce:
4 tablespoons chicken stock
1 tablespoon sherry
1 teaspoon sugar
1 teaspoon cornstarch
2 tablespoons light soy sauce

1. Mix chicken with salt, egg white, and cornstarch. Use hands. Set aside 10 minutes.
2. Combine sauce ingredients. Set aside.
3. Heat oil in wok. Deep-fry cashew nuts in a strainer until golden brown. Drain. Remove.
4. Reheat oil. Deep-fry chicken until color changes. Drain. Remove.
5. Return 2 tablespoons oil to wok. Stir-fry ginger, scallion, and garlic 30 seconds. Add red and green peppers. Stir-fry 30 seconds more.
6. Pour in the sauce mixture. Bring to boil. Pour in chicken. Add cashew nuts. Stir-fry briskly 1 minute.
7. Pour chicken into taro root basket. Serve immediately.

May be prepared in advance through Step 4. May not be frozen.

Serves 4 to 6

Chicken with Fungus and Cucumber   PEKING

Fungus is good for the heart. The cucumber lends a special and unique flavor, as well as crisp texture and color. This is a well-balanced dish.

2 whole chicken breasts, boned, skinned, cut into cubes
1 teaspoon salt
1 egg white
1 tablespoon cornstarch
2 to 4 cups oil for deep-frying
2 slices ginger, minced
1 clove garlic, minced
1 tablespoon cilantro (Chinese parsley), chopped fine
2 tablespoons dried fungus, soaked in boiling water at least 20 minutes

1 cucumber, skin on, cut in half lengthwise, seeded, cut into ¼-inch pieces crosswise

Sauce:
2 tablespoons light soy sauce
1 tablespoon sherry
¼ teaspoon salt
¼ teaspoon sugar
4 tablespoons chicken stock
1 teaspoon cornstarch
2 teaspoons sesame seed oil

1. Mix chicken with salt, egg white, and cornstarch.
2. Heat oil to 375 degrees. Deep-fry chicken until color changes. Drain. Remove.
3. Put ginger, garlic, and cilantro in a bowl. Combine sauce ingredients in another bowl.
4. Reheat 2 tablespoons oil in wok. Stir-fry ginger, garlic, and cilantro 30 seconds. Remove.
5. Reheat 2 tablespoons oil in wok. Stir-fry fungus and cucumber vigorously 1 minute. Pour in sauce. Add ginger, garlic, and cilantro. Bring to boil.
6. Add chicken. Stir-fry until chicken is glazed.

May be prepared in advance. May be frozen.

Serves 4 to 6

Chicken with Five-Spice Powder   ALL REGIONS

Five-spice powder was used as a medicinal aid in China. A blend of five aromatic spices—star anise, fennel, Szechwan peppercorns, cloves, and Chinese cinnamon are ground together into a fine powder. It is helpful for digestion and gives warmth to the body.

1 3-pound fryer, cut into 1½-inch pieces	1 teaspoon five-spice powder
3 tablespoons light soy sauce	¾ cup chicken stock
2 tablespoons oil	1 teaspoon sugar
2 tablespoons onion, chopped fine	1 tablespoon cornstarch, dissolved in 2 tablespoons water

1. Put chicken in bowl with soy sauce. Marinate 1 hour. Drain well. Reserve soy sauce.
2. Heat oil in wok. Stir-fry chicken pieces until brown. Add onion. Stir-fry 1 minute more.
3. Add five spice powder, stock, sugar, and the reserved soy sauce. Cover. Simmer 45 minutes.
4. Bring to high heat. Thicken with dissolved cornstarch. Serve hot.

May be prepared in advance. May be frozen.

Serves 4 to 6

Cooking and life are the same—
you never stop learning and discovering.

Chicken Velvet with Fava Beans   ALL REGIONS

This is a colorful dish; the white chicken velvet is a background for the green fava beans and the red Virginia ham.

1 pound chicken breast, skinned, boned
2 teaspoons salt
1 tablespoon sherry
5 egg whites, beaten slightly stiff
1 cup fava beans, shelled, skins removed or frozen peas, blanched in boiling water 1 minute

2 tablespoons oil
2 cups chicken stock
1 tablespoon cornstarch, dissolved in 1 teaspoon water
2 tablespoons cooked Virginia ham, chopped

1. Mince the chicken or grind in a food processor to a paste. Add 1 teaspoon salt, sherry, and 1 egg white. Mix well. Fold in remaining egg whites, one at a time, mixing well after each addition.
2. Cook fava beans 5 minutes in boiling water. Rinse in cold water. Drain and dry.
3. Heat oil in wok. Stir-fry fava beans 1 minute. Pour in stock. Add remaining salt.
4. Pour in the chicken mixture. Carefully stir-fry 1 minute more. Thicken with dissolved cornstarch. Remove to a serving dish.
5. Sprinkle ham on top. Serve hot.

May be prepared in advance through Step 2. May not be frozen.

Serves 4 to 6

Spicy Chicken   SZECHWAN

Equally delicious served as an appetizer or main dish.

1 pound chicken breast
½ teaspoon salt
4 to 5 tablespoons flour
1 egg
2 cups oil for deep-frying
¼ cup onion, chopped fine
2 scallions, chopped fine
4 slices ginger, chopped
   fine

¼ cup tomato catsup
¼ cup chicken stock
1 tablespoon sugar
1 tablespoon sherry
2 tablespoons chili paste
   with garlic (use 1
   tablespoon, if you prefer
   less spice)

1. Cut chicken into cubes diagonally. Add salt, flour, and egg.
   Mix well with hand.
2. Heat oil in wok. Deep-fry chicken about 1 minute. Drain.
   Remove.
3. Reheat 2 tablespoons oil in wok. Stir-fry onion, scallions,
   and ginger 1 minute. Add catsup, stock, and sugar. Bring to
   boil.
4. Pour in chicken. Add sherry and chili paste with garlic. Stir-
   fry briskly 1 minute.

May be prepared in advance through Step 2. May be frozen.

Serves 4 to 6

Curry Chicken   MADAME WONG'S CREATION

Here again we are using condiments from India for a beautiful Chinese banquet dish.

1 pound chicken breasts,
   boned, skinned
1 teaspoon salt
1 egg white
1 tablespoon cornstarch
2 to 4 cups oil for deep-frying
½ pound string beans, cut
   into 1-inch pieces

Sauce:
1 small onion, chopped fine
2 tablespoons tomato paste
2 tablespoons curry paste
1 tablespoon curry powder
1 teaspoon sugar
¼ cup chicken stock

1. Cut chicken into shreds. Mix with salt, egg white, and cornstarch. Mix well with hand. Set aside.
2. Heat 2 tablespoons oil in wok. Stir-fry onion. Add remaining sauce ingredients. Stir until well mixed. Remove. Set aside.
3. Heat oil for deep-frying. Deep-fry chicken until white. Drain. Remove. Deep-fry string beans 2 minutes. Drain. Remove.
4. Return sauce to wok. Bring to boil. Add chicken and string beans. Stir-fry thoroughly. Remove to a serving platter.

May be prepared in advance through Step 3. May be frozen.

Serves 4 to 6

Don't be proud of your goodness.

Eight Precious Chicken   SHANGHAI

Such a delightful name for a dish. It is equally delightful to taste. You will love the stuffing. Serve with stir-fried broccoli.

1 whole roasting chicken, about 3 pounds
4 ounces pork, shredded
1 egg white
1 tablespoon cornstarch
2 tablespoons oil
1 slice ginger, minced
1 scallion, chopped fine
1 tablespoon sherry
3 tablespoons dark soy sauce
6 water chestnuts, cut in half
6 chestnuts, peeled, cooked in boiling water, cut in half

10 lotus seeds, soaked overnight, then simmered 30 minutes
3 dried black mushrooms, soaked in boiling water 20 minutes, cooked 20 minutes, stems removed, diced
1 cup cooked glutinous rice*
Pinch of salt
2 tablespoons white corn syrup
1 tablespoon sesame seed oil

1. Wipe chicken dry. Mix pork with egg white and cornstarch, using hand.
2. Heat oil in wok. Stir-fry ginger and scallion on low heat until there is an aroma. Add pork. Stir-fry on high heat until color changes. Add sherry, 2 tablespoons soy sauce, water chestnuts, chestnuts, lotus seeds, and mushrooms. Stir-fry until well mixed.
3. Add the above mixture to cooked glutinous rice. Mix well. Add remaining soy sauce.
4. Stuff the chicken with the rice mixture. Close by sewing. Sprinkle with salt. Brush with corn syrup and sesame seed oil. Brush roasting pan with additional sesame seed oil.
5. Roast chicken at 375 degrees 45 to 50 minutes.

---

*To cook the rice: Wash and rinse thoroughly. Add water to 1 inch above the level of the rice. Bring to boil. Cover and simmer 30 minutes. Cool and use for the stuffing mixture.

May be prepared in advance through Step 4. May be frozen.

Serves 4 to 6

Lemon Chicken II   ALL REGIONS

This is a new version of an extremely popular dish. The sauce is simple to prepare.

2 whole chicken breasts,
   boned, skinned
1 teaspoon salt
½ teaspoon pepper
4 tablespoons flour
1 cup sweet rice flour
Cold water
2 to 4 cups oil for deep-frying
1½ tablespoons cornstarch,
   dissolved in 3 tablespoons
   water
2 sliced lemons for garnish

Sauce:
1 large lemon, juice and
   grated rind
6 tablespoons sugar
4 tablespoons white vinegar
1 cup chicken stock

1. Cut each breast into 4 long pieces. Season with salt and pepper. Dredge each piece with flour. Set aside.
2. Finely grate rind from 1 large lemon. Squeeze juice from it. Mix juice and rind with other sauce ingredients. Set aside.
3. For batter mix 1 cup sweet rice flour with cold water. (Should be a little runny.) Add a pinch of salt and pepper.
4. Heat oil in wok to 375 degrees. Dip chicken in batter. Deep-fry until light golden brown. Put on platter. Keep warm.
5. Heat sauce. Stir. Bring to boil. Thicken with dissolved cornstarch.
6. Cut chicken into bite-size pieces. Pour sauce over or serve separately. Garnish with lemon slices.

May be prepared in advance through Step 4. Refry before serving. Do not freeze.

Serves 4 to 6

Sing Fong Chicken CANTON

We call this dish the "King of Kings." It takes time, but the result is worth the effort.

4 cinnamon sticks
6 star anise seeds
1 tablespoon Szechwan
   peppercorns
20 cloves
8 cups water
3 tablespoons salt
1 whole chicken
2 tablespoons honey
¼ cup water
1 tablespoon red wine
   vinegar
2 to 4 cups oil for deep-frying
Cilantro (Chinese parsley) for
   garnish

Dip:
1 tablespoon sesame seed oil
2 tablespoons light soy sauce
½ teaspoon chili oil (see
   Index) or chili paste with
   garlic
2 cloves garlic, minced

1. Wrap cinnamon, star anise seeds, peppercorns, and cloves in a cheesecloth bag and tie tightly. Bring water to a boil. Add spice bag and salt. Cook uncovered 15 minutes.
2. Attach hook* to neck of chicken. Dip chicken, breast down, in spiced water. Spoon water on chicken 3 minutes. Turn off heat. Cover and let chicken stand in water 10 minutes.
3. Lift chicken out of water. Bring water to boil again and return chicken, back first this time. Turn off heat and cover. Let stand 10 minutes.
4. Remove chicken and hang in a windy place for 12 hours.
5. Put honey, water, and vinegar in saucepan. Heat. With hands rub the chicken with this syrup. Rehang chicken 2 hours.
6. Mix dip ingredients together.
7. Heat oil for deep-frying. Holding chicken in a strainer over the oil, baste with hot oil continuously, 15 minutes on each side. Remove to platter. Cut into serving pieces. Garnish with cilantro. Serve with dip.

---

*Top of wire hanger may be bent into "S" shape for use as hook.

May be prepared in advance through Step 6. May be frozen.

Serves 4 to 6

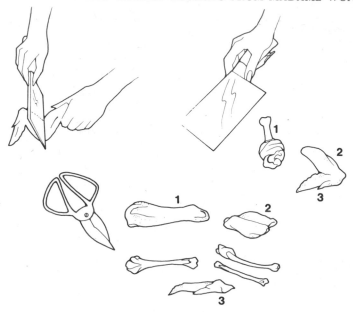

Stuffed Chicken Wings   YANGCHOW

*In Chinese this dish is called "Dragon through Phoenix."
Dragon is the king of animals and Phoenix is the queen. The
chef who created this fantasy developed a very romantic dish.*

½ pound broccoli
1 tablespoon sesame seed oil
12 chicken wings
3 whole bamboo shoots,
    boiled 20 minutes in
    chicken stock
6 dried black mushrooms,
    soaked 20 minutes in
    boiling water, stems
    removed
3 ounces cooked Virginia
    ham

2 tablespoons oil
3 slices ginger, minced
2 cloves garlic, minced
2 scallions, chopped fine
3 tablespoons sherry
2 tablespoons light soy sauce
¾ cup chicken stock
1 tablespoon cornstarch,
    dissolved in 2 tablespoons
    water
1 teaspoon sugar

1. Remove woody part from broccoli. Leave 2 inches of stem
   and flowerette. Blanch 1 minute in boiling water. Drain. Add
   sesame seed oil. Set aside.

2. Cut chicken wings in half. Remove bones with scissors from Sections 1 and 2 of illustrated wing. Discard Section 3 (tip).
3. Cut bamboo shoots, mushrooms, and ham into 24 thick, rectangular pieces.
4. Stuff the 24 boned wing sections, skin side out, with bamboo shoots, mushrooms, and ham.
5. Heat oil in wok. Stir-fry ginger, garlic, and scallions. Add wings. Brown wings slightly on both sides.
6. Add sherry, soy sauce, and stock. Bring to boil. Simmer covered 30 minutes. Thicken with dissolved cornstarch. Add sugar. Garnish with cooked broccoli.

May be prepared in advance. May be frozen.

24 Stuffed Wings

Steamed Chicken II   ALL REGIONS

This dish is delicious when served hot or cold.

6 scallions	1 teaspoon salt
6 slices ginger	1 whole 3-pound chicken
1 tablespoon sherry	4 tablespoons oil

1. Pound 2 scallions and 2 slices ginger with back of knife.
2. Shred remaining scallions and ginger. Set aside.
3. Put the crushed scallions and ginger in a bowl with sherry and salt. Mix well. Rub chicken with this mixture. Place in bowl. Set aside ½ hour.
4. Place bowl with chicken in boiling steamer. Cover and steam 30 minutes.
5. Remove chicken. Let cool. Cut into bite-size pieces.
6. Put chicken on platter. Sprinkle with shredded scallion and ginger.
7. Heat oil in wok. Pour over chicken.
8. Return oil to wok. Heat again. Splash oil on chicken once more.

May be prepared in advance. May be frozen.

Serves 4 to 6

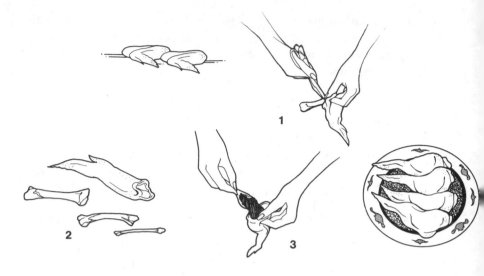

Stuffed Chicken Wings Thai Style   THAILAND

When we teach this dish, it always receives applause.

1½ pounds ground pork
½ pound ground chicken
3 tablespoons cilantro
   (Chinese parsley), chopped
3 tablespoons light soy sauce
1 teaspoon white pepper
2 cloves garlic, minced
1 tablespoon sugar
½ cup vermicelli, soaked in
   boiling water 30 minutes,
   drained
12 chicken wings
Salt
Pepper
Flour
2 to 4 cups oil for deep-frying

Batter:
1½ cups rice flour
1 cup water
½ teaspoon salt
⅛ teaspoon pepper

Cucumber sauce:
4 tablespoons sugar
4 tablespoons white vinegar
½ cup water
½ tablespoon pepper oil (see
   Index) or chili paste with
   garlic
1 tablespoon cornstarch,
   dissolved in 2 tablespoons
   water
¼ cucumber, skin on, cubed

1. Combine all of the sauce ingredients, except for cucumber
   and cornstarch. Heat in saucepan and thicken with dissolved
   cornstarch. Add cucumber at the last minute before serving.

2. Combine pork, chicken, cilantro, soy sauce, pepper, garlic, and sugar. Let stand at room temperature 1 hour. Add vermicelli.
3. To bone chicken wings, start at the large end and carefully push the meat down the bone. Use a scissors or knife to work the meat away from the bone. Bone out the first two joints and leave the tip intact.
4. Mix ingredients of batter together thoroughly.
5. Stuff the ground pork and chicken mixture into the boned wings. Be careful not to stuff them too full. Sprinkle wings with salt, pepper, and a little flour. Dip wings into batter.
6. Heat oil until smoking hot. Fry wings about 5 minutes on each side or until golden brown. Drain on paper towels, slice. Serve with cucumber sauce.

May be prepared in advance. Refry before serving. May be frozen.

Serves 4 to 6

Cooking is like music when properly conducted—
a symphony results.

Wu Lu Chicken   PEKING

This is an unusual chicken dish we had in Peking. It has a delicious, distinctive herb and spice flavoring. It is steamed and then fried.

10 cups water
4 cinnamon sticks
6 star anise seeds
30 whole cloves
2 whole nutmegs, slightly cracked
1 tablespoon Szechwan peppercorns

2 tablespoons salt
1 whole chicken, about 3 pounds
2 tablespoons dark soy sauce
4 tablespoons flour
2 to 4 cups oil for deep-frying

1. Pour water into wok. Add spices and salt. Bring to boil. Simmer 15 minutes.
2. Dip chicken into water. Spoon water onto chicken 3 minutes.
3. Let chicken remain in water 10 minutes. Remove chicken from wok.
4. Bring water to boil again. Return chicken to wok 10 minutes more. Drain. Remove.
5. Steam chicken over boiling water on high heat 35 minutes. Cool.
6. Brush chicken with dark soy sauce. Cut in half and coat heavily with flour.
7. Heat oil for deep-frying. Fry chicken until crispy, breast side down first, 5 minutes each side.
8. Cut into bite-size pieces. Arrange on platter to resemble flattened whole chicken.

May be prepared in advance through Step 6 or frozen after Step 5.

Serves 4 to 6

Sweet Sour Chicken   CANTON

*The Chinese use soy sauce in their sweet sour sauces. Catsup is
used by Westerners.*

1 **pound chicken breast,
   boned, skinned, cut into 1-
   Inch pieces**
1 **teaspoon salt**
1 **egg**
6 **tablespoons cornstarch**
2 **to 4 cups oil for deep-frying**

Sauce:
1 **cup water**
4 **tablespoons sugar**
4 **tablespoons tomato catsup**
4 **tablespoons white vinegar**
2 **tablespoons cornstarch,
   dissolved in 4 tablespoons
   water**
½ **red pepper, cut into 1-inch
   cubes**
½ **green pepper, cut into 1-
   inch cubes**
16 **canned pineapple chunks**

1. Combine chicken, salt, egg, and cornstarch. Mix well with
   hand. Heat oil until it is smoking hot. Drop chicken into oil
   one piece at a time. Deep-fry until crispy, about 3 minutes.
   Remove. Set aside.
2. To make sauce: Pour water, sugar, tomato catsup, and
   vinegar into saucepan. Bring to boil. Stir in dissolved cornstarch. Add peppers and pineapple chunks.
3. Reheat oil until it is smoking hot. Fry chicken 1 minute
   more. Remove to platter. Pour sauce over chicken. Serve hot.

May be prepared in advance through Step 1. May not be frozen.

Serves 4 to 6

Chicken with Green Peas on Fluffy Rice Sticks SHANGHAI

Rice sticks must be deep-fried very, very fast to remain fluffy and white.

2 to 4 cups oil for deep-frying
4 ounces rice sticks (Py Mai
   Fun)
½ pound ground chicken
1 teaspoon salt
Pinch of pepper
2 teaspoons cornstarch
1 egg white
1 box frozen peas

½ teaspoon sugar
1 tablespoon sherry
2 tablespoons chicken stock
1 teaspoon chili paste with
   garlic (optional)
2 tablespoons cooked
   Virginia ham, cut into
   cubes

1. Heat oil in wok. Deep-fry rice sticks quickly, a few at a time, until they puff. Takes about 1 second. Drain. Remove to paper towel.
2. Mix chicken with ½ teaspoon salt, pepper, cornstarch, and egg white. Mix until smooth.
3. Reheat 1 tablespoon oil in wok. Pour in peas. Stir-fry 1 minute. Add remaining salt and sugar.
4. Add chicken, sherry, chicken stock, and chili paste. Stir-fry about 1 minute.
5. Put the chicken and pea mixture in center of platter. Sprinkle ham on top. Garnish platter with rice sticks.

May be prepared in advance through Step 3. May not be frozen.

Serves 4 to 6

Chicken Salad with Rice Sticks   CANTON

This salad received raves in our first book. We have changed the sauce and added sesame seeds. You may also shred ham and mix with the chicken.

4 ounces rice sticks (Py Mai
   Fun)
2 to 4 cups oil for deep-frying
1 whole chicken breast*
½ teaspoon salt
2 tablespoon light soy sauce
1 head lettuce, shredded
½ cup toasted sesame seeds
½ cup preserved red ginger,
   chopped

Sauce;
¼ cup sesame seed oil
Pinch of salt
½ teaspoon sugar
¼ cup red wine vinegar
¼ cup light soy sauce
2 scallions, chopped fine
1 teaspoon hot pepper oil
   (optional)

1. Deep-fry rice sticks quickly, a few at a time, in very hot oil until they puff, about 1 second. Drain. Remove.
2. Rub chicken with salt and soy sauce. Place in shallow pan. Pour 1 tablespoon heated oil over chicken. Roast 45 minutes in 350-degree oven
3. When chicken is cool, discard skin and bones and break meat apart with hands into shreds. Do not cut.
4. Combine first 5 ingredients of sauce in serving bowl. Mix well. Add scallions and hot pepper oil (this will make sauce spicy).
5. Add lettuce, chicken, and sesame seeds to sauce. Toss well. Arrange rice sticks on top. Garnish with preserved red ginger. Serve cold.

----

*You may substitute crab, lobster, shrimp, or barbecued pork for chicken.

May be prepared in advance through Step 4. Only cooked chicken may be frozen.

Serves 4 to 6

Pon Pon Chicken   SZECHWAN

This is a cold dish. Pon Pon means shredded. It is delectable in the summertime.

2 pieces mung bean sheet*
2 cups cold cooked chicken, shredded
1 cucumber, peeled, seeded, shredded
Several sprigs cilantro (Chinese parsley) for garnish

Sauce:
3 tablespoons sesame seed paste or peanut butter
3 tablespoons cold chicken stock
1 tablespoon pepper oil (see Index)
2 tablespoons light soy sauce
2 tablespoons red wine vinegar
1 tablespoon sesame seed oil
½ teaspoon peppercorn salt (see Index)
1 teaspoon sugar
2 cloves garlic, minced fine

1. Soak mung bean sheets in boiling water 5 minutes. Drain. Cover with cold water until cool. Drain again. Cut into thick shreds 2 inches in length.
2. Dilute the sesame seed paste with cold stock. Add remaining sauce ingredients.
3. Remove mung bean sheets to platter. Pour half of the sauce on mung bean sheets. Put shredded chicken and cucumber on mung bean sheets, then pour remaining sauce over. Garnish with cilantro.

---

*You may substitute ½ pound blanched bean sprouts.

May be prepared in advance through Step 2. May not be frozen.

Serves 4 to 6

Deep-Fried Cornish Hen   ALL REGIONS

The hen is so well flavored by the marinade.

3 **Cornish hens, cut into**
   quarters
¾ **to 1 cup cornstarch**
2 **to 4 cups oil for deep-frying**

Marinade:
4 **tablespoons dark soy sauce**
2 **slices ginger, pounded**
2 **scallions, cut into quarters**
1 **teaspoon sugar**
2 **tablespoons sherry**

1. Combine marinade ingredients. Marinate the Cornish hens. Set aside at least 30 minutes.
2. Remove hens. Drain. Dredge all over with cornstarch.
3. Heat oil in wok. Deep-fry hens, one piece at a time until golden brown.
4. Deep-fry once more before serving until very crisp. Cut into bite-size pieces. Serve with peppercorn salt (see Index).

May be prepared in advance through Step 3. May be frozen.

Serves 4 to 6

Wherever you go, whomever you are with, you are as big as the biggest and small as the smallest.

5

Duck and Squab

Duck belongs to the group of foods called Yin because the habitat of the duck is water. In China each region has its own duck. The Peking duck reigns supreme. When preparing duck, try to buy a fresh one in Chinatown. It is more flavorful and fresher than those in local markets. There are many ways of making duck. We are introducing you to some interesting recipes you will surely enjoy.

The Chinese are great lovers of squab as well as duck. We have included two unique squab recipes in this chapter.

93

Braised Duck in Wine   CANTON

The French are known for Duck a l'Orange. The Chinese chefs created their own version. The Chinese eat braised duck by picking at it with their chopsticks.

1 4- to 5-pound duck, cut
   into 2½-inch pieces
1 leek, cut into 1-inch pieces
1 cup sherry
1 orange, skin and seeds
   removed, cut into 1-inch pieces

½ cup water
4 tablespoons dark soy sauce
2 tablespoons sugar
Orange slices for garnish

1. Put duck in large pot or wok. Add leek and sherry. Bring to boil. Add orange, water, soy sauce, and sugar. Bring to boil again.
2. Cover. Simmer 1½ hours. Turn occasionally to prevent burning. Remove grease.
3. Bring to high heat. Baste until glazed.
4. Remove to platter. Garnish with orange slices.

May be prepared in advance. May be frozen.

Serves 4 to 6

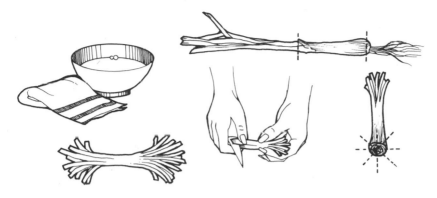

Chinese Roast Duck

The Chinese did not have ovens in their homes so they improvised their own way of preparing this duck dish.

1 duck, about 5 pounds
2 teaspoons salt
1 cup brown sugar
4 cloves garlic, minced
4 tablespoons light soy sauce

2 medium-size sweet
  potatoes, peeled, cut into
  2-inch pieces
1 cup water

1. Rub duck with salt inside and out. Place duck in roasting pan, breast side down.
2. Mix brown sugar, garlic, and soy sauce. Pour on duck.
3. Boil sweet potatoes 3 minutes in water. Set aside.
4. Roast duck in preheated 350-degree oven 30 minutes.
5. Turn duck and roast 30 minutes more. Turn again and roast 1 hour. Add potato and water during last 30 minutes.
6. Skim off fat. Serve with plum sauce or gravy from duck. Garnish with scallion flowerettes.*

---

*All duck recipes may be garnished with scallion flowerettes. Put trimmed scallions in cold water to flower.

May be prepared in advance. May be frozen.

Serves 4 to 6

Crispy Duck II ALL REGIONS

An easy way to make an excellent duck dish.

1 duck, about 5 pounds	2 tablespoons light soy sauce
1 tablespoon salt	1 teaspoon sugar
½ cup flour mixed with 2 teaspoons five-spice powder	2 tablespoons sherry
	4 to 6 cups oil for deep-frying

1. Rub duck inside and out with salt and half the flour mixture.
2. Place duck on platter. Steam 2 hours over boiling water. Remove.
3. Rub soy sauce, sugar, and sherry on duck. Sprinkle remaining flour on duck. Pat well all over. Set aside until the mixture is dry on duck, about 1 hour.
4. Heat oil in wok. Deep-fry duck, turning, until golden brown.
5. Cut into bite-size pieces. Serve with peppercorn salt or plum sauce.

May be prepared in advance. Refry before serving. May be frozen.

Serves 4 to 6

Duck Steamed with Wine   CANTON

Your guests will be impressed by this easy duck recipe.

1 4½-pound duck	2 slices ginger, pounded
4 tablespoons oil	1 teaspoon sugar
1 tablespoon salt	1 tablespoon light soy sauce
1 scallion, cut into quarters	1 cup sherry

1. Wash duck. Dry thoroughly with paper towel inside and out.
2. Heat oil. Fry duck, turning, until light brown. Remove.
3. Rinse duck in cold water. Drain.
4. Rub duck with salt inside and out.
5. Put scallion and ginger inside duck.
6. Place duck in bowl. Sprinkle with sugar. Pour soy sauce and sherry over.
7. Put bowl on rack in boiling steamer. Steam duck on low heat 2 hours or until meat is tender. Serve hot or cold.

May be prepared in advance. May be frozen.

Serves 4 to 6

First we drink the wine, then the wine drinks the wine,
then the wine drinks us.

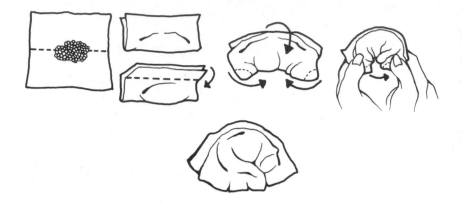

Duck in Casserole with Won Ton   HANGCHOW

This is a famous Hangchow dish. There is a restaurant near the West Lake where Emperor Chien Lung ate 200 years ago. It is called Lui Wai Lui. This dish is one of their specialties. We had it when we were in Hangchow at the very same restaurant.

1 duck, about 5 pounds	1 celery cabbage (1 pound),
2 slices ginger, pounded	cut into 1-inch pieces
1 scallion, cut into quarters	24 boiled won tons
1 tablespoon sherry	4 ounces cooked Virginia
	ham, sliced thin

1. Remove fat from duck. Wash it thoroughly. Pat dry.
2. Place duck in casserole. Add water to cover. Add ginger, scallion, and sherry. Bring to boil. Cover. Simmer 2 hours.
3. Skim off fat. Add celery cabbage. Cook 20 minutes more.
4. Arrange won tons around the sides of duck. Spread ham on top. Cook 5 minutes. May be served directly from casserole.

May be prepared in advance through Step 3. May be frozen after Step 3.

Serves 4 to 6

Won Tons   ALL REGIONS

½ pound ground pork*
¼ teaspoon salt
½ tablespoon light soy sauce
½ tablespoon sherry
2 water chestnuts, chopped fine

1 scallion, chopped fine
½ egg, beaten
2 leaves bok choy** (Chinese green), optional
24 won ton wrappers
4 cups boiling water

1. Combine pork with salt, soy sauce, sherry, water chestnuts, scallion, beaten egg, and bok choy. Mix well. This is the won ton filling.
2. Put 1 teaspoon filling in center of each wrapper. Fold to the center. Gently press edges together. Fold in half again lengthwise; then fold back and bring ends together.
3. Dab a little water on one corner, put two corners one over the other, and press together. Won ton properly made resembles a nurse's cap.
4. Put won tons in boiling water 4 minutes until they float to top. Rinse in cold water. Remove.

---

*Beef, veal, turkey, or chicken may be used in place of pork.
**Dip bok choy into boiling water, boil 1 minute. Drain. Squeeze out water and finely chop.

May be prepared in advance through Step 3. May be frozen after Step 3.

24 Won Tons

Duck with Spinach   PEKING

This dish was eaten by the wife of a famous Chinese statesman in Hong Kong. She enjoyed it so much, she asked to meet the chef who prepared it.

1 **5-pound duck**	3 **tablespoons sugar**
4 **tablespoons light soy sauce**	1 **tablespoon dark soy sauce**
2 **scallions**	¾ **cup chicken stock**
2 **large slices ginger, mashed**	3 **bunches spinach, cleaned,**
5 **cloves garlic**	**stems removed**
3 **star anise seeds**	½ **teaspoon salt**
1 **cup oil**	4 **scallion flowerettes**
3 **tablespoons sherry**	

1. Place duck in pot of boiling water. Keep turning for about 3 minutes. Drain. Remove.
2. Put duck on large plate. Rub 1 tablespoon light soy sauce on front and 1 on back. Place scallions, ginger, garlic, and star anise seeds on same plate. Set aside.
3. A few hours before serving, heat 1 cup oil in a large, heavy pot. Wait until it is sizzling. Put duck in pot breast side down. Turn when browned.* Brown other side. Keep turning to brown all sides. Takes about 25 minutes. Turn heat down. Add scallion, ginger, garlic, and anise when almost browned.
4. Remove duck and oil from pot. Return duck. Add sherry, sugar, dark soy sauce, remaining light soy sauce, and stock. Cover and cook over low heat 1 hour. Turn and baste duck occasionally. Turn heat up. Bring to boil. Baste until glazed.
5. Stir-fry spinach and salt in 2 tablespoons oil. Place spinach on platter.
6. Place duck on cutting board. Remove wings and drumsticks. Chop in pieces to resemble flattened whole duck. Arrange over spinach on platter. Serve with sauce and scallion flowerettes.

---

*Be very careful when turning duck while oil is sizzling.

May be prepared in advance through Step 4. May be frozen after Step 4.

Serves 4 to 6

Fragrant Duck ALL REGIONS

This is another way of braising a duck with sweet potatoes. Taro root is just as good.

1 duck, about 4 to 5 pounds
3 tablespoons dark soy sauce
2 tablespoons oil
1 clove garlic, minced
1 slice ginger, minced
2 star anise seeds
1 tablespoon sherry
1 tablespoon sugar

2 medium sweet potatoes, peeled, cut into 1-inch cubes
1 tablespoon cornstarch, dissolved in 2 tablespoons water
Scallion flowerettes for garnish

1. Rub duck with 1 tablespoon dark soy sauce.
2. Heat oil in wok. Fry duck, turning, until light brown. Remove.
3. In the same oil, stir-fry garlic and ginger 30 seconds. Return duck to wok. Add star anise seeds, sherry, sugar, remaining soy sauce, and water to half cover the duck. Cover and simmer 1½ hours. Skim off fat.
4. Add sweet potatoes. Cook 20 minutes more. Thicken with dissolved cornstarch.
5. Put duck on platter. Garnish with scallion flowerettes.

May be prepared in advance. May be frozen.

Serves 4 to 6

Mock Peking Duck   PEKING

Making Peking Duck is a time-consuming affair. Here is an easy way. Beer is the secret ingredient.

1 5-pound duck	**6 tablespoons hoisin sauce**
12 ounces beer	**6 scallion flowerettes**
6 Chinese pancakes (recipe below)	

1. Wash and clean duck. Pat dry.
2. Hang duck by neck 8 hours in an airy place.
3. Place duck in roasting pan. Rub beer on skin thoroughly.
4. Roast duck in preheated oven, breast side up, at 350 degrees 30 minutes. Turn duck and roast 45 minutes. Turn duck back to its original position and roast 30 minutes more.
5. Use a sharp knife to cut off crispy skin. Serve meat and skin immediately on a prewarmed dish.
6. The duck is eaten rolled in Chinese pancakes that have been brushed with hoisin sauce. Garnish with scallion flowerettes.

May be prepared in advance through Step 3. May not be frozen.

Serves 4 to 6

Chinese Pancakes

These pancakes, served with Mock Peking Duck, are also served with Moo Shu Pork or any shredded meat or vegetable. Adding hoisin sauce to the center of each pancake before filling makes them even more delicious.

1 cup flour	**2 tablespoons sesame seed oil**
½ cup boiling water	**Aluminum foil**

1. Put flour in bowl. Make a well. Add boiling water. Stir quickly with chopsticks or fork until water is absorbed and all flour comes away from side of bowl.
2. Knead dough on lightly floured board until smooth.
3. Put dough in bowl and cover with damp cloth. Let stand 20 minutes.

4. Return dough to floured board. Knead a little more. Make into long, sausagelike roll about 1½ inches in diameter.
5. Cut dough into 8 even pieces. Flatten each into a very thin round cake with palm.
6. Brush one side of each pancake evenly with a little sesame seed oil. Place one on another, oiled sides together, to form 4 stacks.
7. Roll each stack into a 7-inch circle.
8. Heat ungreased frying pan on medium heat. Cook pancake on both sides until it puffs up slightly. Do not brown. Remove.
9. Separate into 2 pancakes. Repeat until all are cooked and separated.
10. Put stack of pancakes in aluminum foil. Fold over the sides to keep cakes from drying out.
11. Place foil-wrapped pancakes in a steamer. Cover and steam over boiling water about 10 minutes.

Note: These pancakes can be kept frozen for months. It is a good idea to make a large quantity so they will be ready whenever you need them.

May be prepared in advance. Resteam before serving. May be frozen. If frozen, thaw out in foil and resteam in foil 20 minutes.

8 Pancakes

Take the time to make the climb up the hill.

Leek Duck   SHANGHAI

This is a variation of Plum Duck. It is simple to prepare.

1 duck, about 4 pounds	4 leeks, cleaned, chopped
2 tablespoons light soy sauce	2 tablespoons sherry
2 tablespoons oil	2 tablespoons cornstarch,
2 slices ginger	dissolved in 2 tablespoons
2 scallions, cut into 1-inch pieces	water (optional)

1. Rub 1 tablespoon soy sauce on duck. Heat oil in wok. Stir-fry ginger and scallion 30 seconds. Add duck and fry until golden brown. Remove duck.
2. Add a little more oil if necessary and stir-fry leeks with scallions and ginger 5 minutes or until leeks are wilted.
3. Stuff duck with the leek mixture.
4. Put duck in wok. Add remaining soy sauce, sherry, and water to half cover the duck. Simmer 1½ hours or until tender.
5. Remove duck. Pour sauce into a bowl. Refrigerate overnight. The next day, skim grease from the top of sauce. Remove leeks from duck.
6. Place duck in wok. Pour sauce and leeks over duck. Heat thoroughly until the sauce is reduced to half. Add dissolved cornstarch, if necessary. Baste duck with sauce.
7. Remove to platter. Break duck apart into serving pieces.

May be prepared in advance. May be frozen.

Serves 4 to 6

Pineapple and Ginger Duck   CANTON

Pineapple is used frequently in Cantonese dishes.

1 **5-pound duck**
2 **teaspoons salt**
6 **slices canned pineapple,**
  cut into quarters
½ **cup preserved red ginger**
1 **cup pineapple juice**

3 **tablespoons syrup (from**
  preserved red ginger)
1 **tablespoon cornstarch,**
  dissolved in 2 tablespoons
  water

1. Rub duck with salt inside and out.
2. Put duck on steamer tray. Steam 1½ hours over boiling water. Cool.
3. Discard skin. Remove all meat from bones. Cut into 2-inch pieces. Arrange meat in center of platter.
4. Arrange slices of pineapple around duck. Put ginger on pineapple.
5. Put pineapple juice and syrup in saucepan. Bring to boil. Thicken with dissolved cornstarch. Pour sauce over duck. Serve immediately.

May be prepared in advance. May not be frozen.

Serves 4 to 6

Pressed Duck   CANTON

This is a popular Cantonese dish. It is interesting to note that it originated in Northern China during the Ming Dynasty (17th century). Later on it moved to the South. This is our simplified version.

1 duck, about 4 to 5 pounds
2 tablespoons light soy sauce
1 teaspoon salt
1 teaspoon sugar
2 slices ginger
1 scallion, cut into thirds
1 star anise seed
2 egg whites, slightly beaten
½ cup water chestnut powder
¼ cup cornstarch
1 tablespoon cornstarch, dissolved in 1 tablespoon water
2 to 4 cups oil for deep-frying

¼ cup almonds, toasted, finely chopped
Lettuce for garnish

Sauce:
1 tablespoon sherry
1 teaspoon white vinegar
1 teaspoon dark soy sauce
3 teaspoons sugar
1 orange, juice only
½ cup chicken stock
1 slice ginger, minced
½ teaspoon orange extract
1 tablespoon plum sauce

1. Wash and clean duck. Remove tips of wings.
2. Rub soy sauce, salt, and sugar on duck. Put ginger, scallion, and star anise seed on duck. Place duck on plate in steamer. Steam over boiling water 1½ hours or until meat is tender. Remove. Cool.
3. Combine sauce ingredients in a bowl. Set aside.
4. Place duck on flat surface. Cut into quarters. Remove breastbone and backbone from duck. Be careful so as not to tear the skin. Leave wings and drumsticks intact.
5. Brush duck with beaten egg white. Sprinkle evenly with water chestnut powder and cornstarch. Steam over boiling water about 20 minutes or until water chestnut powder is transparent. Put on platter to dry and cool.
6. Bring sauce to boil. Add dissolved cornstarch. Keep warm.
7. Heat oil to 375 degrees. Deep-fry duck 5 minutes until crispy and brown.
8. Cut off wings and drumsticks. Chop duck into serving pieces. Sprinkle almonds on top. Garnish with lettuce. Serve with sauce.

May be prepared in advance. Refry before serving. May be frozen.
                                                Serves 4 to 6

West Lake Duck   CANTON

*This recipe is almost as famous as Peking Duck. Because of the
dark soy sauce, this is called "red cooking."*

1 duck, about 4 to 5 pounds
4 tablespoons dark soy sauce
1 tablespoon sherry
2 cloves garlic, minced
½ teaspoon salt
4 tablespoons oil
4 cups chicken stock
10 dried black mushrooms,
   soaked 20 minutes in
   boiling water, stems
   removed

½ cup bamboo shoots,
   shredded
1 tablespoon sugar
2 tablespoons cornstarch,
   dissolved in 4 tablespoons
   water
Lettuce for garnish

1. Marinate duck in the next four ingredients 1 hour. Drain and
   dry. Set marinade aside.
2. Heat oil in wok. Fry duck, turning to brown all sides.
   Remove oil.
3. Put duck in wok with stock, mushrooms, bamboo shoots,
   and marinade.
4. Cover and simmer 1½ to 2 hours. Uncover. Skim off fat.
5. Add sugar. Bring to boil. Thicken with dissolved cornstarch.
6. Place duck and sauce on platter. Garnish with shredded
   lettuce.

May be prepared in advance. May be frozen.

Serves 4 to 6

To create is a gift.

Braised Squab with Oyster Sauce   CANTON

Oyster sauce gives exquisite flavor to squab. This dish has great delicacy. Stir-fried pea pods make a lovely garnish.

2 squabs
2 tablespoons oil
1 clove garlic, minced
1 slice ginger, minced
2 tablespoons oyster sauce
1 tablespoon light soy sauce

1 tablespoon sherry
1 teaspoon sugar
1 cup chicken stock
2 teaspoons cornstarch, dissolved in 4 teaspoons water

1. Cut squabs into quarters.
2. Heat oil in wok. Stir-fry garlic and ginger 30 seconds.
3. Add squab. Fry until brown all over, turn with spatula, about 3 minutes.
4. Add oyster sauce, soy sauce, sherry, sugar, and stock. Cover. Simmer 20 minutes.
5. Bring to boil. Thicken with dissolved cornstarch.

May be prepared in advance through Step 4. May be frozen.

Serves 4 to 6

Braised Squab II   CANTON

Squab cooked in any form is a specialty of Cantonese chefs.

½ teaspoon salt
¼ teaspoon pepper
2 squabs
3 tablespoons dark soy sauce
1 tablespoon sherry
2 tablespoons oil
1 medium-size onion,
  coarsely chopped

1 tablespoon Worcestershire
  sauce
1 teaspoon sugar
1 cup chicken stock
Sliced tomatoes for garnish

1. Sprinkle salt and pepper on squabs.
2. Marinate squabs in 2 tablespoons soy sauce and sherry 15 minutes.
3. Heat oil in wok. Fry squabs, turning, until completely brown. Remove.
4. Use same oil. Fry onion until it is wilted.
5. Return squabs to wok. Add 1 tablespoon soy sauce, Worcestershire sauce, sugar, and stock. Cover. Simmer 25 minutes.
6. Bring to boil. Baste until squabs are glazed. Remove. Cut into quarters.
7. Garnish with tomatoes. Serve immediately.

May be prepared in advance through Step 6. May be frozen after Step 6.

Serves 4 to 6

6

Beef

Chinese have always eaten less beef than Westerners. There is a small population of Muslims in China. They consist of only 1.5 percent of the population. They do not eat pork. Beef is meat for them. Most beef dishes are combined with vegetables and cooked rapidly. This is lower in cholesterol and calories and easier on the pocketbook than Western cooking methods. Today Americans are emulating the Chinese because they are more health conscious. Chinese cooking has increased in popularity. Chinese cuisine supports thousands of restaurants around the world; this includes Samoa and New Guinea.

Beef with Black Bean Chili Sauce   SZECHWAN

For those who enjoy hot dishes, this is an easy one.

1 pound flank steak,
  shredded
1 egg white
1 teaspoon salt
1 tablespoon cornstarch
2 to 4 cups oil for deep-frying
1 pound bok choy, cut into
  1-inch-square pieces
1 teaspoon sugar

2 slices ginger, julienne
1 scallion, chopped fine
1 clove garlic, minced
2 tablespoons black bean
  sauce with chili
½ cup chicken stock
1 tablespoon cornstarch,
  dissolved in 1 tablespoon
  water

1. Mix beef with egg white, ½ teaspoon salt, and cornstarch. Heat oil. Deep-fry beef. Drain. Remove.
2. Reheat 2 tablespoons oil in wok. Stir-fry bok choy 1 minute. Add remaining salt and sugar. Remove to platter.
3. Reheat 2 tablespoons oil in wok. On moderate heat stir-fry ginger, scallion, and garlic. Add black bean sauce with chili and chicken stock. Bring to boil. Thicken with dissolved cornstarch. Add beef and mix well.
4. Pour beef over bok choy.

May be prepared in advance. Reheat by stir-frying. May not be frozen.

Serves 4 to 6

Beef with Bean Sprouts   SHANGHAI

A simple, quick dish.

¾ pound flank steak, julienne
1½ teaspoons cornstarch
1 tablespoon light soy sauce
3½ tablespoons oil
4 cups bean sprouts
1 teaspoon salt

½ teaspoon sugar
1 teaspoon chili paste with garlic
1 teaspoon cornstarch, dissolved in 1 tablespoon water

1. Put meat in a bowl. Add cornstarch, soy sauce, and ½ tablespoon oil. Mix with hands.
2. Wash bean sprouts. Nip off ends. Drain. Set aside.
3. Heat 2 tablespoons oil in wok. Stir-fry beef until color changes. Remove.
4. Heat 1 tablespoon oil in wok. Stir-fry bean sprouts on high heat 1 minute. Add salt and sugar. Add beef. Stir-fry briskly 1 minute more. Add chili paste. Thicken with dissolved cornstarch. Stir until thoroughly heated.

May be prepared in advance through Step 3. May not be frozen.

Serves 4 to 6

A fool at 40 is a fool forever.

Beef with Scrambled Eggs   CANTON

Shredded beef can accompany anything. We were surprised to have this dish in Hong Kong. Quick and easy to prepare.

½ pound flank steak,
   shredded
5 eggs
½ teaspoon salt
3 tablespoons oil
2 scallions, chopped fine
Cilantro (Chinese parsley)

Marinade:
1 slice ginger, minced
½ teaspoon sugar
½ tablespoon sherry
1 tablespoon cornstarch
1 tablespoon light soy sauce
2 tablespoons cold water
1 tablespoon oil

1. Combine marinade ingredients. Marinate beef at least 15 minutes.
2. Beat eggs. Add salt. Mix well.
3. Heat 2 tablespoons oil in wok. Stir-fry beef until color changes. Remove.
4. Mix beef with beaten eggs.
5. Heat remaining oil in wok. Stir-fry scallions. Add the egg and meat mixture. Stir quickly until eggs are set. Remove to platter. Garnish with cilantro.

May be prepared in advance through Step 4. May not be frozen.

Serves 4 to 6

Beef Soochow

This is a simple dish for beginners. The hoisin sauce gives it a rich flavor.

1 pound flank steak, shredded	4 tablespoons hoisin sauce
½ teaspoon salt	1 tablespoon sugar
1 egg white	2 tablespoons chicken stock
1 tablespoon cornstarch	1 tablespoon sherry
2 to 4 cups oil for deep-frying	2 scallions, cut into 1-inch pieces

1. Combine beef with salt, egg white, and cornstarch. Mix well with hand.
2. Heat oil in wok. Deep-fry beef 1 minute. Drain. Remove.
3. Return 1 tablespoon oil to wok. Add hoisin sauce, sugar, stock, and sherry. Bring to boil. Slide beef in. Stir-fry 1 minute. Add scallions. Cook 1 minute more.

May be prepared in advance through Step 2. May be frozen.

Serves 4 to 6

Beef Stewed in Fruit

CANTON

This stew cooks in a casserole. The Chinese use an earthenware pot. The pot is then put on the table for serving.

1 orange	1 tablespoon A.1. Steak
1 tangerine	Sauce
1 pear	¼ teaspoon cinnamon
2 to 3 tablespoons oil	¼ teaspoon anise seed
2 pounds stewing beef, cut	powder
into 1-inch cubes	¼ teaspoon ground cloves
4 cloves garlic, minced	¼ teaspoon pepper
1 slice ginger, minced	½ teaspoon salt
½ tablespoon sugar	Juice of 1 lemon
6 tablespoons sherry	1½ cups boiling water

1. Peel orange and tangerine. Pull sections apart. Remove seeds. Peel pear. Cut into thin slices. Remove pits.
2. Heat oil in wok. Brown beef with garlic and ginger. Add sugar, sherry, A.1. Sauce, and next 5 ingredients.
3. Add orange, tangerine, pear, lemon juice, and boiling water. Simmer 1 to 1½ hours or until beef is tender.

May be prepared in advance. May be frozen.

Serves 4 to 6

Sleep in peace—wake in joy.

Beef with Onion II   ALL REGIONS

In our first book, beef with onion was most popular. This is another version we had in China.

1 **pound flank steak,
   shredded**
1 **small onion, cut into cubes**
2 **tablespoons oil**

Sauce:
4 **tablespoons chicken stock**
1 **teaspoon oyster sauce**
½ **teaspoon sugar**
1 **teaspoon cornstarch**

Marinade:
1 **tablespoon cornstarch**
1 **tablespoon oil**
1 **tablespoon dark soy sauce**
1 **tablespoon light soy sauce**
1 **teaspoon hoisin sauce**
1 **tablespoon sherry**
¼ **teaspoon salt**
Pinch of pepper

1. Combine sauce ingredients. Set aside.
2. Combine marinade ingredients. Marinate beef at least 15 minutes. Before cooking pour off any remaining marinade.
3. Heat oil in wok until it is very hot. Pour in onion. Stir-fry 1 minute. Add beef. Stir-fry 2 minutes more.
4. Stir sauce well. Pour on beef. Stir-fry quickly 1 minute more.

May be prepared in advance through Step 2. May be frozen.

Serves 4 to 6

Beef Stew Szechwan Style   SZECHWAN

A Chinese stew is easy and fun to prepare.

2 pounds stewing beef or
   chuck
2 star anise seeds
4 scallions, cut into quarters
4 slices ginger
2 tablespoons oil
5 cloves garlic, minced
¾ tablespoon Szechwan
   peppercorns

2 teaspoons crushed red chili
   peppers
3 tablespoons light soy sauce
3 tablespoons dark soy sauce
1 tablespoon sherry
½ tablespoon sugar
1 box bean curd (to-fu), cut
   into cubes

1. Cut beef into 1-inch cubes. Blanch 1 minute in boiling water. Drain. Remove. Rinse with water to remove scum.
2. Put beef into pot. Cover with boiling water. Add star anise seeds, scallions, and ginger. Set aside.
3. Heat 2 tablespoons oil in wok. Add garlic (reserve 1 teaspoon) and Szechwan peppercorns. Add crushed red chilis. Cook mixture until very brown. Add light and dark soy sauces and sherry. Cook this sauce over low heat 2 minutes.
4. Strain sauce and add to beef. Cover and simmer 1 hour. Add sugar. Add reserved garlic. Cook 1 to 2 minutes more.
5. Serve over bean curd.

May be prepared in advance through Step 4. May be frozen.

Serves 4 to 6

Braised Beef with Brown Sauce   SZECHWAN

All students love this dish because they can cook it ahead of time.

2 tablespoons oil
2 slices ginger
2 scallions, cut into thirds
1½ pounds stewing beef, cut into 1-inch cubes
1 tablespoon chili paste with garlic
1 tablespoon bean sauce
1 tablespoon tomato catsup

1 tablespoon sherry
3 tablespoons dark soy sauce
½ tablespoon sugar
4 cups chicken stock
2 carrots, cut diagonally into 2-inch pieces
1 tablespoon cornstarch, dissolved in 2 tablespoons water

1. Heat oil in wok. Stir-fry ginger and scallion until there is an aroma. Add beef. Stir-fry 2 minutes.
2. Add chili paste, bean sauce, catsup, sherry, soy sauce, and sugar. Stir-fry on low heat 2 minutes.
3. Add stock. Cook covered on low heat ½ hour. Add carrots. Cook ½ hour more.
4. Bring to boil. Thicken with dissolved cornstarch.
5. Serve in casserole.

May be prepared in advance. May be frozen.

Serves 4 to 6

Beef with Tomato   CANTON

Tomato is a surprise ingredient in Chinese dishes.

1 pound flank steak, shredded	*Sauce:*
½ teaspoon salt	2 tablespoons tomato catsup
1 egg white	1 tablespoon Worcestershire sauce
1 tablespoon cornstarch	1 table light soy sauce
2 tomatoes, medium size	½ tablespoon sugar
2 to 4 cups oil for deep-frying	1 tablespoon A.1. Steak Sauce
1 slice ginger, shredded	

1. Combine sauce ingredients.
2. Mix beef with salt, egg white, and cornstarch. Use hands.
3. Blanch tomatoes in boiling water 2 seconds. Remove skin and cut into 6 wedges each.
4. Heat oil in wok. Deep-fry beef 1 minute. Drain. Remove.
5. Return 2 tablespoons oil to wok. Stir-fry ginger and tomato 1 minute. Add beef. Stir and mix well. Pour in the sauce mixture. Bring to boil. Stir briskly until thoroughly heated and coated with sauce.

May be prepared in advance through Step 4. May not be frozen.

Serves 4 to 6

One who is quick to promise is apt to be quick to forget.

Curry Beef

*During the Ching Dynasty Emperor Chien Lung was a distin-
guished connoisseur of fine foods. The chefs were trying to
please him in every way. They introduced many imported
condiments to China; among them was curry.*

1 **pound flank steak,
  shredded**
1 **tablespoon light soy sauce**
1 **egg white**
1 **tablespoon cornstarch**
2 **to 4 cups oil for deep-frying**
1 **clove garlic, minced**
1 **small onion, cubed**
2 **tablespoons curry powder**
1 **carrot, cut diagonally into
  1-inch pieces, cooked 5
  minutes**

Sauce:
4 **tablespoons chicken stock**
1 **teaspoon cornstarch**
1 **tablespoon light soy sauce**
½ **teaspoon salt**
½ **teaspoon sugar**

1. Combine sauce ingredients.
2. Mix beef with soy sauce, egg white, and cornstarch. Set aside
   at least 15 minutes.
3. Heat oil in wok. Deep-fry beef until color changes. Drain.
   Remove.
4. Reheat 2 tablespoons oil in wok. Stir-fry garlic and onion 1
   minute. Add curry powder. Stir-fry 30 seconds. Add carrot.
   Pour in sauce. Cook on high heat 1 minute. Add beef. Stir-
   fry quickly about 15 seconds. Serve immediately.

May be prepared in advance. May be frozen.

Serves 4 to 6

Dried Spicy Beef   CANTON

In China children enjoy this as a snack. The Chinese people also like to take dried beef as refreshment on long trips.

1 **pound round steak**	*Sauce:*
2 **tablespoons oil**	½ **cup water**
1 **slice ginger**	2 **star anise seeds**
1 **scallion, cut into quarters**	1 **teaspoon cayenne pepper**
	½ **teaspoon salt**
	2 **tablespoons sugar**
	2 **tablespoons dark soy sauce**

1. Combine sauce ingredients in a bowl.
2. Cut beef into ½-inch cubes.
3. Heat oil in wok. Stir-fry ginger and scallion 30 seconds. Add beef. Stir-fry on high heat 1 minute. Add sauce. Bring to boil. Turn heat down. Cover and simmer 45 minutes.
4. Discard ginger, scallion, and star anise seeds. Bring to boil again. Cook until all liquid is evaporated. Stir constantly while cooking.
5. Spread the beef out in a baking pan.
6. Place pan in a 200-degree preheated oven. Bake 1 hour. Turn off heat. Let beef cool in the oven.
7. When cool, put in tightly covered jar and refrigerate.

May be prepared in advance. May be frozen.

Serves 4 to 6

Fried Beef and Chicken   ALL REGIONS

Served frequently by Madame Wong's family.

½ pound flank steak,
  shredded
½ pound chicken breast,
  boned, skinned, shredded
1 teaspoon salt
1 egg white
1 tablespoon cornstarch
2 to 4 cups oil for deep-frying
½ cup bamboo shoots,
  shredded

½ cup green pepper, shredded
½ tablespoon cornstarch,
  dissolved in 1 tablespoon
  water

Sauce:
2 tablespoons bean sauce
½ tablespoon sugar
2 tablespoons sherry
4 tablespoons stock

1. Combine sauce ingredients.
2. Mix beef with ½ teaspoon salt, ½ egg white, and ½ table-spoon cornstarch. Use hands to mix.
3. Mix chicken with remaining salt, egg white, and cornstarch.
4. Heat oil in wok. Deep-fry beef on high heat 1 minute. Drain. Remove.
5. Reheat oil in wok. Deep-fry chicken on moderate heat 1 minute. Drain. Remove.
6. Reheat 2 tablespoons oil in wok. Stir-fry bamboo shoots and green pepper 1 minute. Add sauce. Bring to boil. Add meat and chicken. Stir until thoroughly heated and mixed.

May be prepared in advance through Step 5. May be frozen.

Serves 4 to 6

Fried Beef with Green Pepper   CANTON

Beef with green pepper is a colorful dish. It is so quick—try it when you have unexpected guests.

1 pound beef, shredded	3 tablespoons oil
1 teaspoon salt	2 green peppers, shredded
1 egg white	1 tablespoon sherry
1 tablespoon cornstarch	2 tablespoons light soy sauce

1. Combine beef with ½ teaspoon salt, egg white, and cornstarch. Mix well with hand.
2. Heat 1 tablespoon oil in wok. Stir-fry peppers on high heat 1 minute. Add remaining salt. Stir-fry 30 seconds. Remove.
3. Heat 2 tablespoons oil in wok. Slide beef in. Stir-fry on high heat until color changes. Add peppers, sherry, and soy sauce. Stir-fry thoroughly. Remove to platter.

May be prepared in advance. May not be frozen.

Serves 4 to 6

Be lenient and generous while you can.

Orange or Tangerine Peel Beef   SZECHWAN

This version was created by the chef at the Shanghai Winter Garden Restaurant in Los Angeles. Many students have requested this recipe.

1 **pound flank steak**
1 **tablespoon dark soy sauce**
1 **teaspoon sugar**
1 **egg**
6 **tablespoons flour**
2 to 4 **cups oil for deep-frying**
10 **dried red chili peppers**
¼ **cup dried orange or tangerine peel***
1 **tablespoon cornstarch, dissolved in 1 tablespoon water**

Sauce:
2 **tablespoons frozen orange juice concentrate**
2 **tablespoons dark soy sauce**
4 **tablespoons sugar**
1 **tablespoon tomato catsup**
4 **tablespoons water**
¼ **teaspoon orange extract (optional)**

1. Combine sauce ingredients.
2. Cut beef into thick slices and pound until ⅜ inch thick. Marinate in soy sauce and sugar 10 minutes. Add egg and flour. Mix with hand.
3. Heat oil for deep-frying. Slide beef into oil piece by piece to prevent sticking together. Fry until crispy. Remove. Fry again. Drain. Remove.
4. Reheat 2 tablespoons oil in wok. Stir-fry chili peppers and orange peel until black. Add sauce. Bring to boil. Thicken with dissolved cornstarch. Add beef. Stir-fry 1 minute more. Remove chili peppers before serving.

---

*Orange or tangerine peel: Cut orange or tangerine rind in small pieces. Put in pan in oven at 250 degrees 1 hour or more. May be stored in a covered jar indefinitely.

May be prepared in advance through Step 3. Do second deep-frying just before Step 4. May be frozen.

Serves 4 to 6

Spicy Beef   SZECHWAN

This is a spicy dish that is fun to prepare.

1 **pound flank steak,
   shredded**
4 **tablespoons oil**
10 **whole red chili peppers**
1 **red pepper, shredded**
1 **bunch scallions, green part
   only, cut 2 inches long**
10 **water chestnuts, sliced thin**

Marinade:
1 **teaspoon salt**
1 **tablespoon oil**
1 **tablespoon cornstarch**
1 **egg white**

Sauce:
6 **tablespoons chicken stock**
2 **tablespoons dark soy sauce**
1½ **teaspoons cornstarch**
1 **teaspoon chili paste with
   garlic**
1 **tablespoon sesame seed oil**

1. Combine sauce ingredients in a bowl. Set aside.
2. Combine marinade ingredients. Marinate steak 15 minutes.
3. Heat 2 tablespoons oil to smoking hot. Add meat. Stir-fry until color changes. Drain. Remove.
4. Heat 2 tablespoons oil. Add red chili peppers. Stir-fry until black. Add red pepper, scallions, water chestnuts, and sauce. Bring to boil. Add meat. Stir-fry 1 minute more. Remove dried chili peppers before serving.

May be prepared in advance through Step 1. May not be frozen.

Serves 4 to 6

Beef with Hot Sauce   SZECHWAN

This recipe produces a rich, dark brown, julienned beef, accompanied by fungus and water chestnuts. It is fairly spicy-hot with a moderately sweet and sour sauce just glazing the shreds. An unusual combination of flavors.

1 pound flank steak, julienne
1 egg white
1 tablespoon light soy sauce
1 tablespoon cornstarch
2 to 4 cups oil for deep-frying
2 slices ginger, shredded
1 large clove garlic, minced
1 tablespoon chili paste with garlic
2 tablespoons water chestnuts, shredded
1 tablespoon black fungus, soaked in boiling water 20 minutes, hard parts removed, cut into shreds
2 scallions, chopped, for garnish

Sauce:

2 tablespoons dark soy sauce
½ tablespoon red wine vinegar
1 tablespoon sherry
½ teaspoon salt
2 teaspoons cornstarch
4 tablespoons chicken stock
1 tablespoon sesame seed oil
1 teaspoon sugar

1. Combine sauce ingredients.
2. Mix beef with egg white, light soy sauce, and cornstarch. Set aside 15 minutes.
3. Heat oil in wok. Deep-fry beef until color changes. Drain. Remove.
4. Reheat 2 tablespoons oil in wok on moderate heat. Stir-fry ginger, garlic, and chili paste 30 seconds.
5. Turn heat up to high. Add water chestnuts and fungus. Pour in the sauce mixture. Bring to boil. Pour in beef. Stir-fry briskly.
6. Remove to serving platter and garnish with chopped scallion.

May be prepared in advance through Step 3. May be frozen.

Serves 4 to 6

7

Pork and Lamb

Pork is the meat that is most in demand in China. The flavor is so delicious when mixed with vegetables, noodles, or rice sticks. It is wonderful barbecued, stir-fried, or roasted. In China when you say, "We are eating meat," that means pork. When the Dowager Empress ate pork or any other dish, she used jade chopsticks tipped in gold and ate from jade plates. If the food was greasy, she had plates of gold and silver.

Lamb is a meat that gives heat to the body. The northern regions eat a great deal of it. Mongolian Lamb Pot is the most famous dish in the North.

129

Barbecued Pork Egg Fu Yung   CANTON

Egg Fu Yung was the first Chinese dish introduced to America. You can vary the meat. Use chicken, turkey, crab meat, shrimp, or lobster. All students love our style of making it.

5 eggs
1 teaspoon light soy sauce
1 teaspoon salt
1 teaspoon sherry
2 to 4 cups oil for deep-frying
½ onion, chopped fine
1 scallion, chopped fine
4 water chestnuts, sliced thin
¼ pound fresh mushrooms, sliced thin
½ pound barbecued pork (see Index), shredded
1 cup bean sprouts, chopped

Sauce:
1 cup chicken stock
2 tablespoons light soy sauce
1 tablespoon cornstarch, dissolved in 1 tablespoon water
Pepper to taste

1. Beat eggs in a bowl. Add soy sauce, ½ teaspoon salt, and sherry. Set aside.
2. Heat 2 tablespoons oil in wok. Stir-fry onion, scallion, and water chestnuts 1 minute. Add mushrooms. Stir-fry 30 seconds. Remove. Cool.
3. Heat 2 tablespoons oil in wok. Stir-fry barbecued pork and bean sprouts 1 minute. Remove. Cool.
4. Add all cooled ingredients to the egg mixture. Add remaining salt. Stir gently.
5. To make sauce: Bring stock to boil. Add soy sauce. Thicken with dissolved cornstarch. Season with pepper to taste. Set aside.
6. Heat oil to 400 degrees in wok. Gently put one quarter of the egg mixture into wok with ladle. Deep-fry 1 minute until golden brown. Fold over with spatula and fry the other side 1 minute. Remove to platter and keep warm. Continue to deep-fry the egg mixture, one quarter at a time. Serve with sauce.

May be prepared in advance through Step 5. May not be frozen.

Serves 4

Amoy Pancakes with Pork Filling   AMOY

Amoy is a city south of Fukien. This dish is similar to Moo Shu Pork. It is usually eaten on festival days.

24 Chinese (Shanghai) pancakes*
1 pound pork, julienne
4 tablespoons light soy sauce
2 teaspoons cornstarch
½ pound shrimp, shelled, deveined
6 tablespoons oil
2 tablespoons sherry
1 scallion, shredded
½ cup bamboo shoots, shredded
4 pieces pressed bean curd, shredded
½ pound string beans, shredded
½ pound bean sprouts
½ teaspoon salt
1 teaspoon sugar

1. Mix pork with 1 tablespoon soy sauce and 1 teaspoon cornstarch.
2. Mix shrimp with remaining cornstarch.
3. Heat 2 tablespoons oil in wok. Stir-fry shrimp 1 minute. Add 1 tablespoon sherry. Drain. Remove.
4. Heat 2 tablespoons oil in wok. Stir-fry pork 1 minute. Add remaining sherry. Drain. Remove.
5. Heat 2 tablespoons oil in wok. Stir-fry scallion, bamboo shoots, pressed bean curd, string beans, and bean sprouts. Add salt, remaining soy sauce, and sugar. Cook 2 minutes.
6. Pour in pork and shrimp. Stir-fry briskly until thoroughly heated.
7. Put filling in center of pancake. Turn bottom up before rolling to prevent spilling.

---

*May be purchased in Chinatown. Steam before using.

Note: May be added to pancake if desired:
  ½ cup roasted peanuts, chopped fine
  1 bunch cilantro (Chinese parsley), stems removed
  2 scallions, white part only, minced
  2 tablespoons bean sauce mixed with 2 tablespoons hoisin sauce

May be prepared in advance through Step 6. May be frozen after Step 6. Pancakes may be frozen separately.

Serves 4 to 6

Braised Pork with Eggs   SHANGHAI

For the Chinese, pork means energy food. This dish is so simple, a novice could pose as a chef.

1 pound pork shoulder or leg	2 tablespoons sherry
2 tablespoons oil	4 tablespoons dark soy sauce
2 slices ginger, minced	1 cup water
1 scallion, cut into 1-inch pieces	4 eggs, hard-boiled, shells removed
	1 tablespoon sugar

1. Cut pork into 1-inch cubes.
2. Heat oil. Stir-fry ginger and scallion 30 seconds. Add pork. Stir-fry until color changes. Add sherry, soy sauce, and water.
3. Cover. Simmer 45 minutes.
4. Add whole hard-boiled eggs. Simmer 30 minutes more.
5. Add sugar. Bring to high heat. Baste until sauce is reduced and glazed.
6. Cut eggs in half. Place pork in center of serving plate. Surround with eggs.

May be prepared in advance through Step 4. May be frozen.

Serves 4 to 6

Braised Pork in Brown Sauce   SHANGHAI

This is a rich, traditional dish, easy to prepare. The Chinese love it. So good with rice or buns.

3 pounds boneless pork shank or leg with skin on
6 cups boiling water
2 star anise seeds
2 scallions
1 slice ginger
5 tablespoons dark soy sauce
2 to 4 cups oil for deep-frying

4 to 6 cups water
1 tablespoon sherry
1½ teaspoons salt
1 tablespoon sugar
1 tablespoon cornstarch, dissolved in 1 tablespoon water
2 bunches spinach, cleaned

1. Put pork into a pan of boiling water, skin side down. Add star anise, scallions, and ginger. Boil 30 minutes uncovered. Drain. Dry completely.
2. Marinate pork in dark soy sauce ½ hour. Reserve marinade.
3. Heat oil. Deep-fry pork, skin side down, 3 minutes. Be careful as it splashes. Remove.
4. Soak pork, skin side down, in cold water about 30 minutes.
5. Put pork in wok. Add water to cover three-quarters of the pork. Add soy sauce left from marinade, sherry, and ½ teaspoon salt. Simmer covered 1½ hours. Bring to high heat. Add sugar. Thicken with dissolved cornstarch.
6. Reheat 2 tablespoons oil in pan. Add 1 teaspoon salt. Add spinach. Stir-fry 1 minute. Remove pork to platter. Garnish with spinach.

May be prepared in advance through Step 5. May be frozen after Step 5.

Serves 4 to 6

Fried Pork Loin   SHANGHAI

*The credit for this recipe must be given to a young Japanese,
Kayuhiko Yoshikawa. He worked as a chef at the Chinese
Friends Restaurant in Los Angeles. You will love it—so simple
to prepare.*

1 pound pork loin	1 egg
1 tablespoon light soy sauce	4 tablespoons flour
1 tablespoon dark soy sauce	2 to 4 cups oil for deep-frying
1 tablespoon oyster sauce	Peppercorn salt (see Index)
1 teaspoon curry powder	(optional)
½ teaspoon sugar	

1. Cut pork into pieces ¼ inch thick, 3 inches long, and 1½
   inches wide.
2. Marinate pork in the following seven ingredients. Mix well
   with hand. Refrigerate overnight.
3. Heat oil in wok. Deep-fry pork 5 to 7 minutes. Serve with
   peppercorn salt.

May be prepared in advance. May be frozen.

Serves 4 to 6

Fried Pork with Cucumber   ALL REGIONS

*An unusual combination—pork with cucumber. Easy and quick
to cook and a delight for those who are dieting.*

1 pound lean pork shoulder, leg, or tenderloin, shredded	1 tablespoon sherry
4 tablespoons light soy sauce	2 cups cucumber, skin on, seeded, sliced into 1-inch pieces
1 teaspoon cornstarch	
2 tablespoons oil	½ teaspoon sugar

1. Mix pork with 1 tablespoon soy sauce and cornstarch. Set
   aside 10 minutes.
2. Heat oil in wok. Stir-fry pork on high heat until color
   changes. Add sherry. Stir-fry 30 seconds.
3. Add cucumber, remaining soy sauce, and sugar. Stir-fry
   about 1 minute more. Serve hot.

May be prepared in advance. May not be frozen.

Serves 4 to 6

Garlic Cold Pork   SZECHWAN

This dish always receives tremendous compliments. May be served as an appetizer.

1 pound pork tenderloin
2 slices ginger
1 scallion, cut into quarters

Cucumber garnish:
3 cucumbers, sliced thin
4 tablespoons sugar
4 tablespoons white vinegar

Sauce:
3 cloves garlic, minced
¼ teaspoon salt
1 tablespoon chicken stock
2 tablespoons light soy sauce
1 tablespoon hot pepper oil
  (see Index)
1 tablespoon sesame seed oil

1. Combine sauce ingredients in a bowl. Set aside. Mix cucumbers with sugar and vinegar.
2. Put pork, ginger, and scallion into boiling water to cover. Cook 30 minutes. Remove and cool. When cool, cut the pork into very thin slices.
3. Drain liquid from cucumbers.
4. Arrange pork on platter. Pour sauce over. Garnish with cucumbers.

May be prepared in advance through Step 4. May not be frozen.

Serves 4 to 6

Life is aspiration.

Pork with Fish Sauce   SZECHWAN

Szechwan is a mountainous region far from the coast. Fish is scarce. This sauce is not actually flavored with fish. It is an imaginary name. Any meat can be used.

1 **pound pork loin or butt, julienne**	*Sauce:*
1 **tablespoon light soy sauce**	1 **tablespoon dark soy sauce**
1 **tablespoon cornstarch**	1 **teaspoon red wine vinegar**
2 **tablespoons dried fungus**	2 **teaspoons chili paste with garlic**
4 **tablespoons oil**	
1 **clove garlic, minced**	1 **tablespoon sherry**
1 **slice ginger, minced**	1 **teaspoon sugar**
1 **scallion, cut into quarters**	1 **teaspoon cornstarch**
10 **water chestnuts, shredded**	1 **tablespoon sesame seed oil**

1. Combine sauce ingredients. Set aside.
2. Marinate pork in soy sauce and cornstarch 15 minutes.
3. Soak dried fungus in boiling water 10 minutes. Cut julienne.
4. Heat 2 tablespoons oil in wok. Stir-fry pork 1 minute. Remove.
5. Heat remaining oil in wok. Stir-fry garlic, ginger, and scallion thoroughly. Pour in the sauce mixture. Stir briskly until thoroughly heated. Serve hot.

May be prepared in advance. May be frozen.

Serves 4 to 6

Pork with Black Fungus   ALL REGIONS

Here is a basic Chinese stew. It is rarely served in restaurants. It reheats well. Try using it as a sandwich filling.

1 **pound pork loin, shoulder, or butt**	1 **scallion, cut into thirds**
	1 **tablespoon sherry**
2 **tablespoons dried fungus**	3 **tablespoons dark soy sauce**
1 **tablespoon oil**	1 **cup boiling water**
1 **slice ginger, shredded**	½ **tablespoon sugar**

1. Cut pork into 1½-inch cubes.
2. Soak fungus in boiling water 20 minutes. Discard the hard part.
3. Heat oil. Add ginger and scallion. Stir-fry 30 seconds. Pour in meat. Stir-fry until color changes. Add sherry, soy sauce, and boiling water. When it boils again, turn to low. Cover and simmer 45 minutes. Keep turning and stirring.
4. Add fungus. Let simmer 20 minutes more. Turn occasionally to prevent burning. Turn up heat.
5. Add sugar. Baste until pork is glazed.

May be prepared in advance. May be frozen.

Serves 4 to 6

Pork with Dried Mushrooms   SHANGHAI

A wonderful dish—high in protein.

4 dried black mushrooms
2 bean curd sheets
1 pound lean pork, cut into
   thin slices about 1½ inches
   long
1 tablespoon light soy sauce

1 tablespoon cornstarch
3 tablespoons oil
1 tablespoon sherry
1 tablespoon dark soy sauce
1 teaspoon salt
½ teaspoon sugar

1. Soak mushrooms in boiling water 20 minutes. Using same liquid, cook mushrooms 20 minutes. Drain. Cut into quarters. Remove stems. Reserve liquid.
2. Soak bean curd in boiling water 20 minutes. Drain. Cut into 2-inch pieces.
3. Mix pork with light soy sauce and cornstarch. Use hands.
4. Heat oil in wok until smoking hot. Add pork. Stir-fry until color changes. Add sherry and dark soy sauce. Add mushrooms, bean curd, and mushroom liquid. Add salt and sugar. Cover. Cook 5 minutes.

May be prepared in advance. May be frozen.

Serves 4 to 6

Words without action are death.

Pork with Mustard Green Cabbage   SHANGHAI

Pork predominates in Chinese cuisine more than any other meat. The Chinese cook with pork just as Americans cook with beef. They have the most versatile ways of preparing pork. Here is a family dish you can enjoy with a bowl of rice.

1 pound pork, shredded	1 cup pickled mustard green
2 tablespoons light soy sauce	(snow) cabbage
2 teaspoons cornstarch	2 teaspoons sugar
2 tablespoons oil	2 tablespoons chicken stock
1 cup bamboo shoots, shredded	1 teaspoon sesame seed oil

1. Mix pork with 1 tablespoon light soy sauce and cornstarch. Use hand.
2. Heat oil in wok. Stir-fry pork until meat separates.
3. Add bamboo shoots and mustard green cabbage. Stir-fry 1 minute.
4. Add remaining soy sauce, sugar, and stock. Stir-fry 1 minute.
5. Add sesame seed oil. Stir-fry 1 minute more.

May be prepared in advance. May be frozen.

Serves 4 to 6

Pork with Noodles and Cabbage   SHANGHAI

This is Sylvia's favorite one-dish meal.

1 pound Chinese water
   noodles
1 tablespoon sesame seed oil
1 pound pork, shredded
4 tablespoons light soy sauce
1 tablespoon cornstarch
4 tablespoons oil
1 slice ginger, minced
1 clove garlic, minced
2 carrots, shredded
1 stalk bok choy, shredded
   (optional)

½ head medium cabbage,
   shredded
1 teaspoon salt
½ cup bamboo shoots,
   shredded
6 dried black mushrooms,
   soaked in boiling water 20
   minutes, shredded
1 scallion, shredded
2 eggs, scrambled fine
   (optional)

1. Boil noodles 5 minutes. Drain. Pour cold water over. Add sesame seed oil. Set aside. Soak pork in 2 tablespoons light soy sauce and cornstarch at least 20 minutes.
2. Heat 2 tablespoons oil in wok. Stir-fry pork until color changes. Remove.
3. Heat 2 tablespoons oil in wok. Stir-fry ginger and garlic until there is an aroma. Gradually add carrots, bok choy, cabbage, salt, and bamboo shoots. Stir-fry 7 minutes until cabbage is cooked down. Add remaining soy sauce. Add mushrooms and scallion. Add eggs. Stir-fry until thoroughly mixed.
4. Serve meat and vegetables on top of noodles.

May be prepared in advance through Step 2. May not be frozen.

Serves 4 to 6

Pork with Sweet Rice Cake   SHANGHAI

This is an authentic family dish. It can be served for luncheon or tea.

½ package sweet rice cake
½ pound pork, shredded
½ tablespoon light soy sauce
1 tablespoon cornstarch
4 tablespoons oil
1 slice ginger, shredded
1 scallion, chopped fine

1 pound celery cabbage, shredded
½ cup bamboo shoots, shredded
2 tablespoons dark soy sauce
½ teaspoon sugar

1. Soak the sweet rice cake in water to cover overnight.* Drain. Slice diagonally into ¼-inch pieces.
2. Mix pork with light soy sauce and cornstarch. Heat 2 tablespoons oil in wok. Stir-fry pork until color changes. Remove.
3. Heat 1 tablespoon oil in wok. Stir-fry ginger and scallion. Add celery cabbage and bamboo shoots. Cook 3 minutes. Add pork, dark soy sauce, and sugar. Remove.
4. Heat 1 tablespoon oil in wok. Pour in sweet rice cake. Stir-fry 2 minutes. Add the pork mixture. Stir-fry until thoroughly heated.

---

*If you buy fresh rice cake, it doesn't have to be soaked. Just slice it diagonally into ⅛-inch pieces.

May be prepared in advance. May not be frozen.

Serves 4

Sesame Seed Pork Loin   SHANGHAI

Another simple dish—fun to prepare. Serve it with Three-in-One Vegetables. You can use chicken if you don't eat pork.

1 scallion, cut into thirds	1 pound pork loin, cut into
2 slices ginger	¼-inch slices
1 tablespoon sherry	1 egg white
1 tablespoon light soy sauce	1 tablespoon cornstarch
½ teaspoon sugar	1 cup sesame seeds
½ teaspoon salt	4 tablespoons oil

1. Pound scallion and ginger with cleaver. Add sherry, soy sauce, sugar, and salt. Mix well.
2. Marinate pork in this mixture 1 hour, turning occasionally. Discard ginger and scallion.
3. Combine egg white and cornstarch. Beat well. Brush on meat pieces.
4. Dip pork pieces in sesame seeds. Coat evenly on both sides.
5. Heat oil. Fry pork on moderate heat 5 minutes. Turn once. Drain on paper towel. Serve immediately.

May be prepared in advance. May be frozen.

Serves 4 to 6

Woe be unto the glutton.

Stewed Pork with Brussels Sprouts   ALL REGIONS

Pork always goes well with any vegetable.

1 pound lean pork	1 tablespoon sherry
3 tablespoons dark soy sauce	1 tablespoon sugar
2 tablespoons oil	1 star anise seed
1 scallion, cut into quarters	2 cups water
1 slice ginger, shredded	12 brussels sprouts*

1. Cut pork into 2-inch squares. Marinate in soy sauce 30 minutes. Reserve marinade.
2. Heat oil in wok. Stir-fry scallion and ginger 30 seconds. Add pork. Stir-fry 1 minute. Add marinade, sherry, sugar, star anise seed, and water. Bring to boil. Cover and cook on low heat 30 minutes.
3. Blanch brussels sprouts in boiling water 5 minutes. Drain. Remove.
4. Add brussels sprouts to pork. Cook 2 minutes. Turn up heat. Cook and stir until sauce is glazed.

---

*Cauliflower may be substituted.

May be prepared in advance. May not be frozen.

Serves 4 to 6

Stir-Fried Pork with Broccoli   ALL REGIONS

This is a healthy dish with a small amount of meat to flavor the vegetable.

1½ pounds broccoli
½ pound lean pork, sliced
   thin
1 teaspoon cornstarch
1 tablespoon light soy sauce
4 tablespoons oil

Sauce:
1 teaspoon salt
½ teaspoon sugar
4 tablespoons chicken stock
1 tablespoon light soy sauce
1 teaspoon cornstarch

1. Combine sauce ingredients. Set aside.
2. Wash broccoli. Drain. Separate flowerettes into small pieces. Remove tough skin on stems. Cut stems diagonally into thin slices about 1½ inches long.
3. Mix pork well with cornstarch and soy sauce.
4. Heat 2 tablespoons oil in wok. Stir-fry pork until color changes. Remove.
5. Heat 2 tablespoons oil in wok. Stir-fry broccoli 2 minutes. Add pork. Stir briskly 1 minute. Pour in the sauce mixture. Stir-fry until the sauce is glazed.

May be prepared in advance. May not be frozen.

Serves 4 to 6

Pork Chops Chinese Style   SHANGHAI

Here is an easy recipe for beginners.

4 boneless pork chops	2 tablespoons sesame seed oil
2 tablespoons light soy sauce	4 tablespoons cornstarch
¼ teaspoon white pepper	1 cup oil
1 teaspoon sugar	Cilantro (Chinese parsley)
½ teaspoon salt	(optional)

1. Pound pork chops with cleaver. Combine next five ingredients. Marinate chops. Set aside 30 minutes. Drain.
2. Dredge pork chops with cornstarch.
3. Heat oil in wok or skillet. Fry chops until golden brown. Cook 5 minutes on each side.
4. Drain on paper towel.
5. Place on platter. Garnish with cilantro.

May be prepared in advance. May be frozen.

Serves 4

You cannot buy experience.

Pork Chops with Onion   SHANGHAI

In old China these pork chops were sold on the streets by vendors who sang songs about what they were selling as they tapped out the tune with chopsticks. Serve this typical Shanghai dish with rice or noodles.

4 pork chops   2 medium-size onions, sliced
4 tablespoons dark soy sauce   1 cup water
1 tablespoon cornstarch   ½ tablespoon sugar
2 tablespoons oil

1. Pound chops with back of knife. Mix chops with 1 table-spoon soy sauce and cornstarch. Mix well with hand. Set aside 15 minutes.
2. Heat oil in wok or skillet. Fry chops 2 minutes or until light brown. Remove.
3. In same oil, stir-fry onion until wilted and light brown.
4. Put chops on top of onion. Add remaining soy sauce and 1 cup water. Cover and cook on low heat 20 minutes.
5. Add sugar. Bring to boil. Baste chops until sauce is glazed.

May be prepared in advance through Step 4. May be frozen.

Serves 4

Meatballs with Sweet Sour Sauce   CANTON

Sweet sour sauce is so versatile. Delicious with this Chinese version of meatballs.

1 pound ground pork
1 scallion, chopped fine
1 clove garlic, minced
2 slices ginger, minced
1 egg
1 tablespoon sherry
½ teaspoon salt
1 tablespoon light soy sauce
1 tablespoon sesame seed oil
2 tablespoons cornstarch
2 tablespoons flour
2 to 4 cups oil for deep-frying
2 tablespoons cornstarch, dissolved in 4 tablespoons water
20 brussels sprouts

Sweet Sour Sauce:
4 tablespoons white vinegar
4 tablespoons sugar
4 tablespoons tomato catsup
1 cup water
10 canned pineapple chunks
½ green pepper, cubed (optional)
½ red pepper, cubed (optional)

1. Mix pork with next ten ingredients. Form into 20 balls with tablespoon to shape.
2. Heat oil in wok. Deep-fry meatballs until golden brown.
3. Put brussels sprouts in boiling water 5 minutes. Drain. Set aside.
4. Put all sauce ingredients in saucepan. Bring to boil. Thicken with dissolved cornstarch. Add meatballs and brussels sprouts. Bring to boil again. Serve hot.

May be prepared in advance. May be frozen.

Serves 4 to 6

Pork-Stuffed Cucumber   ALL REGIONS

A good dish for the budget-minded.

4 whole cucumbers, cut into
   1½-inch lengths*
1 tablespoon plus 2
   teaspoons cornstarch
¾ pound ground pork
1 tablespoon chicken stock
1 teaspoon salt
2½ teaspoons sugar
1 tablespoon sherry
1 slice ginger, chopped
½ scallion, chopped

1 tablespoon cornstarch,
   dissolved in 2 tablespoons
   water for sealing
2 tablespoons oil
1 cup chicken stock
1 tablespoon light soy sauce
1 teaspoon black bean sauce
   with chili
½ teaspoon dried red chili
   peppers

1. Remove seeds from cucumbers. Sprinkle 1 tablespoon cornstarch on inside.
2. Mix pork with remaining cornstarch, 1 tablespoon stock, salt,
   ½ teaspoon sugar, sherry, ginger, and scallion. Stuff the
   hollowed cucumber pieces with the pork mixture. Round the
   tops and coat with the sealing cornstarch mixture.
3. Heat 2 tablespoons oil in wok. Brown cucumber sections, no
   more than 10 at a time. (Add more oil, if necessary.) When
   finished, return all cucumber pieces to wok.
4. Add 1 cup stock, soy sauce, and black bean sauce. Cover and
   simmer 20 minutes.
5. Season to taste by adding remaining sugar and chili peppers,
   if desired. Add dissolved cornstarch, if necessary.

---

*five sections per cucumber

May be prepared in advance. May not be frozen.

Serves 4 to 6

Hunan Lamb   HUNAN

Another favorite for lovers of spicy food.

1 pound boned leg of lamb,
  julienne
¼ teaspoon salt
1 egg white
1 tablespoon cornstarch
1 teaspoon oil
2 to 4 cups oil for deep-frying
2 whole bamboo shoots,
  julienne
4 dried black mushrooms,
  soaked in boiling water 20
  minutes, cooked 20
  minutes, stems removed,
  julienne
4 whole dried red chili
  peppers, cut into quarters
4 cloves garlic, minced
1 small leek, julienne
1 tablespoon bean sauce

Sauce:
3 tablespoons sherry
3 tablespoons light soy sauce
1 teaspoon sugar
1 teaspoon sesame seed oil
2 teaspoons cornstarch,
  dissolved in 2 tablespoons
  water

1. Mix lamb with next four ingredients. Set aside.
2. Combine sauce ingredients in a bowl. Set aside.
3. Heat oil in wok. Deep-fry lamb, bamboo shoots, and mushrooms 2 minutes. Drain. Set aside.
4. Return 2 tablespoons oil to wok. Stir-fry chili peppers until dark brown. Add garlic. Stir-fry 1 second. Add leek. Stir-fry until light brown. Add bean sauce. Stir-fry 1 minute.
5. Pour the lamb mixture into wok. Add sauce ingredients. Stir-fry 2 minutes until thoroughly heated. Remove chili peppers before serving.

May be prepared in advance. May be frozen.

Serves 4 to 6

Mongolian Lamb Hot Pot   MONGOLIA

The hot pot originated in the 13th century when the Mongols came from the north and invaded China. It is an interesting style of eating. Everybody participates in the cooking. If you do not have a hot pot, use an electric wok.

Ingredients for Making Sauces:

1 cup sesame seed oil	½ cup salt
1 cup light soy sauce	½ cup garlic, chopped fine
½ cup chili oil	4 scallions, chopped fine
½ cup sesame seed paste	1 cup cilantro (Chinese
½ cup sugar	parsley)

Each person creates his or her own sauces by combining whichever ingredients he or she wishes. It is fun to see who creates the most imaginative sauces.

1 6-pound boned leg of lamb, slightly frozen, sliced very thin	4 ounces vermicelli, soaked in boiling water 10 minutes, drained, cut into thirds with scissors
2 bunches spinach, cleaned	Sesame Seed Cake (see Index)
1 head celery cabbage, shredded	6 to 10 cups chicken stock,* boiling
4 pieces bean curd (to-fu), cut into 9 squares each (1 box)	2 tablespoons sherry
	Sauces (see above)

1. Put sauce ingredients in separate bowls. Have empty individual bowls for each person.
2. Arrange lamb in single layers on large plates.
3. Put spinach, cabbage, bean curd, and vermicelli on separate plates. Place vegetables and lamb around hot pot.
4. Heat Sesame Seed Cake in 350-degree oven 10 minutes. Place on plate around pot also.
5. Place pot in center of table. Put boiling chicken stock and sherry in pot.

---

*The amount depends on size of hot pot.

6. Each person dips his or her own meat and vegetables in boiling liquid and then in sauce creation.

If using hot pot, heat a few charcoal briquets in a foil-lined baking pan under broiler 20 minutes. Then place them side by side in hot pot.

May be prepared in advance through Step 3. May not be frozen.

Serves 8 to 10

Lamb Aspic   HUNAN

Keep this in the refrigerator and enjoy it for a week. Serve as appetizer or as a cold plate.

2 **pounds boned leg of lamb, cut into large chunks**	1 **cup cold water**
2 **tablespoons oil**	1 **tablespoon sugar**
1 **scallion, cut into thirds**	1 **package Knox gelatin**
1 **slice ginger, pounded**	1 **tablespoon sherry**
1 **carrot, cut into 1-inch pieces**	3 **tablespoons dark soy sauce**
2 **star anise seeds**	**Lettuce leaves**
	Bean sauce for dipping

1. Cover lamb with boiling water. Boil 1 minute. Drain. Remove. Reserve water.
2. Heat oil in wok. Stir-fry scallion and ginger 2 seconds. Add lamb, carrot, star anise, and water. Bring to boil. Cover and simmer 1½ hours or until meat is tender.
3. Discard carrot, star anise, ginger, and scallion.
4. Return lamb to wok. Add ½ cup cold water and sugar. Cover and cook 10 minutes on low heat. Remove lamb. Strain liquid.
5. Dissolve gelatin in remaining cold water. Cook over boiling water 5 minutes.
6. Mix the gelatin with sherry, soy sauce, and meat liquid (make sure it is 1 cup).
7. Put meat in loaf pan. Pour in the sauce mixture. Refrigerate at least 4 hours.
8. Cut into rectangular pieces, 2″ × 1″.
9. Serve cold on bed of lettuce. Use bean sauce as dip.

May be prepared in advance. May be frozen.

Serves 4 to 6

8

Fish and Seafood

Fish were throught to be content in their element and free from restraint. Therefore, they became symbolic of harmony and freedom and an evil-averting charm. Artists painted fish, depicting them as good omens for the future. The Chinese believed if they ate fish, they would have prosperity and happiness.

Deep-Fried Fillet of Fish   CANTON

Easy to prepare. You will feel like a professional chef when your guests start to rave.

1 **pound fish fillet (sea bass or red snapper), sliced thin into 1½-inch squares**
½ **teaspoon salt**
¼ **teaspoon black pepper**
½ **teaspoon sesame seed oil**
1⅓ **cups water**
1 **cup flour**
2 to 4 **cups oil for deep-frying**
1 **tablespoon cornstarch, dissolved in 1 tablespoon water**

Sweet Sour Sauce:
½ **cup wine vinegar**
2 **tablespoons tomato catsup**
½ **tablespoon Worcestershire sauce**
6 **tablespoons sugar**

1. Marinate fish with salt, pepper, and sesame seed oil 20 minutes.
2. Add water to flour. Mix thoroughly. Gradually mix in 2 tablespoons oil.
3. Combine sauce ingredients in saucepan. Bring to boil. Add dissolved cornstarch. Stir constantly until smooth and glazy.
4. Heat oil in wok. Coat fish with flour-water-oil batter. Slide fish pieces into 350-degree oil, one piece at a time. Deep-fry until golden brown. Drain. Remove. Serve with Sweet Sour Sauce.

May be prepared in advance through Step 3. May not be frozen.

Serves 4 to 6

Fish and Bean Curd in Oyster Sauce   CANTON

This is a practical daily dish. Bean curd is also a good accompaniment for meat. Here, the ginger, scallion, garlic, and oyster sauce add a wonderful flavor to the delicate fish.

1 **pound fish fillet, cut into 1½-inch pieces**
½ **teaspoon salt**
1 **egg white**
1 **tablespoon cornstarch**
1 **box bean curd (to-fu)**
2 to 4 **cups oil for deep-frying**
1 **slice ginger, minced**
2 **scallions, chopped**
1 **clove garlic, minced**

½ **pound broccoli, flowerettes only**
4 **tablespoons oyster sauce**
1 **tablespoon light soy sauce**
½ **teaspoon sugar**
½ **cup chicken stock**
1 **tablespoon cornstarch, dissolved in 2 tablespoons water**

1. Mix fish with salt, egg white, and cornstarch.
2. Cut bean curd into ½-inch squares.
3. Heat oil for deep-frying. Deep-fry fish 1 minute. Drain. Remove.
4. Reheat 2 tablespoons oil in wok. Stir-fry ginger, 1 scallion, and garlic until there is an aroma. Add broccoli. Stir-fry 1 minute.
5. Add bean curd, oyster sauce, light soy sauce, sugar, and stock. Bring to boil.
6. Put fish on top of the bean curd. Bring to boil again. Thicken with dissolved cornstarch. Baste fish with sauce.
7. Remove to a serving dish. Sprinkle remaining scallion over fish.

May be prepared in advance through Step 5. May not be frozen.

Serves 4 to 6

Fish with Hot Sauce   SZECHWAN

This is a delicate dish—easy to prepare when you are in a hurry.

1 pound fish fillet
1 teaspoon salt
1 egg
4 tablespoons cornstarch or
   flour
2 to 4 cups oil for deep-frying
2 tablespoons cornstarch,
   dissolved in 2 tablespoons
   water
Blanched brussels sprouts

Sauce:
4 tablespoons red wine
   vinegar
4 tablespoons sugar
1 cup water
1 tablespoon light soy sauce
1 teaspoon crushed red
   chili peppers

1. Combine sauce ingredients. Set aside.
2. Cut fish into 1½-inch-square pieces.
3. Mix fish with salt, egg, and 1 tablespoon cornstarch. Coat heavily with remaining cornstarch.
4. Heat oil for deep-frying. Slide pieces of fish into oil one at a time. Fry until crispy. (It may be necessary to fry fish twice.) Remove to a serving platter.
5. Heat sauce. Bring to boil. Thicken with dissolved cornstarch. Pour sauce over fish. Garnish with brussels sprouts.

May be prepared in advance through Step 4. Refry before serving. May not be frozen.

Serves 4 to 6

Good deeds never go in vain.

Hunan Fish

HUNAN

Spicy and delicious.

1 whole fish, about 3 pounds, boned*
1 teaspoon salt
1 tablespoon sherry
1 slice ginger, minced
½ cup cornstarch or flour
2 to 4 cups oil for deep-frying
3 tablespoons cornstarch, dissolved in 3 tablespoons water

Sauce:
2 dried black mushrooms, soaked in boiling water 20 minutes, stems removed, minced
2 cups water
½ cup sugar
½ cup red wine vinegar
1 tablespoon light soy sauce
1 teaspoon dark soy sauce
3 teaspoons crushed red chili peppers
3 slices ginger, minced

1. Make 3 gashes diagonally on each side of fish. Sprinkle with salt, sherry, and ginger. Sprinkle cornstarch or flour on fish inside and out.
2. Combine sauce ingredients. Heat.
3. Heat oil. Deep-fry fish 7 minutes on each side or until crisp. Drain. Remove to a serving platter.
4. Bring sauce to boil. Thicken with dissolved cornstarch. Pour over fish.

---

*It is preferable to bone fish than to buy fillets. To bone, split fish in half along the belly with a sharp knife. Cut along the backbone. Remove backbone from base of tail. Open and score flesh side with diagonal cuts.

May be prepared in advance through Step 3. Refry fish before serving. May not be frozen.

Serves 4 to 6

Steamed Fish   ALL REGIONS

With a minimum of time, effort, and seasonings the Chinese make the best use of fish. Try it, you will love it, and it will turn out to be a masterpiece.

2 to 3 pounds whole fish (red snapper, sea bass, or flounder)
1½ tablespoons sherry
3 tablespoons oil

3 slices ginger, shredded
3 scallions, shredded
4 tablespoons light soy sauce
¾ teaspoon sugar

1. Make 3, deep, diagonal gashes on each side of fish. Sprinkle fish with sherry inside and out. Put fish on a plate. Let stand 5 minutes.
2. In a steamer bring water to a boil. Steam fish 15 to 20 minutes. Test for tenderness by poking a wooden chopstick all the way through the gill area.
3. Heat oil in wok. Add ginger. Cook on low heat 1 minute. Add scallions, soy sauce, and sugar. Cook 1 minute more.
4. Place fish on a serving platter. Pour sauce over fish.

May be prepared in advance through Step 1. May not be frozen.

Serves 4 to 6

The food of life comes from the heart.

Steamed Fish with Black Bean Sauce   CANTON

The Chinese excel in preparing steamed fish.

1 whole red snapper (about 3
   pounds), cleaned, scaled
2 tablespoons fermented
   black beans
2 scallions, shredded into
   1½-inch-long pieces
4 slices ginger, shredded

2 teaspoons salt
1 teaspoon sugar
2 tablespoons sherry
1 tablespoon light soy sauce
2 tablespoons oil
   Cilantro (Chinese parsley),
    for garnish

1. Make 3, deep, diagonal gashes on each side of fish..
2. Chop the black beans. Place half of black beans, scallions, and ginger on a long plate to be used in the steamer. Place fish on top.
3. Sprinkle fish with salt and sugar. Pour sherry, soy sauce, and oil over. Cover fish with remaining black beans, scallions, and ginger.
4. Steam 20 minutes over briskly boiling water. Fish is finished when a chopstick will easily pierce the gill area. Remove to platter. Garnish with cilantro.

May be prepared in advance through Step 3. May not be frozen.

Serves 4 to 6

Steamed Fish with Hot Sauce   CANTON

The Cantonese people are known for making this. There is no food more delicate than a fresh fish properly steamed.

1 whole fish, about 1½ pounds
2 tablespoons oil
12 cloves garlic, minced
2 slices ginger, minced
2 teaspoons crushed red chili peppers
2 scallions, chopped fine

2 tablespoons A.1. Steak Sauce
2 tablespoons light soy sauce
2 tablespoons oyster sauce
2 tablespoons bean sauce
2 tablespoons hoisin sauce
2 teaspoons sugar
½ cup scallions, for garnish

1. Gash fish deeply in 3 places on each side. Place fish on platter ready for steaming.
2. Bring water to boil in bottom half of steamer. Steam fish 10 minutes.
3. Heat 2 tablespoons oil in wok. Stir-fry garlic, ginger, red chili peppers, and scallions 30 seconds. Add next six ingredients. Bring to boil just before pouring over fish.
4. Pour sauce over fish. Sprinkle scallions on top. Serve immediately.

May be prepared in advance through Step 1. May not be frozen.

Serves 4 to 6

Three-Colored Fish Slices   YANGCHOW

An elegant fish dish.

1½ pounds fish fillet
1 egg white
1 teaspoon salt
Pinch of black pepper
1½ tablespoons cornstarch
2 to 4 cups oil for deep-frying
1 pound string beans, cut
   into 1-inch pieces
1 scallion, minced
1 slice ginger, minced
1 tablespoon sherry

1 teaspoon sesame seed oil
2 tablespoons chicken stock
1 teaspoon cornstarch,
   dissolved in 2 teaspoons
   water
3 tablespoons catsup
Pinch of crushed red chili
   peppers
1 tablespoon curry paste or
   powder

1. Slice fish diagonally into 1-inch pieces, ¼ inch thick. Mix with egg white, ½ teaspoon salt, pepper, and cornstarch. Use hands.
2. Heat oil. Deep-fry string beans. Drain. Add ½ teaspoon salt. Arrange on serving platter in letter "Y" shape.
3. Deep-fry fish 1 minute or until it turns white. Drain. Remove.
4. Reheat 2 tablespoons oil in wok. Stir-fry scallions and ginger. Add sherry, sesame seed oil, 1 tablespoon chicken stock, and dissolved cornstarch. Stir-fry 1 minute. Add fish. Stir-fry 1 minute more.
5. Put one-third of the fish on the platter in one section of the "Y." Reserve two-thirds of fish in a bowl.
6. Heat 1 tablespoon oil in wok. Add catsup and crushed red chili peppers. Add one-third reserved fish. Stir-fry until fish is coated. Remove to second section of the "Y." Clean wok.
7. Heat 1 tablespoon oil in wok. Add curry paste or powder and remaining stock. Add last third of fish. Stir-fry until evenly coated. Remove to last section of the "Y."

May be prepared in advance through Step 3. May not be frozen.

Serves 4 to 6

Green Peppers Stuffed with Seafood   CANTON

Try a different garnish each time you make this dish. It's fun.

¼ pound fish fillet
½ pound medium shrimp, shelled, deveined
½ teaspoon salt
1 egg white
1 teaspoon plus 3 tablespoons cornstarch
1 slice ginger, chopped fine
1 scallion, chopped fine
Pinch of black pepper
3 green peppers

Cilantro (Chinese parsley), minced cooked Virginia ham, or black sesame seeds for garnish
2 tablespoons oil
1½ tablespoons fermented black beans, mashed to a paste
½ teaspoon sugar
1 cup chicken stock
1 tablespoon cornstarch, dissolved in 2 tablespoons water

1. Mince fish and shrimp together. Add salt, egg white, 1 teaspoon cornstarch, ginger, scallion, and pepper. Mix well with hand. Set aside.
2. Cut peppers in half. Remove seeds. Cut each pepper into 8 squares. Dry well. Sprinkle with remaining cornstarch on the inside. Fill with the seafood mixture. Smooth the top. Press garnish onto top.
3. Heat 1 tablespoon oil in skillet. Brown stuffed peppers 4 at a time, shrimp side down 2 minutes. Turn. Fry 1 minute more. Remove.
4. Heat remaining oil in skillet. Add black bean paste. Stir-fry on low heat. Add sugar and stock. Add stuffed peppers. Cook 3 minutes. Thicken with dissolved cornstarch.
5. Put peppers on platter. Pour any remaining sauce over.

May be prepared in advance through Step 3. May not be frozen.

Serves 4 to 6

Abalone with Oyster Sauce CANTON

A number of students went fishing and caught fresh abalone. We created this dish and they raved—"heavenly!"

1 **pound abalone (about 2 pieces), shelled, cleaned**	*Sauce:*
2 **tablespoons cornstarch**	3 **tablespoons oyster sauce**
3 **tablespoons oil**	1 **tablespoon light soy sauce**
1 **slice ginger, minced**	1 **tablespoon sugar**
1 **clove garlic, minced**	1 **teaspoon cornstarch**
1 **scallion, chopped fine**	1 **tablespoon sherry**
10 **lettuce leaves**	2 **tablespoons chicken stock**

1. Combine sauce ingredients.
2. Slice abalone crosswise into ¼-inch-thick pieces. Pound. Sprinkle cornstarch on both sides.
3. Heat 2 tablespoons oil to smoking hot. Fry abalone 30 seconds on each side. Remove. Set aside.
4. Heat 1 tablespoon oil in wok. Stir-fry ginger, garlic, and scallion 30 seconds. Add sauce. Bring to boil. Put abalone in sauce. Cook 30 seconds.
5. Arrange abalone on platter. Pour sauce over fish. Garnish with lettuce leaves. Serve immediately.

May be prepared in advance through Step 2. May not be frozen.

Serves 4 to 6

Heaven does not permit an endless road to any one of us.

Clams in Black Bean Sauce   CANTON

Clams are considered a Chinese delicacy.

24 small live clams
1½ tablespoons fermented
   black beans
2 cloves garlic
3 tablespoons oil
2 slices ginger, minced
1 scallion, chopped fine
1 tablespoon light soy sauce
1 tablespoon sherry
1 teaspoon sugar
1 cup chicken stock

2 teaspoons cornstarch,
   dissolved in 4 teaspoons
   water
2 teaspoons sesame seed oil
½ teaspoon crushed chili
   peppers (optional)
1 teaspoon pepper oil (see
   Index) (optional)
3 tablespoons cilantro
   (Chinese parsley), chopped

1. Soak clams in slightly salted water to cover 2 hours. Rinse fermented black beans. Mash fermented black beans with garlic.
2. Heat oil in wok. Add ginger and scallion. Add fermented black bean and garlic paste. Stir until there is an aroma.
3. Turn heat up. Add clams. Pour in soy sauce, sherry, sugar, and stock. Cover. Cook only 4 minutes, until clams open.
4. Thicken with dissolved cornstarch. Add sesame seed oil. Add the optional chili pepper and pepper oil. Baste clams with sauce.
5. Sprinkle cilantro on top.

May be prepared in advance through Step 2. May be frozen.

Serves 4 to 6

Oysters with Scallions and Ginger   CANTON

Another wonderful dish from the Mon Kee Restaurant in Los Angeles.

1 pound fresh oysters, shelled, cleaned, rinsed in cold water
1 tablespoon cornstarch
2 to 4 cups oil for deep-frying
4 scallions, green part only, cut into 2-inch pieces

4 slices ginger, shredded
1 clove garlic, minced
3 tablespoons oyster sauce
1 tablespoon light soy sauce
1 tablespoon sherry
1 tablespoon chicken stock
1 teaspoon sugar (optional)

1. Put oysters in strainer. Dip in and out of boiling water 10 seconds. Drain. Dry well. Oysters should be firm and color should be grayish-white.
2. Mix oysters with cornstarch.
3. Heat oil in wok. Deep-fry oysters 1 minute. Drain. Remove.
4. Reheat 2 tablespoons oil in wok. Stir-fry scallions, ginger, and garlic 30 seconds. Add oyster sauce, soy sauce, sherry, and chicken stock. Bring to boil. Add oysters and sugar. Stir until thoroughly heated.

May be prepared in advance through Step 3. May not be frozen.

Serves 4 to 6

Fried Oysters   CANTON

Use this as an hors d'oeuvre or main dish.

12 oysters
½ teaspoon salt
6 cups boiling water
¼ teaspoon black pepper
2 to 4 cups oil for deep-frying
Peppercorn salt (see Index)

Batter:
½ cup flour
¼ cup cornstarch
1 teaspoon salt
2 teaspoons baking powder
½ cup water
1 egg, well beaten
1 tablespoon oil

1. Drain oysters. Sprinkle with salt. Rub gently. Pour oysters into a strainer. Rinse under gentle stream of cold water until they are no longer slippery.
2. Dip strainer of oysters in and out of the boiling water 10 seconds. Oysters should look grayish-white and be firm. Drain thoroughly. Sprinkle with black pepper.
3. To prepare the batter: Put flour and cornstarch in a bowl. Add salt, baking powder, and water. Stir in a circular motion. Add egg. Stir again. Add oil and stir until batter is smooth. Consistency should be like pancake batter.
4. Put oysters in batter.
5. Heat oil. Deep-fry oysters at 375 degrees 2 minutes until golden brown and crispy. Drain. Remove.
6. Put on platter. Serve with peppercorn salt as a dip.

May not be prepared in advance. May not be frozen.

Serves 4 to 6

Crab Meat with Straw Mushrooms — YANGCHOW

These mushrooms are a novelty to Westerners. So delicious combined with crab meat. An unusual delicacy.

2 tablespoons oil
2 slices ginger, chopped fine
1 scallion, chopped fine
½ pound fresh crab meat
1 can straw mushrooms
1 cup chicken stock
½ teaspoon salt
1 tablespoon sherry

1 tablespoon cornstarch, dissolved in 2 tablespoons water
1 egg white, beaten to soft peaks
Black pepper to taste
1 tablespoon cooked Virginia ham, chopped fine (optional)

1. Heat oil in wok. Add ginger and scallion. Stir-fry 30 seconds. Add crab meat and mushrooms. Stir-fry 1 minute.
2. Pour in stock. Bring to boil. Add salt, sherry, and dissolved cornstarch.
3. Add beaten egg white. Cook 1 minute. Season with black pepper.
4. Sprinkle ham over.

May not be prepared in advance. May not be frozen.

Serves 4 to 6

Grasp the good, discard the bad.

Ginger Crab   CANTON

A mouth-watering dish from the southern part of China. The secret of making it perfect is very fast stirring.

4 tablespoons oil
2 fresh crabs, cut into 2-inch pieces
2 cloves garlic, minced
8 slices ginger, minced
4 scallions (white part only), chopped fine

3 tablespoons oyster sauce
2 tablespoons light soy sauce
1 teaspoon sugar
2 cups chicken stock
1 tablespoon cornstarch, dissolved in 1 tablespoon water

1. Heat 2 tablespoons oil in wok until smoking hot. Pour in crab sections. Stir-fry until color changes. Remove.
2. Heat 2 tablespoons oil in wok. Stir-fry garlic, ginger, and scallion 30 seconds. Add oyster sauce, soy sauce, sugar, and stock. Add crab pieces. Cover. Steam 5 minutes.
3. Thicken with dissolved cornstarch. Baste crab with sauce.
4. Remove to platter. Serve immediately.

May not be prepared in advance. May not be frozen.

Serves 4 to 6

Lobster with Sweet Sour Hot Sauce   CANTON

Here you can see the Chinese using imported ingredients in their recipes.

2 lobster tails (1 pound each)
1 teaspoon salt
1 tablespoon flour
2 to 4 cups oil for deep-frying
2 cloves garlic, minced
2 tablespoons onion, chopped fine
1 scallion, minced
1 slice ginger, minced

Sauce:

4 tablespoons chicken stock
6 tablespoons tomato catsup
2 tablespoons sherry
2 tablespoons A.1. Steak Sauce
2 tablespoons Worcestershire sauce
4 tablespoons sugar
4 tablespoons red wine vinegar
1 tablespoon chili oil

1. Combine sauce ingredients. Set aside.
2. Cut each lobster tail in half lengthwise. Cut into quarters in width. This makes 16 pieces. Sprinkle with salt and flour.
3. Heat oil in wok. Deep-fry lobster pieces 2 minutes. Drain. Remove.
4. Reheat 2 tablespoons oil in wok. Stir-fry garlic, onion, scallion, and ginger 30 seconds. Add the sauce mixture. Bring to boil. Pour in lobster. Stir-fry briskly 1 minute more.

May be prepared in advance through Step 3. May not be frozen.

Serves 4 to 6

Lobster with Green Peppers and Chili Flakes   SZECHWAN

An elegant and spicy company dish.

2 uncooked lobsters, cut into
   large pieces
1 teaspoon salt
4 tablespoons flour
2 to 4 cups oil for deep-frying
5 cloves garlic, minced
2 slices ginger, minced
1 teaspoon crushed red chili
   peppers

1 green pepper, cut into 1-
   inch squares
1 small onion, cut into 1-
   inch squares
1 teaspoon dark soy sauce
1 teaspoon sugar
2 teaspoons cornstarch,
   dissolved in 4 tablespoons
   chicken stock
1 scallion, chopped

1. Sprinkle lobsters with salt and flour. Heat oil for deep-frying
   until smoking hot. Slide lobster pieces into oil. (Be sure the
   pieces are very dry and coated with flour.) Cook until all of
   the meat is white. Drain. Remove.
2. Reheat 2 tablespoons oil in wok. Add garlic, ginger, and chili
   peppers. Fry until there is an aroma. Add green pepper and
   onion. Stir-fry 1 minute. Add soy sauce, sugar, and dissolved
   cornstarch.
3. Pour in lobster. Stir-fry until well mixed. Sprinkle with
   scallions. Stir-fry 1 second. Remove to platter.

May not be prepared in advance. May not be frozen.

Serves 4 to 6

Scallops with Black Bean Sauce   CANTON

Cantonese chefs reign supreme in the creation of seafood dishes.

1 **pound scallops, cut in half
diagonally**
1 **tablespoon cornstarch**
2 **tablespoons fermented
black beans**
1 **clove garlic, minced**
2 **tablespoons water**
2 **to 4 cups oil for deep-frying**
1 **orange, cut into ½-inch
slices, for garnish**

Sauce:
½ **teaspoon salt**
1 **teaspoon sugar**
1 **tablespoon sherry**
2 **tablespoons chicken stock**
1 **teaspoon chili oil**

1. Combine sauce ingredients. Set aside.
2. Rinse scallops in cold water. Drain on paper towel. Dry
   thoroughly. Mix with cornstarch. Use hands. Blend well. Set
   aside.
3. Pound black beans with back of knife or cleaver. Add garlic.
   Add water slowly. Mix well. Set aside.
4. Heat oil in wok. Deep-fry scallops on moderate heat 1
   minute. Drain. Remove.
5. Reheat 1 tablespoon oil in skillet. Stir-fry the black bean
   mixture until there is an aroma, about 1 minute. Add sauce.
   Bring to boil. Spread the scallops evenly in the pan. Heat
   quickly 1 minute.
6. Remove to platter. Garnish with orange slices.

May be prepared in advance through Step 4. May not be frozen.

Serves 4 to 6

Scallops with Beef in Satay Sauce   CANTON

The combination of seafood and beef with this sauce is a treat to the palate.

1 pound flank steak,
   shredded
1½ teaspoons salt
1 egg white
1 tablespoon cornstarch
½ pound scallops, cut in half
2 tablespoons flour
2 to 4 cups oil for deep-frying
½ cup snow peas, strings
   removed
1 clove garlic, minced
1 slice ginger, chopped fine
1 scallion, chopped fine

Satay sauce:
6 tablespoons chicken stock
1 teaspoon red wine vinegar
1 teaspoon cornstarch
2 tablespoons dark soy sauce
Pinch of sugar
2 tablespoons satay sauce

1. Combine sauce ingredients. Set aside.
2. Mix beef with 1 teaspoon salt, egg white, and cornstarch. Mix scallops with flour and ½ teaspoon salt.
3. Deep-fry beef in smoking hot oil 1 minute. Drain. Remove. Lower the heat. Deep-fry scallops 1 minute. Drain. Remove.
4. Reheat 1 tablespoon oil in wok. Stir-fry snow peas 1 minute. Remove.
5. Reheat 1 tablespoon oil in wok. Stir-fry garlic, ginger, and scallions 30 seconds. Pour in the satay sauce mixture. Bring to boil. Add beef, scallops, and snow peas. Stir-fry quickly. Remove to a platter and serve immediately.

May be prepared in advance through Step 3. May not be frozen.

Serves 4 to 6

Scallops with Hot Sauce   SZECHWAN

So many students request recipes using scallops. This one is a favorite.

1 pound scallops, cut in half
1 teaspoon salt
1 tablespoon cornstarch
2 to 4 cups oil for deep-frying
2 cloves garlic, minced
1 scallion, cut into 1-inch pieces
1 slice ginger, minced
½ pound broccoli flowerettes
4 water chestnuts, sliced thin
¼ green pepper, shredded
1 tablespoon dried fungus, soaked in boiling water 20 minutes, stems removed
Black pepper to taste

Sauce:
½ teaspoon crushed red chili peppers
2 teaspoons sugar
2 teaspoons cornstarch
2 tablespoons white vinegar
1 tablespoon light soy sauce
½ cup chicken stock
1 tablespoon sherry

1. Mix scallops with salt and cornstarch.
2. Combine sauce ingredients. Set aside.
3. Heat oil. Deep-fry scallops 1 minute. Drain. Remove.
4. Reheat 2 tablespoons oil in wok. Stir-fry garlic, scallion, and ginger 30 seconds. Add broccoli, water chestnuts, green pepper, and fungus. Stir-fry 1 minute more. Pour in sauce. Bring to boil. Add scallops. Season with pepper to taste.

May be prepared in advance through Step 3. May not be frozen.

Serves 4 to 6

How can you beat a dog that licks your hand?

Three-Flavored Scallops with Ponzu Vinegar   SZECHWAN

Scallops, shrimp, and chicken are coated with a delicate lemon sauce. An outstanding company dish.

½ pound large scallops, cut in half
½ pound large shrimp, shelled, deveined, cut in half lengthwise
½ pound chicken breast, boned, skinned, shredded
1 teaspoon salt
1 egg white
2 tablespoons cornstarch
2 to 4 cups oil for deep-frying
½ cup snow peas, strings removed
1 slice ginger, minced
1 clove garlic, minced
2 scallions, chopped fine

4 dried black mushrooms, soaked in boiling water 20 minutes, cooked 20 minutes, stems removed, shredded
¼ cup bamboo shoots, shredded
¼ cup water chestnuts, sliced thin
1 tablespoon cornstarch, dissolved in 1 tablespoon water

Sauce:
½ cup water
¼ cup sugar
¼ cup Ponzu vinegar*
1 teaspoon crushed red chili peppers

1. Combine sauce ingredients. Set aside.
2. Mix scallops, shrimp, and chicken with salt, egg white, and cornstarch. Use hand for mixing.
3. Heat oil in wok for deep-frying. On medium heat fry scallops, shrimp, and chicken in 2 batches 1 minute each. Drain. Remove. Deep-fry snow peas 30 seconds. Drain. Remove.
4. Return 2 tablespoons oil to wok. Add ginger, garlic, and scallions. Stir-fry 30 seconds. Add mushrooms, bamboo shoots, and water chestnuts. Stir-fry 2 minutes. Add sauce. Bring to boil. Thicken with dissolved cornstarch. Add seafood, chicken, and snow peas. Stir-fry until thoroughly heated, about 2 minutes. Remove to a serving platter.

---

*White vinegar may be substituted.

May be prepared in advance through Step 3. May not be frozen.

Serves 4 to 6

Braised Shrimp SHANGHAI

You must use quick movements to make a success of this dish. Shrimp should be firm and crisp.

1 pound medium-size shrimp, shelled, deveined, cut in half crosswise	*Sauce:*
	½ teaspoon salt
	½ teaspoon sugar
1 teaspoon salt	1 tablespoon sherry
1 egg white	1 teaspoon cornstarch,
1 tablespoon cornstarch	dissolved in 2 tablespoons
2 to 4 cups oil for deep-frying	chicken stock
	1 teaspoon sesame seed oil

1. Combine sauce ingredients. Set aside.
2. Wash shrimp. Change water many times until water is clear. Then soak shrimp in salt water (1 teaspoon salt) to cover 30 minutes. Dry shrimp on paper towel.
3. Place shrimp in bowl. Add egg white and cornstarch. Use hand to mix. Set aside at least 30 minutes.
4. Heat oil in wok to moderate heat. Add shrimp. Stir quickly to separate. Drain. Remove.
5. Reheat 2 tablespoons oil in wok. Add shrimp. Pour in sauce. Stir until thoroughly heated. Sauce will thicken and form a clear glaze.

May be prepared in advance through Step 4. May not be frozen.

Serves 4 to 6

Chiao's Shrimp   PEKING

A popular dish created by Chef Ling Chiao.

1 pound large shrimp,
   cleaned, deveined
Salt and pepper to taste
2 tablespoons cornstarch
2 eggs, beaten, plus ½
   tablespoon water
½ cup oil plus 4 tablespoons
2 bunches spinach, washed,
   drained*

2 tablespoons roasted
   almonds, minced
1 scallion, minced

Sauce:
1 slice ginger, minced
2 cloves garlic, minced
¼ cup sherry
4 tablespoons catsup
¾ cup chicken stock

1. Slit shrimp and open lengthwise. Leave tails on. Flatten and
   pound. Put 3 diagonal gashes on each half with wrong side of
   knife. Do not go too deep.
2. Place shrimp on flat surface. Add salt and pepper. Strain
   cornstarch over shrimp to cover.
3. Put each shrimp in the egg and water mixture.
4. Heat ½ cup oil to moderate heat in skillet. Saute shrimp,
   inside first, until color changes. Turn over. Remove. Keep
   warm. Clean pan.
5. Heat 2 tablespoons oil to moderate heat in same skillet. Stir-

*Leeks may be substituted.

fry ginger and garlic 30 seconds. Add remaining sauce ingredients. Bring to boil. Turn down heat. Leave in pan.
6. Heat 3 tablespoons oil in wok. Stir-fry spinach, add a little salt. Place on platter. Put shrimp on top. Pour sauce over.
7. Garnish with almonds and scallion.

May be prepared in advance through Step 2. Stack shrimp and wrap in wax paper. May not be frozen.

Serves 4 to 6

Crystal Shrimp SZECHWAN

A crispy, crunchy banquet dish. A gourmet's delight.

1 **pound shrimp, shelled, deveined, dried thoroughly**	1 **slice ginger, minced**
1 **teaspoon salt**	6 **tablespoons tomato catsup**
1 **egg white**	1 **tablespoon sugar**
¾ **to 1 cup cornstarch**	2 **tablespoons chicken stock**
2 **to 4 cups oil for deep-frying**	1 **teaspoon pepper oil (see**
1 **scallion, minced**	**Index)**

1. Mix shrimp with salt, egg white, and cornstarch until heavily coated. Shrimp should separate and not stick together. Shake off excess cornstarch before frying.
2. Heat oil in wok. Deep-fry shrimp. Add one by one. Do not slide in together. Fry about 1 minute. Drain. Remove.
3. Deep-fry again 30 seconds. Drain. Remove.
4. Return 2 tablespoons oil to wok. Stir-fry scallion and ginger until there is an aroma. Add catsup, sugar, stock, and pepper oil. Bring to boil.
5. Pour fried shrimp into sauce. Put on platter and serve immediately.

May be prepared in advance through Step 2. May be frozen.

Serves 4 to 6

Fried Shrimp with Walnuts   SHANGHAI

Only the Chinese would think of combining shrimp and walnuts.

1 **pound large shrimp (16 to 20), shelled, deveined, cut in half crosswise**
½ **teaspoon salt**
1 **teaspoon cornstarch**
½ **cup carrots and peas (frozen)**
2 **to 4 cups oil for deep-frying**
1 **cup shelled walnuts**
1 **slice ginger, chopped fine**
1 **scallion, chopped fine**

Sauce:
1 **tablespoon sherry**
4 **tablespoons chicken stock**
1 **teaspoon cornstarch**
½ **teaspoon salt**
Few drops of sesame seed oil

1. Wash shrimp thoroughly. Wipe dry with paper towel. Mix shrimp with salt and cornstarch. Combine sauce ingredients in a bowl. Set aside.
2. Plunge carrots and peas into boiling water 1 minute. Drain. Remove.
3. Heat oil in wok. Deep-fry shrimp 1 minute until color turns pink. Drain. Set aside.
4. Deep-fry walnuts 3 minutes. (Place in large strainer to prevent scattering.) Drain. Remove.
5. Reheat 2 tablespoons oil in wok. Stir-fry ginger and scallions 30 seconds. Add carrots and peas. Stir-fry 1 minute.
6. Pour in shrimp. Stir-fry shrimp 1 minute on high heat. Pour in sauce. Stir-fry 1 minute. Add walnuts. Stir-fry quickly. Serve immediately.

May be prepared in advance through Step 4. May not be frozen.

Serves 4 to 6

Shrimp with Broccoli   CANTON

Broccoli is a wonderful source of vitamin B. Combined with shrimp—a healthy dish.

1 **pound medium shrimp, shelled, devcined**	*Sauce:*
½ **teaspoon salt**	2 **tablespoons light soy sauce**
1 **tablespoon cornstarch**	1 **tablespoon sherry**
2 to 4 **cups oil for deep-frying**	1 **teaspoon sugar**
1 **clove garlic, minced**	4 **tablespoons chicken stock**
1 **slice ginger, minced**	1 **teaspoon cornstarch**
2 **stalks broccoli, peeled***	2 **teaspoons sesame seed oil**

1. Mix shrimp with salt and cornstarch. Use hands.
2. Combine sauce ingredients. Set aside.
3. Heat oil in wok. On moderate heat deep-fry shrimp until color changes. Drain. Remove.
4. Reheat 2 tablespoons oil in wok. Stir-fry garlic and ginger 30 seconds. Add broccoli. Stir-fry 1 minute.
5. Pour in the sauce mixture. Bring to boil. Pour in shrimp. Stir-fry 1 minute more.

---

*Use flowerettes and thin, diagonal slices of stalk.

May be prepared in advance through Step 3. May not be frozen.

Serves 4 to 6

Shrimp with Cashew Nuts   SZECHWAN

Students love this. It is so easy to prepare.

1 **pound shrimp, shelled,
   deveined**
½ **teaspoon salt**
1 **tablespoon cornstarch**
2 to 4 **cups oil for deep-frying**
½ **cup cashews**
10 **whole dried red chilies**
1 **scallion, cut into 1-inch
   pieces**
1 **clove garlic, minced**
½ **onion, cubed**
1 **green pepper, cubed**

Sauce:
¼ **cup chicken stock**
2 **tablespoons light soy sauce**
1 **teaspoon red wine vinegar**
1 **teaspoon cornstarch,
   dissolved in 2 teaspoons
   water**

1. Combine sauce ingredients. Set aside.
2. Mix shrimp with salt and cornstarch.
3. Heat oil. Deep-fry shrimp until color changes. Drain. Remove. Deep-fry cashews in large strainer until light brown (30 seconds). Drain. Remove.
4. Reheat 2 tablespoons oil in wok. Fry chilies until dark brown. Add scallion and garlic. Stir-fry 30 seconds. Add onion. Stir-fry 1 minute. Add green pepper. Stir-fry 30 seconds more. Remove chilies.
5. Pour in sauce. Bring to boil. Add shrimp and nuts. Mix until shrimp and nuts are glazed. Remove to serving platter.

May be prepared in advance through Step 3. May not be frozen.

Serves 4 to 6

Shrimp with Fava Beans SHANGHAI

This is an impressive company dish.

1 pound shrimp, shelled,
  deveined, cut in half
  lengthwise
½ teaspoon salt
1 tablespoon cornstarch
2 to 4 cups oil for deep-frying
1 pound fava beans

½ cup water
2 teaspoons cornstarch,
  dissolved in ¼ cup chicken
  stock
2 tablespoons cooked
  Virginia ham, minced

1. Mix shrimp with salt and cornstarch. Heat oil. Deep-fry shrimp until color changes. Drain. Set aside.
2. Shell fava beans. Remove inner skin.
3. Return 1 tablespoon oil to wok. Add ½ cup water. Add beans. Cook 2 to 3 minutes on high heat. Remove. Drain.
4. Reheat 1 tablespoon oil in wok. Stir-fry beans 1 minute. Add dissolved cornstarch. Bring to boil. Add shrimp. Stir-fry thoroughly 1 minute. Sprinkle with ham. Remove to serving platter.

May be prepared in advance through Step 2. May not be frozen.

Serves 4 to 6

Don't judge the tree until you see the fruit.

Slippery Shrimp   SZECHWAN

A favorite dish—easy, delicious, and attractive to the eye.

1½ pounds shrimp, shelled,
   deveined, cut in half
   lengthwise
1 teaspoon salt
1 egg white
6 tablespoons cornstarch
2 to 4 cups oil for deep-frying
1 slice ginger, minced
2 cloves garlic, minced
1½ tablespoons cornstarch,
   dissolved in 3 tablespoons
   water
2 scallions, chopped fine

Sauce:
4 tablespoons catsup
1 teaspoon pepper oil (see
   Index)
Pinch of crushed red chili
   peppers
1½ tablespoons sugar
2 scallions, chopped fine
1 cup water

1. Mix shrimp with salt, egg white, and 1 tablespoon cornstarch. Set aside 10 minutes. Coat shrimp heavily with remaining cornstarch. Place shrimp in a strainer and shake off excess cornstarch. Shrimp must be very dry.
2. Combine sauce ingredients in a bowl. Heat 1 tablespoon oil in saucepan. Stir-fry ginger and garlic 30 seconds. Add sauce ingredients and bring to boil. Thicken with dissolved cornstarch. Sprinkle scallions on top.
3. Heat remaining oil in wok. Deep-fry shrimp 1 minute. Drain. Remove. Heat oil again. Deep-fry shrimp again until crispy. Drain. Remove to platter. Pour hot sauce over shrimp. Serve immediately.

May be prepared in advance through first deep-frying in Step 3. May not be frozen.

Serves 4 to 6

Prawns in the Shell, Szechwan Style   SZECHWAN

This is an exquisite dish for the buffet table.

10 jumbo prawns
2 to 4 cups oil for deep-frying
½ onion, minced
2 scallions, minced
4 slices ginger, minced
2 tablespoons tomato catsup

¼ cup chicken stock
2 tablespoons chili paste
  with garlic
1 tablespoon sherry
1 tablespoon sugar

1. Wash prawns. Remove feet. Make a cut in the shell along the back. Remove the black vein. Pat dry.
2. Heat oil. Deep-fry prawns until color changes. Drain. Remove.
3. Reheat 2 tablespoons oil in wok. Stir-fry onion, scallion, and ginger 1 minute. Add catsup, stock, and chili paste. Bring to boil.
4. Pour in prawns. Add sherry and sugar. Stir-fry briskly on high heat 1 minute. Remove to platter.

May be prepared in advance through Step 3. May not be frozen.

Serves 4 to 6

Shrimp Balls with Pea Pod Leaves   SHANGHAI

Pea pod leaves are rarely seen in markets in America. Once in a while, you can find them in Chinatown. Watercress is a good substitute. Shrimp balls and pea pod leaves or watercress is a delicate, subtly flavored combination.

1 pound shrimp, shelled, deveined, ground
1 egg
1 teaspoon salt
1 teaspoon cornstarch
Pinch of black pepper
1 tablespoon sherry
1 slice ginger, minced
4 water chestnuts, minced
2 scallions, chopped fine

2 to 4 cups oil for deep-frying
1 bunch pea pod leaves (watercress or spinach), leaves only
1 cup chicken stock
1 tablespoon cornstarch, dissolved in 2 tablespoons water
Pinch of sugar (optional)

1. Mix shrimp, egg, ½ teaspoon salt, cornstarch, pepper, sherry, ginger, water chestnuts, and scallions with chopsticks until the consistency is such that the mixture adheres to the chopsticks (food processor can be used).
2. Form the shrimp mixture into balls with a wet tablespoon and the palm of your hand.
3. Heat oil in wok for deep-frying. Fry shrimp balls 2 minutes. Drain. Remove.
4. Reheat 1 tablespoon oil in wok until very hot. Add remaining salt. Add pea pod leaves. Stir-fry 1 minute. Remove.
5. Reheat 1 tablespoon oil in wok. Add shrimp balls, stock, and pea pod leaves. Bring to boil. Thicken with dissolved cornstarch. Add sugar.

May be prepared in advance through Step 3. May not be frozen.

Serves 4 to 6

Squid Stir-Fried with Pork SHANGHAI

So delicious when complimented with rice.

2 pounds squid
1 pound pork, shredded
½ teaspoon salt
1 egg white
1 tablespoon cornstarch
2 to 4 cups oil for deep-frying
2 scallions, cut into 1-inch pieces

1 can pickled snow cabbage
(mustard green)
1 teaspoon sugar
½ teaspoon crushed red chili
peppers
1 teaspoon light soy sauce

1. Clean squid by cutting open and removing ink sac and cuttlebone. Remove skin and score squid diagonally on the inner side and cut into quarters or in half, depending on size of squid. Drain and pat dry with paper towels. (A teaspoon of cornstarch may be added to absorb extra water.) Squid must be very dry.
2. Mix pork with salt, egg white, and cornstarch.
3. Heat oil in wok. Deep-fry pork until color changes. Drain. Set aside. Deep-fry squid 30 seconds. Drain. Set aside.
4. Reheat 2 tablespoons oil in wok. Stir-fry scallions 1 minute. Add snow cabbage, sugar, and crushed red chili peppers. Stir-fry until mixed. Add pork. Stir-fry briskly. Add soy sauce and squid. Stir-fry about 1 minute. (Squid will curl up when cooked.) Remove to platter.

May be prepared in advance through Step 3. May be frozen.

Serves 4 to 6

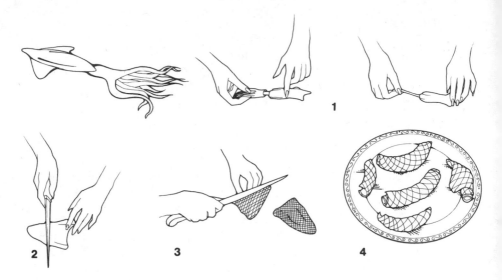

Squid in Hot Sauce   SZECHWAN

This is a beautiful dish, the white squid embellished with green pepper. Those who are calorie conscious can enjoy this with no feeling of guilt.

2   pounds squid
2 to 4 cups oil for deep-frying
1   medium onion, cut into cubes
1   green pepper, cut into small cubes
2   teaspoons crushed red chili peppers

Sauce:
2   tablespoons light soy sauce
1   tablespoon sherry
1   tablespoon red wine vinegar
2   tablespoons chicken stock
1   tablespoon sugar
1   teaspoon cornstarch
4   cloves garlic, minced
2   slices ginger, shredded
2   scallions, shredded

1. Clean squid by cutting open and removing ink sac and cuttlebone. Remove skin and score squid diagonally on the inner side and cut into quarters or in half, depending on size of squid. Drain and pat dry with paper towels. (A teaspoon

of cornstarch may be added to absorb extra water.) Squid must be very dry.

2. Combine sauce ingredients. Cook in a saucepan until thickened.

3. Heat oil in wok. Oil must be very hot and squid must be absolutely dry. Cook squid by immersing in hot oil. Remove with a strainer immediately.

4. Reheat 1 tablespoon oil in wok. Add onion. Stir-fry 1 minute. Add green pepper and crushed red chili peppers. Stir-fry 1 minute more. Add sauce. Bring to boil. Add squid. Stir-fry until glazed. (Squid will curl up when cooked.) Remove to a platter and serve immediately.

May be prepared in advance through Step 2. May not be frozen.

Serves 4 to 6

Stop feeling sorry for yourself.

9

Vegetables

The poverty of the Chinese may have resulted in their becoming culinary experts. They made use of every growing plant. Today one can prepare a Chinese meal to fit into a very limited budget. The mixture of vegetables cut up with meat or fish can create an elegant, well-balanced meal. Vegetables cooked by themselves are either steamed or rapidly stir-fried. This quick cooking retains the vitamins and nutritional value of the vegetable.

Agar Agar Salad   ALL REGIONS

The Chinese use agar agar just as Westerners use lettuce in salads.

1 **tablespoon dry Chinese mustard**	*Sauce:*
2 **tablespoons cold water**	2 **tablespoons sesame seed paste**
½ **ounce agar agar**	2 **tablespoons white vinegar**
1 **large cucumber, cut in half lengthwise**	2 **tablespoons light soy sauce**
1 **cup cooked chicken, shredded**	1 **teaspoon salt**
2 **tablespoons cooked ham, shredded**	1 **tablespoon sesame seed oil**

1. Mix mustard thoroughly with cold water. Set aside at least 15 minutes. Mix sauce ingredients together.
2. Using scissors, cut agar agar into pieces 1½ inches long. Seed and shred cucumber. Leave skin on.
3. Soak agar agar in warm water 15 minutes. Squeeze dry. Put on platter in a circle.
4. Arrange cucumber on top of agar agar. Put chicken on top of cucumber. Spread ham on top of chicken. Refrigerate.
5. Pour sauce and mustard on salad. Toss just before serving.

May be prepared in advance through Step 4. May not be frozen.

Serves 4 to 6

Chicken and Vegetable Salad   SHANGHAI

You can use any leftover meat to produce this lightly seasoned salad. The pungent smell of the sesame seed oil makes this dish special.

3 tablespoons oil
3 small cucumbers, skin and
   seeds removed, cut into 1-
   inch cubes
½ pound cabbage, cut into 1-
   inch cubes
1 green pepper, cut into ½-
   inch cubes
1 cup cooked chicken, cut
   into ½-inch cubes

Sauce:
1 teaspoon sugar (optional)
2 tablespoons red wine
   vinegar
2 tablespoons light soy sauce
1 teaspoon pepper oil
   (optional)
1 tablespoon sesame seed oil

1. Combine sauce ingredients. Set aside.
2. Heat oil in wok. Stir-fry cucumbers, cabbage, and green pepper on high heat 1 minute. Remove.
3. Put chicken in bowl. Add the vegetables and sauce. Mix well.
4. Chill in refrigerator before serving.

May be prepared in advance. May not be frozen.

Serves 4 to 6

The glory of life is being useful.

Cucumber Salad   ALL REGIONS

A cool and multicolored, yellow, green, red, and white summer salad.

2   cucumbers, washed, peeled
1   tablespoon oil
2   eggs, beaten
½ pound ham, cooked,
    shredded
2   cooked chicken breasts,
    boned, skinned, shredded

Sauce:
3   tablespoons light soy sauce
3   tablespoons red wine
    vinegar
1   teaspoon dry mustard
    powder
2   tablespoons sesame seed
    oil
1   teaspoon chili paste with
    garlic

1. Combine sauce ingredients. Set aside.
2. Cut cucumbers in half lengthwise. Remove seeds. Cut into 1-inch pieces. Shred lengthwise.
3. Grease skillet with oil. Pour in beaten eggs. Fry egg on each side like a pancake. Remove. Cut pancake in thirds lengthwise. Shred crosswise.
4. Arrange egg, cucumber, ham, and chicken shreds next to each other on round platter.
5. Pour sauce over and toss just before serving.

May be prepared in advance through Step 4. May not be frozen.

Serves 4 to 6

Pickled Cucumber with Pineapple   CANTON

This is a refreshing side dish for summer.

4 cucumbers	1 small can sliced pineapple
1 teaspoon salt	or ½ fresh pineapple and
4 tablespoons white vinegar	½ teaspoon salt
4 tablespoons sugar	

1. Cut cucumbers lengthwise. Leave skin on. Scoop out seeds. Cut into thin slices crosswise. Sprinkle with salt. Set aside for 1 hour. Drain liquid.
2. Add vinegar and sugar to cucumber.
3. When using canned pineapple, cut each piece into 8 pieces. Mix with cucumber, sugar, and vinegar. Put in refrigerator at least 1 hour before serving.
4. When using fresh pineapple, peel, remove brown spots, and slice. Cut each slice into 8 pieces. Sprinkle with ½ teaspoon salt. Set aside 1 hour. Pour off liquid. Use as garnish around cucumbers.

May be prepared in advance. May not be frozen.

Serves 4 to 6

Mushrooms with Brown Sauce   ALL REGIONS

These dried black mushrooms are considered a delicacy in China. Your guests will enjoy having them as an unusual hors d'oeuvre.

24 medium dried black mushrooms	3 tablespoons dark soy sauce
	2 tablespoons oil
Boiling water to cover	1 tablespoon sugar

1. Wash mushrooms. Soak in water 30 minutes. Remove stems. Save water.
2. Put mushrooms with same water to cover in a saucepan. Pour carefully for there is residue at the bottom.
3. Cook mushrooms in this water with soy sauce and oil. Simmer covered 1 hour or until mushrooms are tender. Stir occasionally.
4. Bring to high heat. Add sugar. Cook until gravy coats the mushrooms.

May be prepared in advance. May not be frozen.

Serves 4 to 6

Braised Mushrooms and Spinach   SHANGHAI

This is a work of art. Dark brown on the surface and jade green underneath. A wonderful contrast of flavors and textures.

4 tablespoons oil	2 tablespoons dark soy sauce
24 small dried black mushrooms, soaked 20 minutes in boiling water, simmered 1 hour, stems removed	1 tablespoon sugar
	½ cup chicken stock
	½ teaspoon salt
	2 bunches spinach, cleaned, stems removed

1. Heat 2 tablespoons oil in wok. Add mushrooms, soy sauce, sugar, and stock. Cook on high heat until glazed and mushrooms have absorbed the liquid. Remove.
2. Heat 2 tablespoons oil in wok. Add salt. Pour in spinach. Stir with chopsticks until just wilted. Drain thoroughly.
3. Using chopsticks, remove spinach to a round plate. Arrange in a small mound. Arrange mushrooms, smooth sides up, on top of spinach. The mushrooms will cover the spinach. Serve hot or cold.

May be prepared in advance. May not be frozen.

Serves 4 to 6

Assorted Vegetables

An original dish by Madame Wong. Vegetarians love it.

4 tablespoons oil
1 teaspoon salt
1 carrot, sliced diagonally
1 stalk broccoli, cleaned, sliced diagonally
1 cup bok choy, cut into 1-inch pieces
1 cup snow peas, strings removed
½ cup straw mushrooms
½ cup fresh mushrooms, sliced
½ cup dried black mushrooms, soaked 20 minutes in boiling water, shredded

½ cup baby corn, cut in half
½ red pepper, cubed
2 fried bean curd cakes, cut into quarters
2 tablespoons light soy sauce
½ cup chicken stock
1 tablespoon cornstarch, dissolved in 1 tablespoon water
1 tablespoon sesame seed oil

1. Heat 2 tablespoons oil in wok. Add salt. Stir-fry carrot, broccoli, and bok choy. Add snow peas. Stir one minute more. Remove.
2. Heat 2 tablespoons oil. Stir-fry remaining vegetables and soy bean cakes 1 minute. Return first batch of vegetables to wok.
3. Add soy sauce and stock. Bring to boil. Thicken with dissolved cornstarch. Add sesame seed oil.

May be prepared in advance. May not be frozen.

Serves 4 to 6

Fava Beans   ALL REGIONS

This is a great favorite of the Chinese. Fava beans resemble lima beans. They are in season during May and June. The Chinese cook them in large quantities and enjoy them as a complete meal.

3 tablespoons oil
2 pounds fava beans, shells
   removed

1 cup water
1 teaspoon salt
2 tablespoons sugar

1. Heat oil in wok. Stir-fry beans 30 seconds. Add water.
2. Add salt and sugar. Cover. Simmer 10 minutes. Serve hot or cold.

May be prepared in advance. May not be frozen.

Serves 4 to 6

Deep-Fried Zucchini and Eggplant   SYLVIA'S CREATION

Use this as a vegetable dish or as an appetizer.

2 zucchini
1 eggplant
3 tablespoons flour
Pinch of salt and pepper

1 cup sweet rice flour
Cold water
2 to 4 cups oil for deep-frying

1. Diagonally slice zucchini and eggplant into ½-inch pieces. Leave skin on.
2. Dust with flour. Add salt and pepper.
3. Combine sweet rice flour and cold water to make a batter. Should be slightly runny. Dip vegetable pieces into batter.
4. Heat oil in wok. Deep-fry zucchini and eggplant, a few pieces at a time until crisp. Drain on paper towels. Serve hot.

May be prepared in advance through Step 2. May not be frozen.

Serves 4 to 6

Stuffed Eggplant SHANGHAI

This is the creation of Chef Ling Chiao. Veal or chicken may be substituted for pork.

10 oriental eggplants
20 scallion stalks for ties
4 tablespoons oil
2 large slices ginger, minced
3 cloves garlic, minced
3 scallions, chopped fine
1¼ pounds pork
2 tablespoons sherry

¼ cup light soy sauce
¾ cup chicken stock
2 teaspoons sugar
2 tablespoons cornstarch, dissolved in 2 tablespoons water
1 tablespoon sesame seed oil

1. Split eggplant in half lengthwise. Blanch in boiling water 1 minute. Blanch scallion stalks until soft. Drain. Remove.
2. Heat 1 tablespoon oil in wok. Stir-fry ginger, garlic, and chopped scallions until there is an aroma. Remove. Mix with pork.
3. Make a sandwich with two halves of eggplant, using pork mixture as filling. Tie each sandwich together with two scallion stalks.
4. Heat 3 tablespoons oil in skillet. Put in eggplant sandwiches. Brown 2 minutes on each side.
5. Add sherry, soy sauce, stock, and sugar. Cover. Simmer 30 minutes.
6. Uncover. Bring sauce to boil. Thicken with dissolved cornstarch. Add sesame seed oil.
7. Put on platter. Pour sauce over.

May be prepared in advance through Step 5. May not be frozen.

Serves 10

Eggplants don't grow on melon vines.

Nun's Pillow   CANTON

This is a famous dish in Chinese monasteries. The nuns ate only vegetables. In this recipe of vegetables the package looks like a pillow, thus the name.

4 pieces of dried bean curd sheet*	¼ cup bamboo shoots, chopped fine
1 pound bok choy	4 tablespoons light soy sauce
5 tablespoons oil	¼ pound bean sprouts
4 dried black mushrooms, soaked in boiling water 20 minutes, cooked 20 minutes, stems removed, chopped fine	½ teaspoon salt
	1 tablespoon cornstarch, dissolved in 2 tablespoons water
	1½ to 2 cups chicken stock
	1 teaspoon sugar

1. Pour boiling water over bean curd sheets to soften. Drain. Remove. Cut into 4-inch squares. Cover with towel. Set aside.
2. Boil bok choy in boiling water 2 minutes. Drain. Squeeze out water. Chop fine.
3. Heat 2 tablespoons oil in wok. Stir-fry bok choy 1 minute. Add mushrooms and bamboo shoots. Add 2 tablespoons soy sauce. Stir-fry 2 minutes. Remove to plate.
4. Heat 1 tablespoon oil. Stir-fry bean sprouts 30 seconds. Add salt. Remove.
5. Combine bok choy mixture with bean sprouts to make filling.
6. Use bean curd sheet as wrapper. Scoop 1½ tablespoons of mixture onto each bean curd square. Wrap like an egg roll.** Seal the end of each package with dissolved cornstarch.
7. Heat remaining oil. Fry packages on both sides. Add more oil if necessary.
8. Add stock to half cover the packages. Add 2 tablespoons soy sauce and sugar. Cover and cook over low heat 40 minutes. Serve hot or cold.

---

*If bean curd sheets are not available, use cabbage leaves. Secure with toothpick. Cook 10 minutes only.
**See egg roll illustration on page 24.

May be prepared in advance. May be frozen.

12 Packages

Our Special Broccoli ALL REGIONS

Every student loves this dish. They consume it as a meal by itself.

1½ pounds broccoli
3 tablespoons oil
½ teaspoon salt
½ cup chicken stock
½ teaspoon sugar

½ tablespoon cornstarch, dissolved in 1 tablespoon water
1 tablespoon sesame seed oil

1. Separate broccoli flowerettes. Remove tough skin and leaves from stalks. Cut stalks diagonally into slices about 1½ inches long. Wash and drain.
2. Heat oil in wok. Add salt. Stir-fry broccoli 2 minutes. Add stock and sugar. Bring to boil. Thicken with dissolved cornstarch. Add sesame seed oil.

May be prepared in advance through Step 1. May not be frozen.

Serves 4 to 6

Pea Pods with
Szechwan Preserved Vegetable ALL REGIONS

Pea pods or snow peas, as they are sometimes called, are considered a sophisticated vegetable by the Chinese.

2 tablespoons oil
½ teaspoon salt
1 pound pea pods, strings removed

½ cup Szechwan preserved vegetable, minced
1 teaspoon sugar
1 tablespoon sherry

1. Heat oil in wok. Add salt. Add pea pods and Szechwan preserved vegetable. Stir-fry 1 minute.
2. Add sugar and sherry. Stir-fry 1 minute more on high heat.

May not be prepared in advance. May not be frozen.

Serves 4 to 6

Three-in-One Vegetables   ALL REGIONS

Healthy, quick-cooked vegetables with a spicy sauce. Delicious with Three-Flavored Scallops with Ponzu Vinegar.

1 **pound broccoli**	½ **cup chicken stock**
2 **carrots**	1 **large clove garlic, minced**
½ **small head celery cabbage**	1 **teaspoon sugar**
2 **tablespoons oil**	2 **teaspoons sesame seed oil**
2 **teaspoons chili paste with**	2 **teaspoons cornstarch,**
garlic	**dissolved in 4 teaspoons**
½ **teaspoon salt**	**water**
1 **tablespoon sherry**	

1. Remove stalks from broccoli;* save for use in another recipe. Separate flowerettes into small pieces. Cut carrots diagonally into ¼-inch pieces. Cut cabbage into 1½-inch-square pieces.
2. Heat oil in wok. Add chili paste with garlic. Stir-fry 30 seconds. Add vegetables and salt. Stir-fry 1 minute.
3. Add sherry, stock, garlic, sugar, and sesame seed oil. Stir-fry 1 minute. Bring to boil. Thicken with dissolved cornstarch. Serve immediately.

---

*See Broccoli Stalks with Sesame Seed Oil in Dim Sum chapter.

May be prepared in advance through Step 1. May not be frozen.

Serves 4 to 6

Pea Pods with Triple Mushrooms   ALL REGIONS

The jade-colored pea pods combined with three varieties of mushrooms make an exquisite dish—so easy to prepare.

4 tablespoons oil
6 fresh mushrooms, sliced
½ can straw mushrooms (16-ounce can), drained
6 dried black mushrooms, soaked in boiling water 20 minutes, cooked 20 minutes, stems removed, sliced thin

1 pound pea pods, strings removed
½ teaspoon salt
1 teaspoon sugar
1 tablespoon sherry
1 tablespoon sesame seed oil

1. Heat 2 tablespoons oil in wok until it is smoking hot. Add all mushrooms. Stir-fry 1 minute. Remove.
2. Heat remaining oil in wok. Add pea pods. Stir-fry 1 minute. Pour in mushrooms. Add salt, sugar, and sherry. Stir-fry briskly until thoroughly heated. Add sesame seed oil. Stir-fry 1 second more.

May not be prepared in advance. May not be frozen.

Serves 4 to 6

True words are more valuable than gold.

Hot Spicy Cabbage   SZECHWAN

If this is too spicy for you, put in only five chili peppers.

4 tablespoons oil
1 clove garlic, minced
10 dried red chili peppers
1 large head cabbage, cut
   into 2-inch pieces
4 tablespoons red wine vinegar

2 tablespoons light soy sauce
2 tablespoons sugar
½ teaspoon salt
1 teaspoon cornstarch,
   dissolved in 2 teaspoons
   water

1. Heat oil in wok. Stir-fry garlic 30 seconds. When oil is smoking hot, add chili peppers. Stir-fry until brown.
2. Add cabbage. Stir-fry 2 minutes.
3. Add vinegar, soy sauce, sugar, and salt. Thicken with dissolved cornstarch. Remove peppers before serving.

May be prepared in advance. May not be frozen.

Serves 4 to 6

Shanghai-Style Celery Cabbage with
Bean Curd Sheet   SHANGHAI

This dish will give you renewed energy.

2 ounces bean curd sheet
3 tablespoons oil
1½ pounds celery cabbage,
   cut into 1½-inch pieces
½ teaspoon salt
4 dried black mushrooms,
   soaked 20 minutes in
   boiling water, cooked 20

minutes, stems removed,
cut into quarters
3 tablespoons dark soy sauce
1 tablespoon sugar
1 tablespoon cornstarch,
   dissolved in 1 tablespoon
   water
2 tablespoons sesame seed oil

1. Soak bean curd sheet in boiling water about 10 minutes. Tear into small pieces. Drain. Remove.
2. Heat oil in wok. Add cabbage and salt. Stir-fry 1 minute. Add bean curd, mushrooms, soy sauce, and sugar. Stir-fry 3 minutes. Thicken with dissolved cornstarch. Add sesame seed oil.

May be prepared in advance. May not be frozen.

Serves 4 to 6

Stir-Fried Chinese Cabbage ALL REGIONS

Green vegetables that are stir-fried quickly in oil always retain their color.

1½ pounds Chinese cabbage or bok choy	1 teaspoon salt
4 tablespoons oil	½ cup water
	1 teaspoon sugar

1. Discard outer leaves of cabbage. Cut cabbage into quarters lengthwise.
2. Heat oil in wok until it is smoking hot. Stir-fry cabbage 1 minute.
3. Add salt and water. Cook covered 3 minutes.
4. Remove cover. Bring to high heat. Add sugar. Cook 1 minute. Stir constantly. Serve hot or cold.

May be prepared in advance. May not be frozen.

Serves 4 to 6

Spicy Sweet Sour Cabbage SZECHWAN

The Chinese serve this as a cold plate. A super salad to serve if you like a spicy flavor.

1 pound celery cabbage	3 tablespoons white vinegar
1½ teaspoons salt	4 tablespoons sugar
4 slices ginger, thinly shredded	1 tablespoon pepper oil (see Index)
1 tablespoon oil	

1. Discard core of cabbage. Cut cabbage into pieces 2 inches in length.
2. Put cabbage in a bowl. Sprinkle with salt. Let stand 4 hours.
3. Squeeze liquid from cabbage with hands. Place in container. Distribute ginger evenly on cabbage.
4. Heat oil in wok. Add vinegar, sugar, and pepper oil. Turn off heat as soon as sugar is dissolved. Pour over cabbage. Cover and refrigerate. Serve cold.

May be prepared in advance. May not be frozen.

Serves 4 to 6

Asparagus with Braised Black Mushrooms   SHANGHAI

An elegant company dish.

½ pound asparagus
20 medium dried black
  mushrooms, soaked 20
  minutes in boiling water,
  stems removed
3 tablespoons oil
1 tablespoon dark soy sauce
2 teaspoons sugar

2 cups chicken stock
20 small fresh mushrooms,
  cleaned
2 tablespoons oyster sauce
1 tablespoon light soy sauce
1 tablespoon cornstarch,
  dissolved in 2 tablespoons
  water

1. Wash asparagus. Discard hard ends. Leave asparagus whole. Cook in boiling water 3 minutes. Drain. Remove. Arrange in center of platter. Keep warm.
2. Heat 1 tablespoon oil in wok. Add dried mushrooms, dark soy sauce, 1 teaspoon sugar, and 1 cup stock. Cook uncovered on low heat 20 minutes. Turn heat up. Cook until liquid is glazed. Arrange mushrooms on one side of serving platter.
3. Heat remaining oil in wok. Stir-fry fresh mushrooms 2 minutes. Arrange on other side of the platter.
4. Heat remaining stock in wok. Add oyster sauce, light soy sauce, and remaining sugar. Bring to boil. Thicken with dissolved cornstarch.
5. Pour the sauce over asparagus and mushrooms. Serve immediately.

May not be prepared in advance. May not be frozen.

Serves 4 to 6

Stir-Fried Asparagus with Shrimp ALL REGIONS

Pink shrimp and green asparagus—a beautiful color combination.

1 pound medium-size shrimp, shelled, deveined, cut in half crosswise	1 slice ginger, minced
	1 clove garlic, minced
½ teaspoon salt	½ teaspoon sugar
1 teaspoon cornstarch	1 tablespoon light soy sauce
½ pound asparagus	4 tablespoons chicken stock
3 tablespoons oil	1 tablespoon sesame seed oil

1. Mix shrimp with salt and cornstarch. Set aside.
2. Wash asparagus. Discard tough ends. Roll cut into 1-inch pieces.
3. Heat 1 tablespoon oil in wok. Stir-fry shrimp 30 seconds. Drain. Remove.
4. Heat remaining oil in wok. Add ginger and garlic. Stir-fry 30 seconds. Add asparagus. Stir-fry 1 minute. Add shrimp, sugar, soy sauce, and stock. Stir-fry vigorously 1 minute. Add sesame seed oil.
5. Remove to platter. Serve immediately.

May be prepared in advance through Step 2. May not be frozen.

Serves 4 to 6

Learn the art of enjoying yourself.

Stir-Fried Asparagus with
Fermented Black Beans   CANTON

Fermented black bean is a wonderful seasoning for Chinese dishes. It gives excellent flavor to asparagus.

1 pound asparagus	1 scallion, cut into 1-inch
2 tablespoons fermented	pieces
black beans, chopped	½ teaspoon sugar
1 clove garlic, minced	¼ cup chicken stock
1 tablespoon water	1 teaspoon cornstarch,
2 tablespoons oil	dissolved in 2 teaspoons
1 slice ginger, chopped fine	water

1. Wash asparagus. Discard tough ends. Roll cut into 1-inch pieces.
2. Pound fermented black beans with garlic and water in a small bowl.
3. Heat oil in wok. Stir-fry ginger, scallion, and the black bean mixture until there is an aroma. Pour in asparagus. Stir-fry 2 minutes. Add sugar and stock. Bring to boil. Thicken with dissolved cornstarch. Serve immediately.

May be prepared in advance through Step 2. May not be frozen.

Serves 4 to 6

Stir-Fried Asparagus   ALL REGIONS

We love this asparagus just as much as Our Special Broccoli.

1 pound asparagus	½ tablespoon cornstarch,
2 tablespoons oil	dissolved in 1 tablespoon
1 teaspoon salt	water
¼ cup chicken stock	1 tablespoon sesame seed oil
½ teaspoon sugar	

1. Wash asparagus in cold water.
2. Roll cut into 1-inch pieces. Discard the hard part.
3. Heat oil in wok to smoking hot. Pour in asparagus. Stir rapidly 1 minute. Add salt, stock, and sugar. Bring to boil. Thicken with dissolved cornstarch. Add sesame seed oil.

May be prepared in advance through Step 2. May not be frozen.

Serves 4 to 6

Szechwan Pickled Vegetables   SZECHWAN

Here is a traditional recipe. In China every housewife knows how to pickle vegetables. It is ideal for today's world of dieters—low in calories, easy to do, any vegetable can be used. Serve it as an appetizer or side dish.

1 pound cabbage	1 cup boiling water
½ cup string beans	1 tablespoon Szechwan
2 small cucumbers	peppercorns
1 carrot	4 whole dried chili peppers
½ cup cauliflower flowerettes	3 cups cold water
2 tablespoons salt	2 tablespoons gin

1. Remove outer leaves from cabbage. String and nip off ends of beans. Cut cabbage, beans, and cucumbers into 1½-inch pieces. Cut carrot in half lengthwise and cut into 1-inch pieces crosswise.
2. Dissolve salt in boiling water in 2-quart jar. Stir until completely dissolved. Add peppercorns and chili peppers. Stir well.
3. Add cold water and stir. Add gin.
4. Add vegetables. Stir well with chopsticks. Press the vegetables down so that they are completely covered by brine.
5. Cover jar. Refrigerate 4 to 5 days.

Note: Keep liquid in refrigerator. When reusing, add 2 teaspoons salt. Refill with your own desired vegetables. After adding fresh vegetables twice, replace chili peppers and add 1 tablespoon gin. Always use clean chopsticks or spoon for removing vegetables.

May be prepared in advance. May not be frozen.

Serves 4 to 6

Vegetables of Harmony and Peace   ALL REGIONS

Here is a healthy and easily digestible dish. It is often eaten on festival days.

3 **egg pancakes (see recipe below)**	2 **carrots, julienne**
6 **ounces vermicelli (cellophane noodles)**	2 **tablespoons Szechwan preserved vegetable, washed, julienne**
2 **tablespoons oil**	2 **tablespoons sliced canned mushrooms (optional)**
1 **slice ginger, minced**	3 **tablespoons oyster sauce**
1 **clove garlic, minced**	1 **tablespoon light soy sauce**
1 **scallion, chopped fine**	1 **tablespoon sesame seed oil**
1 **pound spinach, washed**	

1. Make egg pancakes. Set aside.
2. Soak vermicelli in hot water 20 minutes. Drain. Cut with scissors into pieces 4 inches long.
3. Heat oil. Stir-fry ginger, garlic, and scallion on low heat until there is an aroma. Add spinach. Stir-fry until wilted.
4. Add carrots, preserved vegetable, and mushrooms.
5. Add vermicelli. Stir-fry, mixing all ingredients well.
6. Add oyster sauce, soy sauce, and sesame seed oil. Add half the shredded pancake. Stir and mix.
7. Place on platter. Top with remaining shredded pancake.

May be prepared in advance through Step 4. May not be frozen.

Serves 4 to 6

Learning is an endless occupation.

Egg Pancake

6 teaspoons oil
3 eggs

1 tablespoon cornstarch, dissolved in 2 tablespoons water

1. Grease 8-inch skillet with 2 teaspoons oil.
2. Mix eggs with dissolved cornstarch.
3. Heat skillet to moderate heat. Pour one-third of the egg mixture into pan. When it is set, turn it over and then remove.
4. Repeat with the remaining mixture, making 3 thin pancakes. Oil skillet each time.
5. Place pancakes one on top of another. Cut into 3 long pieces. Shred on short side.

Yard Beans, Ninpoo Style   NINPOO

When you visit Chinatown, you cannot resist buying yard beans. They are also called long beans. Here is a much requested recipe.

1 pound yard beans
1 tablespoon sesame seed oil*
1 tablespoon oil

½ tablespoon sugar
3 tablespoons dark soy sauce
1 tablespoon honey

1. Cut yard beans into 1-inch pieces. Put in wok. Add remaining ingredients except honey.
2. Cook 1 hour covered on low heat. Bring to high heat. Reduce all liquids. Add honey. Stir well.

---

*One more teaspoon of sesame seed oil may be added at end if desired.

May be prepared in advance. May not be frozen.

Serves 4 to 6

Yard Beans with Chicken   CANTON

Yard beans resemble the Western-style string beans. They are 14 inches long and rich in vitamin B.

1　pound chicken breast, boned, skinned, julienne
½ teaspoon salt
1　tablespoon cornstarch
5　tablespoons oil
1　slice ginger, julienne
1　pound yard beans, cut into 1½-inch pieces

Sauce:
4　tablespoons chicken stock
1　tablespoon sherry
½ teaspoon salt
1　teaspoon sugar
1　teaspoon cornstarch, dissolved in 2 teaspoons water

1. Combine sauce ingredients. Set aside. Mix chicken with salt, cornstarch, and 1 tablespoon oil. Set aside.
2. Heat 2 tablespoons oil in wok. Add ginger. Stir-fry 30 seconds. Add yard beans. Stir-fry 1 minute more. Remove.
3. Heat remaining oil in wok. Stir-fry chicken 1 minute. Add yard beans. Pour in sauce. Stir-fry briskly until completely glazed.

May be prepared in advance through Step 2. May not be frozen.

Serves 4 to 6

Yard Beans with Pork

ALL REGIONS

This is a traditional Chinese family dish.

2 tablespoons oil	1 tablespoon sherry
1 scallion, cut into quarters	3 tablespoons dark soy sauce
1 slice ginger, pounded	1 pound yard beans, cut into
1 pound lean pork, cut into	1½-inch pieces
1-inch cubes	½ tablespoon sugar

1. Heat oil in wok. Stir-fry scallion and ginger 30 seconds. Add pork. Stir-fry until color changes. Add sherry and 1 tablespoon soy sauce. Add water to half cover. Bring to boil. Cover and simmer 15 minutes.
2. Add beans, remaining soy sauce, and sugar. Cook covered on low heat 45 minutes more.
3. Bring to boil. Baste until sauce is glazed. Serve hot or cold.

May be prepared in advance. May be frozen.

Serves 4 to 6

Vermicelli with Red and Green Peppers

ALL REGIONS

A low-calorie dish.

4 ounces vermicelli	1 cup green pepper, shredded
2 tablespoons oil	3 tablespoons dark soy sauce
2 slices ginger, minced	1 teaspoon chili paste with
2 scallions, chopped fine	garlic
1 clove garlic, minced	½ teaspoon salt
1 cup red pepper, shredded	1 teaspoon sugar

1. Soak vermicelli in boiling water 30 minutes. Cut into thirds with scissors. Drain. Set aside.
2. Heat 1 tablespoon oil in wok. Stir-fry ginger, 1 scallion, and garlic on moderate heat 30 seconds. Add red and green peppers. Stir-fry 1 minute more. Remove.
3. Heat remaining oil in wok. Add vermicelli, soy sauce, chili paste, salt, and sugar. Stir-fry on high heat 2 minutes. Add the pepper mixture. Mix well. Garnish with remaining scallion.

May be prepared in advance through Step 2. May not be frozen.

Serves 4 to 6

10

Bean Curd

DRIED BEAN CURD

The value of bean curd is finally being recognized outside of China. It is pure protein, contains no fat, and has only three hundred calories a pound. Having no flavor of its own, it is a wonderful food to mix with various sauces, scramble in eggs, crumble in salads, and add to soups. Children love it, old people digest it easily. It is called a "food for all ages." Centuries ago dried bean curd was an offering to the gods at gravesites.

213

Bean Curd with Leek   ALL REGIONS

A well-known dish. Leek contains a great deal of vitamin C.

2 boxes bean curd (to-fu, 4 pieces in a box), drained
6 tablespoons oil (may need more)
1 small can whole mushrooms
5 tablespoons light soy sauce
1 cup chicken stock

3 leeks, cleaned, cut into 1-inch pieces
1 scallion, chopped fine
1 tablespoon sesame seed oil
2 tablespoons cornstarch, dissolved in 3 tablespoons water

1. Carefully cut all 8 pieces of bean curd in half horizontally so that they will have half the thickness. Then cut into 1½-inch-thick slices on the short side. Saute in 4 tablespoons oil in skillet. Brown on both sides, turning once. Shake pan to keep from sticking.
2. Put bean curd, mushrooms, soy sauce, and stock in saucepan. Cook ½ hour covered.
3. Heat 2 tablespoons oil in wok. Add leeks, scallion, and sesame seed oil. Stir-fry until leeks are wilted.
4. Add the bean curd mixture to the leek mixture. Gently stir-fry. Thicken with dissolved cornstarch.

May be prepared in advance through Step 3. May not be frozen.

Serves 4 to 6

Bean Curd with Fresh Mushrooms   SHANGHAI

This is a magnificent dish for the calorie conscious.

4 pieces bean curd (to-fu, 4 pieces in a box)
3 tablespoons oil
½ pound fresh mushrooms, sliced
1 clove garlic, minced
1 scallion, cut into 1-inch pieces

3 tablespoons light soy sauce
1 cup chicken stock
1 tablespoon cornstarch, dissolved in 2 tablespoons water

1. Cut each piece of bean curd into 9 cubes. Set aside.
2. Heat 1 tablespoon oil in wok. Add mushrooms. Stir-fry on high heat 30 seconds. Remove.
3. Heat remaining oil in wok. Stir-fry garlic and scallion 30 seconds. Add bean curd, soy sauce, stock, and mushrooms. Bring to high heat. Thicken with dissolved cornstarch.

May be prepared in advance through Step 2. May not be frozen.

Serves 4 to 6

A soft answer takes away wrath.

Fried Bean Curd with Vermicelli and Spinach   SHANGHAI

The little pockets in this nutritious dish look appealing and interesting.

1 or 2 packages vermicelli
½ pound ground pork
1 tablespoon light soy sauce
1 tablespoon sherry
1 teaspoon cornstarch
1 package fried bean curd (6 in package), each piece cut in half
1 tablespoon cornstarch, dissolved in 1 tablespoon water

4 tablespoons oil
2 cups chicken stock
2 tablespoons dark soy sauce
1 teaspoon chili paste with garlic
½ teaspoon salt
2 bunches spinach, washed, stems removed

1. Soak vermicelli in hot water 30 minutes. Drain. Cut into thirds with scissors.
2. Mix pork with light soy sauce, sherry, and cornstarch.
3. Make a slit in each piece of bean curd (12 pieces). Stuff with pork. Coat pork with dissolved cornstarch to seal.
4. Heat 2 tablespoons oil. Fry the bean curd, meat side down, until brown. Cook 1 minute. Add chicken stock and dark soy sauce. Cook 10 minutes. Add chili paste. Cook 2 minutes. Add vermicelli. Bring to boil. Remove to platter.
5. Heat 2 tablespoons oil until smoking hot. Add salt. Add spinach. Stir-fry 1 second. Garnish platter with spinach.

May be prepared in advance through Step 3. May not be frozen.

12 Bean Curd Pieces

Yangchow Bean Curd   YANGCHOW

Bean curd is available in many forms but fresh to-fu is the most popular for Westerners.

4 tablespoons oil
1 pound leek, cleaned, cut into 1-inch pieces
2 boxes bean curd (to-fu, 4 pieces in a box), cubed
4 tablespoons dark soy sauce
1 cup chicken stock
1 tablespoon cornstarch, dissolved in 1 tablespoon water

1 tablespoon pepper oil (see Index) or 1 teaspoon chili paste with garlic (optional)
½ cup dried shrimp, soaked in sherry to cover until soft (optional)

1. Heat 2 tablespoons oil in wok. Stir-fry leek until it is wilted. Drain. Remove.
2. Heat remaining oil in wok. Slide in bean curd. Add soy sauce and stock. Bring to boil. Thicken with dissolved cornstarch. Place leek on top. At this point you may add pepper oil or chili paste with garlic and dried shrimp. Stir gently 1 minute.

May be prepared in advance through Step 1. May not be frozen.

Serves 4 to 6

Bean Curd with Shrimp   SZECHWAN

Bean curd is so healthy and economical, it will soon be the food of the world.

1 box bean curd (to-fu, 4
   pieces in a box)
½ pound medium shrimp,
   shelled, deveined, cut in
   half crosswise
¼ teaspoon salt
1 teaspoon cornstarch
4 tablespoons oil
1 slice ginger, chopped fine
1 scallion, cut into quarters

1 tablespoon sherry
3 tablespoons light soy sauce
1 cup chicken stock
1 teaspoon chili paste with
   garlic
1 clove garlic, minced
2 teaspoons cornstarch,
   dissolved in 4 teaspoons
   water

1. Cut each piece of bean curd into 9 cubes. Set aside.
2. Mix shrimp with salt and cornstarch.
3. Heat 2 tablespoons oil in wok. Stir-fry ginger and scallion 30 seconds. Put in shrimp. Stir-fry 1 minute. Add sherry. Stir 30 seconds more. Remove to plate.
4. Heat remaining oil in wok. Slide in bean curd. Add soy sauce, stock, chili paste with garlic, and minced garlic. Add shrimp. Bring to boil. Thicken with dissolved cornstarch. Gently stir and heat thoroughly.

May be prepared in advance through Step 3. May not be frozen.

Serves 4 to 6

Fish-Stuffed Bean Curd   CANTON

Another easy family dish that is low in calories.

½ pound fish fillet
½ teaspoon salt
1 egg white
1 teaspoon cornstarch
¼ teaspoon white pepper
½ scallion, minced
1 slice ginger, minced
1 box bean curd (to-fu, 4 pieces in a box)

2 tablespoons cornstarch, dissolved in 2 tablespoons water
2 tablespoons oil
1 tablespoon sherry
½ cup chicken stock
2 tablespoons oyster sauce
2 cloves garlic, minced
1 scallion, cut in 1-inch pieces

1. Finely chop fish or grind in food processor.
2. Mix fish with salt, egg white, cornstarch, pepper, scallion, and ginger.
3. Cut each piece of bean curd into 2 triangles (8 triangles). On the cut edge carve a hole with a small spoon. Stuff with the fish mixture so that the mixture bulges out slightly. Coat stuffed side with dissolved cornstarch to seal the mixture in.
4. Heat oil in wok. Brown bean curd triangles. Add sherry, stock, oyster sauce, and garlic. Bring to boil. Cook 3 minutes.
5. Thicken with dissolved cornstarch. Add scallion.

May be prepared in advance through Step 3. May not be frozen.

Serves 4 to 6

Don't waste tears on anything that can't cry over you.

Beef with Snow-in-White Bean Curd   SHANGHAI

The snow cabbage gives extra fine flavor to bean curd and the beef makes this dish mouth watering.

1   box bean curd (to-fu, 4
   pieces in a box)
½ pound flank steak,
   shredded
½ teaspoon salt
½ tablespoon cornstarch
4   tablespoons oil
1   slice ginger, chopped fine
1   scallion, cut into 1-inch
   pieces

½ cup snow cabbage,
   chopped coarsely
1   tablespoon sherry
2   tablespoons light soy sauce
1   teaspoon sugar
1   cup chicken stock
1   tablespoon cornstarch,
   dissolved in 2 tablespoons
   water

1. Cut each piece of bean curd into 9 cubes. Set aside.
2. Mix beef with salt, cornstarch, and 1 tablespoon oil. Set aside 5 minutes.
3. Heat 2 tablespoons oil in wok. Stir-fry ginger and scallion 30 seconds. Pour in beef. Stir-fry 1 minute. Add snow cabbage. Stir-fry 1 minute more. Add sherry. Cook 30 seconds. Remove.
4. Heat remaining oil in wok. Pour in bean curd. Add soy sauce, sugar, and stock. Add the beef mixture. Stir gently. Bring to boil. Thicken with dissolved cornstarch. Serve immediately.

May be prepared in advance through Step 3. May be frozen.

Serves 4 to 6

Sun Ya Bean Curd with Minced Pork   CANTON

There are many ways of cooking bean curd. It all depends on the creativity of the chef. Sun ya means elegant new gathering place.

1 box bean curd (to-fu, 4
  pieces in a box)
1½ teaspoons salt
5 tablespoons oil
1 pound spinach, washed,
  stems removed
1 slice ginger, minced
1 scallion, minced

1 clove garlic, minced
1 pound pork, minced
½ cup chicken stock
2 tablespoons dark soy sauce
1 teaspoon pepper oil (see
  Index) (optional)
1 tablespoon cornstarch,
  dissolved in 2 tablespoons
  water

1. Cut each piece of bean curd into 9 cubes. Sprinkle with ½ teaspoon salt. Drain on paper towel.
2. Heat 2 tablespoons oil in wok. Fry bean curd on high heat until light brown, about 2 minutes. Turn. Fry 2 minutes more. Remove. Keep warm.
3. Heat 2 tablespoons oil in wok with 1 teaspoon salt. Stir-fry spinach until just wilted. Remove. Drain. Keep warm.
4. Heat 1 tablespoon oil in wok. Stir-fry ginger, scallion, and garlic 30 seconds. Add pork. Stir-fry until color changes. Add stock, soy sauce, and pepper oil. Bring to boil. Thicken with dissolved cornstarch.
5. Pour the meat mixture in center of a large round platter. Surround with a ring of bean curd cubes and then a ring of spinach.

May be prepared in advance through Step 3. May not be frozen.

Serves 4 to 6

Three-Flavored Bean Curd   SHANGHAI

We love this for lunch when we go to Chinatown.

4 ounces shrimp, shelled,
    deveined, cut in half
4 ounces chicken fillet,
    shredded
4 ounces flank steak,
    shredded
½ teaspoon salt
1 egg white
1 tablespoon cornstarch
2 to 4 cups oil for deep-frying
1 scallion, cut into 1-inch
    pieces
1 slice ginger, shredded
1 clove garlic, minced
½ cup snow peas, strings
    removed

4 dried black mushrooms,
    soaked in boiling water 20
    minutes, simmered 20
    minutes, stems removed,
    cut into quarters (if
    mushrooms are large, cut
    smaller)
1 package bean curd strips,
    soaked in boiling water at
    least 20 minutes

Sauce:
½ cup chicken stock
1 tablespoon light soy sauce
2 tablespoons dark soy sauce
1 tablespoon sherry
1 teaspoon sugar
2 teaspoons cornstarch
1 teaspoon chili paste with
    garlic

1. Combine sauce ingredients. Set aside.
2. Combine shrimp, chicken, and beef in a bowl. Add salt, egg white, and cornstarch. Mix well with hand. Set aside 10 minutes.
3. Heat oil. Deep-fry the meat mixture 1 minute. Drain. Remove.
4. Reheat 2 tablespoons oil in wok. Stir-fry scallion, ginger, and garlic 30 seconds. Add snow peas, mushrooms, and bean curd. Stir-fry 1 minute.
5. Pour in sauce. Bring to boil. Add the meat mixture. Stir-fry quickly until thoroughly heated.

May be prepared in advance through Step 4. May not be frozen.

Serves 4 to 6

11

Noodles

When Marco Polo visited China, the legend goes that he brought spaghetti back to Italy. He loved the noodles and the great variety of dishes using them. Many humble shops in China served only noodles with different toppings.

You can also serve noodles to your guests with various toppings. Use your leftovers and serve over noodles—a wonderful, economical, and healthy one-dish meal.

Barbecued Pork Lo Mien   CANTON

Always remember to heat barbecued pork in aluminum foil for 20 minutes in oven after it has been removed from freezer.

½ pound Chinese fresh-water noodles
½ cup cold water
1 tablespoon sesame seed oil
2 tablespoons oil
1 slice ginger, shredded
1 clove garlic, minced
1 scallion, cut into 1-inch pieces

½ pound barbecued pork (see Index), shredded
1 tablespoon sherry
½ pound bean sprouts
1 tablespoon light soy sauce
2 tablespoons oyster sauce
½ teaspoon salt
½ teaspoon sugar

1. Drop noodles into boiling water. Cook about 4 minutes. Add ½ cup cold water. Bring to boil 1 minute. Rinse with cold running water. Drain. Mix with sesame seed oil. Set aside.
2. Heat oil in wok. Stir-fry ginger, garlic, and scallion 30 seconds. Add pork. Stir-fry 1 minute. Add sherry. Stir 30 seconds.
3. Add bean sprouts. Stir-fry 30 seconds. Pour in soy sauce, oyster sauce, salt, and sugar. Add noodles. Stir-fry briskly 3 minutes or until the mixture is thoroughly heated. Pour onto platter. Serve immediately.

May be prepared in advance through Step 2. May not be frozen.

Serves 4 to 6

Cold Noodles   ALL REGIONS

Cold noodles are served very often in China. They are a refreshing summer dish.

1 pound Chinese fresh-water noodles
¼ cup cold water
1 tablespoon sesame seed oil
½ pound bean sprouts
1 green pepper, shredded
2 eggs
1 tablespoon oil
1 cup cooked chicken, shredded

½ cup cooked Virginia ham, shredded

Sauce:
4 tablespoons sesame seed oil
1 tablespoon chili paste with garlic
2 tablespoons light soy sauce

1. Combine sauce ingredients. Set aside.
2. Drop noodles into boiling water to cover. Cook about 4 minutes. Add ¼ cup cold water. Bring to boil 1 minute. Rinse with cold water immediately. Drain. Mix with sesame seed oil. Set aside.
3. Plunge bean sprouts and shredded green pepper into boiling water 1 minute. Drain. Remove.
4. Beat eggs. Heat oil in skillet. Pour half of beaten eggs into skillet and fry like a pancake. Repeat. Shred pancakes crosswise.*
5. Put noodles on serving plate. Put bean sprouts, green pepper, shredded chicken, ham, and egg on top of noodles.
6. Pour sauce over noodles before serving.

---

*See Index for Vegetables of Harmony and Peace, another egg pancake recipe, if you like.

May be prepared in advance through Step 5. May not be frozen.

Serves 4 to 6

Chicken Noodle Soup   YANGCHOW

This is a classic noodle recipe, very well flavored. It is a cure-all when one is sick.

½ pound Chinese fresh-water
  noodles
¼ cup cold water
6 cups chicken stock
¼ pound bok choy, cut into
  small cubes
1 cup cooked chicken, cut
  into small cubes

¼ cup cooked Virginia ham,
  cut into small cubes
  (optional)
1 tablespoon light soy sauce
½ teaspoon salt
Pinch of white pepper

1. Drop noodles into boiling water to cover. Cook 4 minutes. Bring water to boil. Add ¼ cup cold water. Bring to boil again. Drain.
2. Bring stock to boil. Add bok choy, chicken, ham, soy sauce, and salt. Cook 2 minutes.
3. Remove noodles to tureen. Pour in stock. Place chicken and the bok choy mixture on top. Sprinkle with white pepper.

May be prepared in advance. May be frozen.

Serves 4 to 6

You have to laugh a little, cry a little—
that is the charm of life.

Rice Sticks in Vegetable Soup   FUKIEN

This soup can be served by itself as a luncheon dish or light supper.

½ **pound rice sticks (Py Mai Fun)**	2 **zucchini, sliced**
2 **tablespoons oil**	6 **cups chicken stock**
6 **fresh mushrooms, sliced**	1 **teaspoon salt**

1. Soak rice sticks in boiling water 5 minutes. Drain. Remove.
2. Heat oil. Stir-fry mushrooms and zucchini 1 minute. Remove.
3. Bring stock to boil. Add salt. Pour in rice sticks and vegetables. Bring to boil again. Rice sticks expand after cooking. May be necessary to add stock. Serve immediately.

May be prepared in advance. May be frozen.

Serves 4 to 6

Rice Sticks with Chicken and Ham   FUKIEN

You can create many toppings for rice sticks. A delicious light meal.

½ **pound rice sticks (Py Mai Fun)**	½ **pound chicken breast, boned, skinned, sliced thin**
6 **cups chicken stock**	½ **teaspoon salt**
1 **pound bok choy or spinach, shredded**	1 **ounce cooked Virginia ham, sliced thin**

1. Soak rice sticks in boiling water 5 minutes. Drain. Remove.
2. Bring stock to boil. Add bok choy. Cook 5 minutes. Add sliced chicken. Cook 2 minutes more.
3. Pour in rice sticks. Add salt. Bring to boil. Rice sticks will expand after cooking. Add more stock, if necessary. Arrange ham on top. Serve in tureen or individual bowls.

May be prepared in advance through Step 2. May not be frozen.

Serves 4 to 6

Da Lu Noodles   SHANTUNG

Here is a famous Shantung dish called Da Lu Noodles. Da Lu means big sauce.

6 medium shrimp, shelled, deveined
2 cups broccoli
1 pound Chinese fresh-water noodles
½ cup cold water
6 cups chicken stock
¼ cup bamboo shoots, shredded
6 dried black mushrooms, soaked in boiling water 20 minutes, cooked 20 minutes, stems removed, cut into quarters

½ cup pork, shredded
½ pound chicken breast, boned, skinned, shredded
3 tablespoons light soy sauce
3 tablespoons cornstarch, dissolved in 3 tablespoons water
2 eggs, beaten
1 tablespoon sesame seed oil

Marinade:
1 teaspoon sherry
2 teaspoons cornstarch
1 teaspoon light soy sauce

1. Combine marinade ingredients. Cut shrimp in half lengthwise. Marinate 10 minutes.
2. Remove woody part of broccoli. Slice stalk into 1-inch pieces. Pull flowerettes apart.
3. Drop noodles into boiling water. Cook 4 minutes. Add ½ cup cold water. Bring to boil 1 minute. Drain thoroughly. Put in tureen.
4. Bring stock to boil. Add shrimp, broccoli, bamboo shoots, mushrooms, pork, and chicken. Bring to boil again. Stir constantly. Add soy sauce. Thicken with dissolved cornstarch.
5. Add the beaten egg slowly, stirring constantly in a circle. Add sesame seed oil.
6. Pour the Da Lu sauce over the noodles.

May be prepared in advance through Step 2. May not be frozen.

Serves 4 to 6

Madame Wong's Birthday Noodles   SHANGHAI

This is the noodle dish my family chef cooked for me until I was married. Every Shanghai family knows this as Lu Tse Mien. This means noodles with sauce.

3 tablespoons oil
1 slice ginger, minced
1 scallion, cut into 1-inch pieces
½ pound pork or chicken, diced
1 tablespoon sherry
3 tablespoons light soy sauce
4 pieces baked brown bean curd, diced
4 dried black mushrooms, soaked in boiling water 20 minutes, cooked 20 minutes, stems removed, diced
¼ cup bamboo shoots, diced
6½ cups chicken stock
1 pound Chinese fresh-water noodles

1. Heat 2 tablespoons oil in wok. Stir-fry ginger and scallion 30 seconds. Add pork. Stir-fry until color changes. Add sherry and 1 tablespoon soy sauce. Stir 30 seconds. Remove.
2. Heat 1 tablespoon oil in wok. Stir-fry bean curd, mushrooms, and bamboo shoots 1 minute. Add pork, ½ cup stock, and remaining soy sauce. Cook on low heat 5 minutes.
3. Drop noodles into boiling water. Cook 4 minutes. Drain. Remove.
4. Bring remaining stock to boil. Add noodles. Bring to boil again. Serve noodles and stock in individual bowls. Serve the meat mixture on top.

May be prepared in advance through Step 3. May not be frozen.

Serves 4 to 6

Mee Krob   THAILAND

Fantastic. Incredible. The most famous dish in Thai cooking.

1 pound shrimp, shelled,
  deveined, cut in half
  lengthwise
1 teaspoon salt
1 tablespoon cornstarch
2 to 4 cups oil for deep-frying
½ pound rice sticks
2 scallions, chopped fine
½ pound pork, julienne
1 tablespoon light soy sauce

Sauce:
½ cup onion, minced
4 cloves garlic, minced
2 tablespoons bean sauce
2 tablespoons tomato paste
⅔ cup sugar
¼ cup tamarind water*
¼ cup fish sauce
½ cup fresh lemon juice
1 tablespoon lemon peel, julienne
¼ teaspoon crushed red chili
  peppers

1. Mix shrimp with salt and cornstarch.
2. Heat oil in wok. Deep-fry rice sticks. Drain on paper towel. Deep-fry shrimp. Drain. Set aside.
3. Reheat 2 tablespoons oil in wok. Add half of the chopped scallions. Stir-fry 30 seconds. Add pork. Stir-fry until color changes. Add soy sauce. Stir-fry to mix. Set aside.
4. To make the sauce: Reheat 3 tablespoons oil in a saucepan. Add onion and garlic. Stir 1 minute. Add bean sauce and tomato paste. Bring sauce to boil. Add sugar, tamarind water, and fish sauce. Turn down heat. Cover and simmer 25 minutes. Stir in lemon juice, lemon peel, and crushed chili peppers. Cover and simmer 4 minutes more or until syrupy. Cool. Refrigerate. Sauce will thicken (must be cold before using).
5. To assemble Mee Krob: Crush rice sticks. Place a quarter of the rice sticks in a deep bowl. Pour ½ cup sauce over. Toss rice sticks gently and thoroughly. Add another quarter of the rice sticks. Add ½ cup sauce. Toss again. Repeat until all of the rice sticks and sauce are used.
6. Reheat pork and shrimp together in wok. Put on top of rice sticks. Sprinkle remaining scallion over.

---

*To make tamarind water: Use 1 teaspoon concentrated tamarind, dissolved in ¼ cup water. Tamarind concentrate may be purchased in Chinese or Indian markets.

May be prepared in advance through Step 4. May not be frozen.

Serves 4 to 6

Yangchow Noodles in Casserole   YANGCHOW

This dish has no peer. A supreme one-dish meal.

½ pound Chinese fresh-water noodles
¼ pound chicken breast, boned, skinned, cut into thin slices
¼ pound pork, cut into thin slices
¼ pound shrimp, shelled, deveined, cut in half
1 teaspoon salt
1 egg white
1 tablespoon cornstarch
2 to 4 cups oil for deep-frying
1 clove garlic, minced

1 scallion, cut into 1-inch pieces
1 slice ginger, minced
4 dried black mushrooms, soaked in boiling water 20 minutes, cooked 20 minutes, stems removed, cut in half
¼ cup bamboo shoots, sliced
½ cup pea pods, strings removed, cut in half diagonally
2 tablespoons soy sauce
1 tablespoon sherry
4 cups chicken stock

1. Drop noodles into boiling water. Cook 4 minutes. Rinse with cold water. Drain. Remove.
2. Put chicken, pork, and shrimp in a bowl. Add salt, egg white, and cornstarch. Mix well with hand. Set aside.
3. Heat oil in wok. Deep-fry the meat mixture 1 minute. Drain. Remove.
4. Return 2 tablespoons oil to wok. Add garlic, scallion, and ginger. Stir-fry 30 seconds. Add mushrooms, bamboo shoots, and pea pods. Stir-fry 1 minute. Add the meat mixture, soy sauce, and sherry. Stir briskly 1 minute more. Remove.
5. Bring stock to boil. Add noodles, and the meat and vegetable mixture. Bring stock to boil again. Turn down heat. Cover. Simmer 2 minutes.
6. Put noodles in casserole. Arrange meat and vegetables on top. Pour stock around noodles. Serve hot.

May be prepared in advance through Step 4. May not be frozen.

Serves 4 to 6

Toppings for Noodles

Noodles and toppings are served in separate serving dishes or serving bowls. Individual portions of noodles are placed in bowls with or without hot chicken stock and the topping is placed over the noodles. Toppings may also be served over pan-fried noodles without the chicken stock.

To cook noodles: Bring water to boil. Add Chinese fresh-water noodles. Stir to separate. Cook 4 minutes. When it comes to a boil, add ½ cup cold water. Noodles are done when they float. Drain. Pour 1 tablespoon sesame seed oil over noodles and mix well. Serve with toppings in bowls alone or with hot chicken stock.

I. Stir-Fried Shrimp   SHANGHAI

We had this in Shanghai—irresistible.

1½ pounds shrimp, shelled,
   deveined
1½ teaspoons salt
1 egg white
2 teaspoons cornstarch
2 to 4 cups oil for deep-frying
½ teaspoon sugar
1 tablespoon sherry

½ teaspoon sesame seed oil
1½ teaspoons cornstarch,
   dissolved in 2 tablespoons
   chicken stock
Red wine vinegar to taste
½ cup pickled snow cabbage
   (optional)

1. Mix shrimp with 1 teaspoon salt, egg white, and cornstarch. Let stand 1 hour in refrigerator.
2. Heat oil in wok. Deep-fry shrimp until color changes. Drain. Remove.
3. Reheat 2 tablespoons oil in wok. Add shrimp, ½ teaspoon salt, and sugar. Add sherry and sesame seed oil.
4. Pour dissolved cornstarch slowly over shrimp until it forms a clear glaze. Serve on top of noodles with red wine vinegar and/or pickled snow cabbage.

May be prepared in advance through Step 1. May not be frozen.

Serves 4 to 6

II. Chicken with Snow Cabbage   SHANGHAI

1 pound chicken breast,
  skinned, boned, shredded
½ teaspoon salt
1 egg white
1 tablespoon cornstarch
2 to 4 cups oil for deep-frying
1 slice ginger, shredded
1 clove garlic, shredded
1 scallion, cut into 1-inch
  pieces

¼ cup pickled snow cabbage
¼ cup snow peas, strings
  removed, cut in half
½ teaspoon sugar
4 cups bean sprouts, heads
  and tails removed
1½ tablespoons light soy
  sauce
1 tablespoon sherry
1 scallion, chopped

1. Mix chicken with salt, egg white, and cornstarch. Use hand
   to mix. Set aside 30 minutes.
2. Heat oil in wok. Deep-fry chicken until color changes. Drain.
   Remove.
3. Reheat 2 tablespoons oil in wok. Stir-fry ginger, garlic, and
   scallion 1 minute. Add pickled snow cabbage and snow peas.
   Add sugar. Stir-fry until mixed. Remove.
4. Reheat 2 tablespoons oil in wok. Stir-fry bean sprouts 1
   minute. Add snow cabbage and snow peas. Stir-fry 1 minute.
   Add chicken, soy sauce, and sherry. Mix well. Serve over
   noodles with chopped scallion as a garnish.

May be prepared in advance through Step 2. May not be frozen.

Serves 4 to 6

III. Szechwan Red Cooked Spicy Beef   SZECHWAN

This is a well-known Szechwan dish. Good with rice and especially good over noodles.

2 tablespoons oil
1 teaspoon Szechwan peppercorns
2 scallions, cut into 1-inch pieces
3 slices ginger
1 clove garlic, minced
1 pound stewing beef (chuck), cubed

3 tablespoons dark soy sauce
3 tablespoons sherry
1 tablespoon sugar
1 tablespoon chili paste with garlic
3½ cups boiling water
2 star anise seeds
¼ cup frozen peas, defrosted

1. Heat oil in wok. On moderate heat stir-fry peppercorns 1 minute until brown. Discard peppercorns.
2. Turn heat high. Stir-fry scallions, ginger, garlic, and beef until color of beef changes. Add soy sauce, sherry, sugar, and chili paste. Add boiling water and star anise. Bring to boil. Simmer covered 2 hours.
3. Add peas. Serve over noodles. Add extra chili paste if more spice desired.

May be prepared in advance. May be frozen through Step 2.

Serves 4 to 6

Pan-Fried Noodles   SHANGHAI

These noodles may be topped with a variety of sauces. Try creating your own. It's fun.

1 pound Chinese fresh-water noodles
½ cup cold water

1 tablespoon sesame seed oil
3 tablespoons oil

1. Drop noodles into boiling water to cover. Cook about 4 minutes. Add ½ cup cold water. Bring to boil 1 minute. Rinse with cold water. Drain. Mix with sesame seed oil.
2. Heat oil in wok. Add half the noodles. Do not stir. Let noodles brown on bottom (about 5 minutes). Turn noodle cake over. Brown other side. Remove to platter. Repeat with remaining half. Pour topping over.

May be prepared in advance through Step 1. May not be frozen.

Serves 4 to 6

Three-Flavored Pan-Fried Noodles CANTON

Pan-fried noodles make every dinner party successful.

1 pound Chinese fresh-water noodles
1 tablespoon sesame seed oil
¼ pound flank steak, shredded
¼ pound medium shrimp, shelled, deveined, dried thoroughly, cut in half crosswise
½ pound chicken breast, boned, skinned, shredded
1 teaspoon salt
1 egg white
1 tablespoon cornstarch
2 to 4 cups oil for deep-frying
½ pound bok choy (Chinese green), cut into 2-inch pieces

2 tablespoons bamboo shoots, shredded
4 tablespoons water chestnuts, sliced thin
4 dried black mushrooms, soaked in boiling water 20 minutes, stems removed, cut into quarters
4 fresh mushrooms, sliced
3 tablespoons light soy sauce
½ cup chicken stock
1 tablespoon cornstarch, dissolved in 1 tablespoon water
Red wine vinegar

1. Bring 4 cups water to boil. Add noodles. Cook 4 minutes. Rinse in cold water. Drain well. Toss with sesame seed oil.
2. Combine beef, shrimp, and chicken with salt, egg white, and cornstarch. Mix well with hand.
3. Heat oil in wok. Deep-fry the meat mixture until color changes. Drain. Remove to a bowl.
4. Reheat 2 tablespoons oil in wok. Stir-fry bok choy, bamboo shoots, water chestnuts, and mushrooms 2 minutes. Add the meat mixture, soy sauce, and stock. Thicken with dissolved cornstarch. Remove.
5. Reheat 3 tablespoons oil in skillet. Add noodles. Do not stir. Let noodles brown on bottom (5 minutes). Turn noodle cake over. Brown other side in same manner. Remove to warm platter. Pour the meat mixture over. Serve with red wine vinegar.

May be prepared in advance through Step 3. May not be frozen.

Serves 4 to 6

Three-Flavored Seafood on Pan-Fried Noodles   CANTON

An outstanding topping for noodles.

4 cups water
1 pound Chinese fresh-water
   noodles
1 tablespoon plus 1 teaspoon
   sesame seed oil
2 to 4 cups oil for deep-frying
4 ounces shrimp, shelled,
   deveined
4 ounces scallops
1 tablespoon flour
4 ounces squid, cleaned;
   skin, ink sac, and cuttle
   bone removed
1 slice ginger, minced
1 clove garlic, minced
1 scallion, minced

1 cup broccoli flowerettes
½ cup celery, shredded
4 fresh mushrooms, sliced
   thin
1 teaspoon red wine vinegar
   (optional)
1 teaspoon chili paste with
   garlic (optional)

Sauce:
2 tablespoons light soy sauce
1 tablespoon oyster sauce
½ cup chicken stock
1 tablespoon sherry
½ teaspoon sugar
2 teaspoons cornstarch

1. Bring 4 cups water to boil. Add noodles. Cook 4 minutes. Rinse in cold water. Drain well. Toss with 1 tablespoon sesame seed oil.
2. Cut each shrimp in half lengthwise. Cut scallops in half. Mix scallops with flour in a bowl. Score squid on the inside in a diamond-shaped pattern, cutting at a 45-degree angle. Cut into 1½-inch pieces.
3. Combine sauce ingredients in a bowl. Set aside.
4. Heat 3 tablespoons oil in skillet. Fry noodles until light brown on the bottom, about 5 minutes. Turn noodle cake over. Brown other side in the same manner. Remove to a platter. Put in warm oven until topping is ready.
5. Heat oil in wok. Deep-fry shrimp until color changes. Drain. Set aside. Deep-fry scallops 30 seconds. Drain. Set aside. Deep-fry squid until they curl into rolls. Drain. Remove.
6. Reheat 2 tablespoons oil in wok. Stir-fry ginger, garlic, and scallion 30 seconds. Turn up heat. Pour in broccoli, celery, and mushrooms. Stir-fry 1 minute. Pour in sauce. Bring to

boil. Pour in seafood. Stir-fry thoroughly. Add 1 teaspoon sesame seed oil. Stir-fry to mix well. Pour the seafood mixture over noodles. If more spice is desired, serve with red wine vinegar or chili paste with garlic.

May be prepared in advance through Step 3. May not be frozen.

Serves 4 to 6

Noodles in Broth with Ham and Chicken   SHANGHAI

Noodles are symbolic of longevity. They are always served on birthdays.

1 **pound Chinese fresh-water noodles**
¼ **cup cold water**
2 **tablespoons oil**
1 **pound bok choy, shredded**
1 **teaspoon salt**
¼ **cup cooked Virginia ham, shredded**

2 **cups cooked chicken, shredded**
4 **dried black mushrooms, soaked in boiling water 20 minutes, stems removed, cooked 20 minutes, shredded**
10 **cups boiling chicken stock**

1. Drop noodles into boiling water to cover. Cook about 4 minutes. Add ¼ cup cold water. Bring to boil 1 minute. Rinse with cold water immediately. Drain.
2. Heat oil in wok. Stir-fry bok choy 2 minutes. Add salt. Add ham, chicken, and mushrooms. Stir-fry until thoroughly heated.
3. Put noodles in tureen or individual bowls. Pour stock over. Add meat and vegetables.

May be prepared in advance through Step 1. May not be frozen.

Serves 10

Rice Sticks with Chicken and Snow Cabbage   FUKIEN

Rice sticks are easily digested. The light texture blends wonderfully with the tender chicken and crispy bean sprouts.

½ pound rice sticks (Py Mai
  Fun)
1 pound chicken breast,
  boned, skinned, cut
  julienne
1 teaspoon salt
1 egg white
1 tablespoon cornstarch
2 to 4 cups oil for deep-frying

2 scallions, cut into 1-inch
  pieces
½ cup snow cabbage,
  chopped fine
½ pound bean sprouts
2 tablespoons light soy sauce
1 teaspoon chili paste with
  garlic
Pepper to taste

1. Soak rice sticks in boiling water 5 minutes. Rinse. Drain. Must be thoroughly dry.
2. Mix chicken with ½ teaspoon salt, egg white, and cornstarch.
3. Heat oil in wok. Deep-fry chicken until it turns white. Drain. Remove. Set aside.
4. Reheat 2 tablespoons oil in wok. Stir-fry scallions, snow cabbage, and bean sprouts vigorously 1 minute. Remove.
5. Reheat 2 tablespoons oil in wok. Stir-fry rice sticks 1 minute. Add the snow cabbage mixture and chicken. Stir-fry 1 minute. Add soy sauce, remaining salt, and chili paste with garlic. Stir-fry briskly 1 minute more. Sprinkle with pepper.

May be prepared in advance. May not be frozen.

Serves 4 to 6

12

Rice

In China the proper way of serving rice is in a small bowl. The bowl must be raised to the mouth with the left hand, while using chopsticks with the right hand to put the rice into one's mouth. A person who lets his bowl sit on the table and eats by picking up lumps of rice from the bowl is expressing extreme dissatisfaction. If this person is a guest in someone's home, he or she would be considered insulting to the host.

Rice is always steamed and cooked in its own pot; just as the wok is not supposed to be used for rice, the rice pot is not used for other ingredients. Fan means grain and starchy foods. T'sai represents vegetables and meat. A balanced meal should have fan and t'sai ingredients included. Children are taught at an early age not to leave a single grain of fan in their bowls.

Basic Rice Recipe   ALL REGIONS

People ask Madame Wong why her rice is so fluffy. Here is the secret. It is the old method of cooking rice. No matter what amount of rice you cook, here is the direct way.

2 cups long-grain rice
Water

1. Wash rice with hands 5 times until water is clear. Pour into saucepan.
2. Now, measure with index finger to see if the water is one knuckle above the rice (1 inch). This is the exact amount of water that is needed.
3. Bring rice to boil. Let cook until all of the water is evaporated (about 4 minutes).
4. Cover. Simmer 30 minutes.

Serves 4 to 6

Chicken and Chinese Sausage Rice   CANTON

A famous Cantonese rice dish.

½ **pound chicken breast,**
  boned, skinned, cut into 1-
  inch pieces
2 cups long-grain rice
2 Chinese sausages, cut into
  1-inch pieces
4 dried black mushrooms,
  soaked in boiling water 20
  minutes, stems removed,
  cut in half

Marinade:
1 tablespoon sherry
2 tablespoons light soy sauce
½ **teaspoon salt**
½ **teaspoon sugar**

1. Combine marinade ingredients. Marinate chicken 1 hour. Reserve marinade.
2. Wash rice. Rinse thoroughly in cold water. Cover with water to reach 1 inch above rice. Bring rice to boil on high heat. Boil until water is evaporated.
3. Arrange chicken, sausages, and mushrooms on top of rice. Pour marinade over. Cover. Simmer 20 minutes.

May be prepared in advance. May be frozen.

Serves 4 to 6

Vegetable Rice with Yam   ALL REGIONS

This rice is very aromatic with bok choy and yam. All country people know how to prepare this. They eat it as a meal in itself.

2 **cups short-grain rice**
4 **tablespoons oil**
1 **pound bok choy, cut into**
   1-inch pieces
1½ **teaspoons salt**
2 **cups yams, peeled, cut into**
   1-inch pieces

1. Wash rice thoroughly in cold water 5 times. Place in pot and cover with water 1 inch above rice.
2. Heat oil in wok. Stir-fry bok choy on high heat. Add salt. Stir-fry 2 minutes.
3. Bring rice to boil. Add vegetable and yams. Cover. Simmer 30 minutes.
4. Toss ingredients thoroughly before serving.

May be prepared in advance. May be frozen.

Serves 8

Diligence makes you rich, laziness makes you poor.

Rice with Pork and Peas   ALL REGIONS

Another rice dish the country people relish.

½ pound pork or ham, diced
1 tablespoon dark soy sauce
1 tablespoon sherry
2 teaspoons cornstarch
2½ tablespoons oil
¼ cup bamboo shoots, diced

4 dried black mushrooms, soaked in boiling water 20 minutes, stems removed, diced
1 pound fresh peas, shelled (optional)
2 tablespoons light soy sauce
2 cups long-grain rice

1. Marinate pork in dark soy sauce, sherry, cornstarch, and ½ tablespoon oil 30 minutes. Reserve marinade.
2. Heat remaining oil in wok. Stir-fry pork 2 minutes. Add bamboo shoots, mushrooms, and peas. Add light soy sauce. Stir briskly 1 minute. Remove. Set aside.
3. Wash rice in cold water. Place in pot. Cover with water 1 inch above rice.
4. Bring rice to boil on high heat. Boil until water has evaporated. Put pork and vegetables on rice. Pour the marinade over the rice. Cover and simmer 20 minutes.

May be prepared in advance. May be frozen.

Serves 4 to 6

Quick Lunch Rice

Serve hot rice and spoon any topping mixture, such as curry beef, over the rice. In China this is a well-known lunch dish.

½ cup small shrimp, shelled, deveined
¼ teaspoon salt
½ teaspoon cornstarch
3 tablespoons oil
2 scallions, chopped fine
½ cup barbecued pork (see Index), sliced thin
4 dried black mushrooms, soaked in boiling water 20 minutes, cooked 20 minutes, stems removed, cut in half

1 carrot, cut diagonally, cooked 5 minutes
1 broccoli stalk, cut into 1-inch pieces
1 cup chicken stock
3 tablespoons light soy sauce
½ teaspoon sugar
1 tablespoon cornstarch, dissolved in 2 tablespoons water
1 tablespoon sesame seed oil
4 cups hot, cooked rice

1. Mix shrimp with salt and cornstarch.
2. Heat 1 tablespoon oil in wok. Stir-fry shrimp 30 seconds. Remove.
3. Heat 2 tablespoons oil in wok. Stir-fry scallions, barbecued pork, mushrooms, carrot, and broccoli 2 minutes. Add stock, soy sauce, and sugar. Bring to boil. Thicken with dissolved cornstarch. Stir in sesame seed oil.
4. Serve the hot rice on individual plates. Spoon the meat-vegetable mixture over the rice.

May be prepared in advance through Step 2. May not be frozen.

Serves 4 to 6

Fried Rice with Raisins and Ham   ALL REGIONS

A wonderful way to use leftover rice.

4 tablespoons oil
2 eggs, beaten
4 cups cold, cooked rice
2 scallions, cut into small
   pieces
½ cup black seedless raisins

¾ cup cooked ham, cut into
   small cubes
1 cup frozen peas, blanched
   in boiling water 1 minute
2 tablespoons light soy sauce
1 tablespoon dark soy sauce

1. Heat 2 tablespoons oil in wok. Scramble eggs very fine. Remove.
2. Heat 2 tablespoons oil in wok. Stir-fry rice on high heat. Break up lumps by pressing rice against pan. Turn quickly and constantly.
3. Add scallions, raisins, ham, peas, and eggs. Add light and dark soy sauce. Heat and mix thoroughly.

May be prepared in advance. May be frozen.

Serves 4 to 6

Jade Fried Rice   ALL REGIONS

The color green always connotes jade to the Chinese. An imaginative chef saw the bok choy and gave this dish its wonderful name.

2 teaspoons salt
½ pound bok choy, cut into
   large pieces
4 tablespoons oil
2 eggs, beaten

2 scallions, chopped fine
4 cups cooked rice
½ cup cooked ham, cut into
   small cubes

1. Sprinkle 1 teaspoon salt on bok choy. Set aside 10 minutes. Squeeze dry. Chop fine.
2. Heat 1 tablespoon oil in wok. Pour in beaten eggs. Scramble fine. Remove.
3. Heat 1 tablespoon oil in wok. Stir-fry bok choy 1 minute. Remove.

4. Heat 2 tablespoons oil in wok. Stir-fry scallions 5 seconds. Pour in rice. Stir constantly to break up lumps. Add remaining salt. Continue stirring until rice becomes hot. Pour in ham, scrambled eggs, and bok choy. Stir briskly 1 minute.

May be prepared in advance. May be frozen.

Serves 4 to 6

Turkey Fried Rice   MADAME WONG'S CREATION

Fried rice became popular due to the frugality of the Chinese.

3 **tablespoons oil**	4 **cups cooked rice**
½ **green pepper, cubed**	1 **tablespoon dark soy sauce**
½ **red pepper, cubed**	2 **tablespoons light soy sauce**
1 **cup leftover turkey meat, cubed**	2 **scallions, chopped fine**

1. Heat 1 tablespoon oil in wok. Stir-fry green and red peppers 30 seconds. Add turkey. Stir-fry 1 minute. Remove. Set aside.
2. Heat 2 tablespoons oil in wok. Stir-fry cooked rice. Stir constantly to break up lumps. Add dark soy sauce and light soy sauce. Continue stirring until rice becomes hot. Add scallions, peppers, and turkey. Stir-fry until thoroughly heated and mixed.

May be prepared in advance. May not be frozen.

Serves 4 to 6

Near neighbors are better than distant relatives.

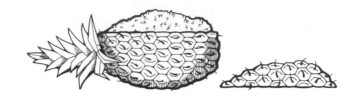

Pineapple Fried Rice   CANTON

This is an exquisite dish. So exotic—fried rice with pineapple.

1 fresh pineapple
8 medium shrimp, shelled,
  deveined, cut crosswise
  into ½-inch pieces
1 teaspoon salt
1 teaspoon cornstarch

4 tablespoons oil
3 eggs, beaten with ¼
  teaspoon salt
4 cups cooked rice
2 scallions, chopped fine

1. Cut off one-third of the pineapple lengthwise for use as a cover. Remove leaves. Reserve leaves for garnish. Scoop out all pulp from top and bottom. Cut 1 cup pineapple into 1-inch cubes. Set aside. (Use remaining pineapple for another dish.)
2. Mix shrimp with ¼ teaspoon salt and cornstarch.
3. Heat 1 tablespoon oil in wok. Pour in shrimp. Stir-fry briskly about 1 minute until they are pink. Remove. Set aside.
4. Heat 1 tablespoon oil in skillet. Scramble eggs fine.
5. Heat 2 tablespoons oil in wok. Add rice. Stir-fry 1 minute. Add remaining salt and scallions. Stir rapidly. Add eggs and shrimp. Stir thoroughly 1 minute. Add pineapple. Stir-fry quickly.
6. Fill the pineapple shell with the rice mixture. Cover. Wrap in aluminum foil. Preheat oven to 350 degrees. Bake 10 minutes.
7. Place leaves at one end of platter. Unwrap pineapple and place on platter. Serve immediately.

May be prepared in advance through Step 5. May not be frozen.

Serves 4 to 6

Yangchow Fried Rice   YANGCHOW

Yangchow is famous for its outstanding chefs. This is one of their specialities.

½ cup small shrimp, shelled, deveined
1¼ teaspoons salt
1 teaspoon cornstarch
6 tablespoons oil
2 eggs, beaten
½ tablespoon sherry
1 cup bean sprouts
4 cups cooked rice

½ cup cooked chicken breasts, cut into small cubes
½ cup barbecued pork (see Index) or cooked ham, cut into small cubes
1 scallion, chopped
¼ cup frozen peas, blanched 1 minute in boiling water, rinsed in cold water

1. Mix shrimp with ¼ teaspoon salt and cornstarch.
2. Heat 2 tablespoons oil in wok. When very hot, pour in beaten egg. Scramble fine. Set aside.
3. Heat 1 tablespoon oil in wok. Stir-fry shrimp 30 seconds. Add sherry. Stir-fry 30 seconds more. Remove. Set aside.
4. Heat 1 tablespoon oil until smoking hot. Stir-fry bean sprouts 30 seconds. Remove.
5. Heat remaining oil in wok. Add rice. Stir constantly on moderate heat, breaking up lumps with spatula. Add remaining salt. Continue stirring until rice is hot. Pour in chicken, pork, and scrambled eggs. Stir-fry to mix.
6. Add shrimp, scallion, peas, and bean sprouts. Stir-fry until thoroughly heated and mixed.

May be prepared in advance through Step 3. May not be frozen.

Serves 4 to 6

13

Desserts

During the Sung Dynasty (960–1279 A.D.) sugar cane became an important crop. However, one writer was supposed to have written the following. "Sweet things are preferred by barbarians and country folk." The most desirable of all desserts were the fresh fruits. There were many varieties of peaches, plums, pears, and apricots, but there seemed to be just one variety of apple. These fruits were eaten betwcen courses as well as at the conclusion of a meal. Only the wealthy could afford fresh fruits. Even today a beautiful bowl of fresh fruit after a delicious Chinese meal creates excitement.

Almond Cookies   CANTON

There are many different recipes for almond cookies. This was given to us by a dear Chinese friend, Madame Lee. We think they are the best we have ever tasted.

2 cups flour	½ cup brown sugar
½ teaspoon baking soda	½ cup granulated sugar
¾ teaspoon baking powder	½ teaspoon almond extract
1 egg	Blanched almonds
½ pound margarine or butter	1 or 2 beaten egg yolks

1. Sift flour, baking soda, and baking powder together.
2. Beat egg and margarine together. Add sugars and almond extract. Mix well.
3. Mix dry ingredients with egg and sugar mixture until well blended.
4. Roll 1 tablespoon batter in a ball for each cookie. Place on Teflon cookie sheet.
5. Press almond in middle.
6. Brush with beaten egg yolk.
7. Bake 15 to 20 minutes in a 350-degree oven. Cool on rack.

May be prepared in advance. May be frozen.

36 Cookies

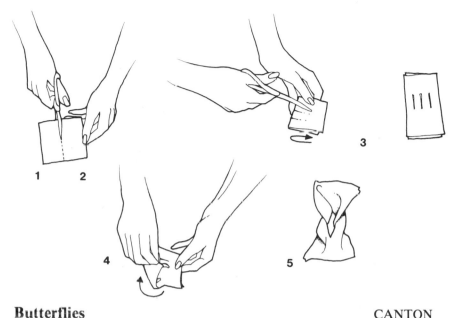

Butterflies   CANTON

Let your family help you make these. A good time will be had by all.

½ package won ton wrappers   1 cup water
2 to 4 cups oil for deep-frying   Toasted sesame seeds
2 cups sugar*

1. Cut each won ton wrapper in half. Place one half on top of the other. Fold in half lengthwise.
2. Cut three 1-inch slits lengthwise.
3. Pull double thickness carefully through center slit.
4. Heat oil to 375 degrees. Fry butterflies until light brown. Drain on paper towels.
5. Boil sugar with water in clean wok until crystalized. Brush grains of sugar from side of wok constantly with brush dipped in cold water.
6. When syrup turns light brown, dip butterflies in one by one, quickly. (Make more syrup if necessary.) Remove to greased plate. Sprinkle with sesame seeds.

—————
*Steps 5 and 6 may be eliminated. Sprinkle with powdered sugar instead.

May be prepared in advance. May be frozen.

About 30 Butterflies

Engagement Cake   SHANGHAI

In China when a couple becomes engaged, they send these cakes to all their friends as an announcement of this important occasion. Try it if you wish to be very Chinese.

1½ cups sweet rice flour
¾ cup sugar
1 cup water
2 tablespoons light corn
   syrup

5 tablespoons corn oil
½ cup walnuts, chopped
½ cup candied fruitcake mix,
   chopped*

1. Grease an 8-inch-square pan with oil.
2. Mix the rice flour and sugar with water. Add corn syrup and 4 tablespoons oil. Add nuts and fruit. Mix well. Pour into pan.
3. Steam 45 minutes over boiling water. Cool. Cut cake into small squares. Pan-fry cake squares in 1 tablespoon hot oil until golden brown.

---

*You can use raisins or any dried fruit.

May be prepared in advance. May be frozen.

Serves 4 to 6

Fruit Crescent Cookies

You can create your own filling recipe. Any dried fruit will be delicious.

½ cup seedless raisins
3 ounces dried apricots
4 ounces dried peaches
¼ cup shredded coconut
¾ cup walnuts

½ cup brown sugar
¼ cup granulated sugar
1 package shao mai or won ton wrappers*
2 to 4 cups oil for deep-frying

1. Put first seven ingredients in blender or food processor. Chop fine.
2. Place wrapper on flat surface. Place 1 heaping teaspoon of mixture in center of wrapper.
3. Fold top of wrapper down. Seal edges with water.
4. Heat oil to 400 degrees. Put a few crescents in, one at a time. Fry until golden brown. Drain. Remove.

---

*If using won ton wrappers, trim corners so that shape will be round.

May be prepared in advance (reheat in oven). May be frozen. Reheat before serving.

56 Cookies

Spilled water never returns to the pan.

Sesame Cookies   CANTON

Make some sesame cookies of your own and surprise your friends. They won't stop eating them.

2 cups flour	1 egg
½ teaspoon baking powder	1 teaspoon vanilla extract
½ teaspoon baking soda	
½ pound butter or margarine	*Coating:*
½ cup brown sugar	1 egg, slightly beaten
½ cup white sugar	Toasted sesame seeds

1. Sift flour, baking powder, and baking soda together.
2. Cream together butter and brown sugar. Add white sugar gradually. Add egg and vanilla. Mix. Add dry ingredients. Mix together to form a ball.
3. Refrigerate dough 3 to 4 hours.
4. Form dough into small balls (about the size of a walnut). Dip balls into slightly beaten egg and then into sesame seeds. Place on Teflon baking sheet. Press slightly to flatten.
5. Preheat oven to 350 degrees. Bake 15 minutes or until golden brown. Cool.

May be prepared in advance. May be frozen.

48 Cookies

Sesame Seed Balls   CANTON

This is a traditional Cantonese snack served during Chinese New Year. Symbolically it means prosperity piling up endlessly. The Chinese love to hear good wishes and happy greetings.

2 cups glutinous rice flour	½ can red bean paste
¾ cup dark brown sugar	Sesame seeds
¾ cup boiling water	2 to 4 cups oil for deep-frying

1. Put flour in bowl.
2. Dissolve sugar in boiling water.
3. Pour sugar water into flour until dough is well blended.
4. Shape dough into a cylinder about 12 inches long. Cut into 12 pieces.
5. Shape bean paste into 12 pieces, slightly smaller than dough.
6. Flatten the dough into 3-inch rounds.
7. Put bean paste ball in center of dough. Working around, seal the edges together. Roll with palm to form round balls.
8. Dampen the balls with a little water. Roll balls onto sesame seeds.
9. Heat oil to 325 degrees. Fry balls 4 to 5 at a time. When they float, move them around with chopsticks or back of spoon. Fry 8 to 10 minutes. Drain on paper towel.

May be prepared in advance. May be frozen.

12 Balls

Sweet Red Bean Paste Pancakes   ALL REGIONS

The Chinese eat a great deal of red beans because they are high in protein and rich in vitamin B.

1 egg, beaten
1 cup milk
1 cup flour
1 teaspoon vanilla
2 to 4 cups oil for deep-frying
1 cup sweet red bean paste*

1 tablespoon cornstarch, dissolved in 2 tablespoons water
2 tablespoons powdered sugar

1. Mix the first four ingredients into a smooth batter.
2. Heat 1 tablespoon oil in a 7- or 8-inch skillet. Pour in a fourth of the batter. Whirl the pan around to make a thin pancake. Remove. Continue with remaining batter.
3. Put 2 tablespoons red bean paste in the center of each pancake. Spread paste 5 inches wide and 2 inches long. Seal the edges with dissolved cornstarch. Fold the pancake like an envelope. Tuck in the ends.
4. Heat oil in wok to smoking hot. Deep-fry pancakes 2 minutes or until golden brown and crispy. Drain. Remove.
5. Cut each pancake into quarters. Sprinkle with powdered sugar.

------

*One cup pureed dates may be substituted.

May be prepared in advance through Step 3. May be frozen after Step 3.

Serves 4 to 6

Water Chestnut Cake

CANTON

Water chestnuts are used as a medicinal aid. When children became ill, they were given water chestnuts boiled in water to reduce their fever.

2½ cups water	6 fresh water chestnuts, skin
1 cup sugar	removed, chopped fine
¾ cup water chestnut powder	1 tablespoon oil

1. Combine 2 cups water with sugar. Bring to boil.
2. Mix water chestnut powder with remaining water. Slowly add boiling sugar syrup. Stir constantly until the mixture is transparent. Add chopped water chestnuts. Mix well.
3. Pour the whole mixture into a greased 9″ × 5″ rectangular cake pan. Let cool thoroughly. Then, refrigerate 1 hour.
4. Cut the cake into pieces 1 inch wide and 2 inches long.
5. Heat oil in skillet. Fry the cakes on moderate heat, a few at a time, until light brown on both sides.

May be prepared in advance through Step 4. May be frozen after Step 4.

Serves 4 to 6

Fruits on the Skewer

ALL REGIONS

Fruit was the favorite dessert of Emperor Chien Lung.

12 green grapes	12 fresh, whole strawberries
12 lychee nuts, canned	¼ cantaloupe, cut into 1-inch
12 pieces pineapple, fresh or	squares (12 pieces)
canned, cut into 1-inch	¼ honeydew melon, cut into
chunks	1-inch squares (12 pieces)
12 loquats, canned	

1. Have 12 skewers ready.
2. Put one piece of each fruit on each skewer.
3. Refrigerate 2 hours.

May be prepared in advance. May not be frozen.

Serves 4 to 6

Fried Bananas   SHANGHAI

This is a fruity and creamy dessert.

4 bananas
4 tablespoons red bean paste
⅔ cup flour
1 tablespoon cornstarch
⅔ cup water

1½ teaspoons baking powder
2 to 4 cups oil for deep-frying
2 tablespoons powdered
    sugar

1. Peel bananas. Cut in half lengthwise.
2. Spread 1 teaspoon red bean paste on half of each banana. Cover with remaining banana halves to make sandwiches. Cut each into thirds crosswise.
3. Combine flour and cornstarch in a bowl. Add water. Mix into a smooth batter. Add baking powder. Stir thoroughly.
4. Drop bananas into batter.
5. Heat oil to 350 degrees. Drop bananas into oil. Deep-fry until light brown (about 2 minutes).
6. Remove to platter. Sprinkle with powdered sugar.

May be prepared in advance through Step 2. May not be frozen.

Serves 4 to 6

Mango Mousse   ALL REGIONS

A refreshing, light dessert.

3 mangoes
1 6-ounce package apricot or
    orange gelatin

½ cup heavy cream
Whole strawberries (optional)

1. Peel mangoes and cut into chunks. Reserve one mango for garnish.
2. Follow instructions for dissolving gelatin using only 1 cup of cold water.
3. Put mangoes in blender or food processor. Puree. Remove to bowl.
4. Blend dissolved gelatin and cream. Add to pureed mangoes. Mix well.
5. Pour into mold. Refrigerate at least 4 hours.
6. Unmold. Garnish with reserved mango and strawberries.

May be prepared in advance. May not be frozen.

Serves 4 to 6

Toffee Apple   PEKING

This is a famous dessert of Peking. It is most interesting to serve. When the fruit is dipped in ice water, it becomes crackly on the surface and soft on the inside.

1 cup flour	½ cup water
⅔ cup water	2 tablespoons toasted sesame
3 apples	seeds (see Index)
6 cups oil for deep-frying	Ice water
1 cup sugar	

1. Place flour in a bowl. Gradually add water. Stir until smooth.
2. Cut each apple into quarters. Peel and core. Put apples in batter. Coat evenly.
3. Heat oil in wok to 350 degrees. Put apples in oil one by one. Deep-fry until light brown (about 2 minutes). Drain. Set aside for second frying.
4. Put sugar and ½ cup water in second wok or large saucepan. Bring to boil until sugar is dissolved. Cook the mixture until the color turns to light brown. Test with chopstick by dropping a little syrup in ice water. It will form a hard ball. Turn heat down.
5. Reheat oil in first wok to smoking hot. Refry the apples 1 minute. Drain. Pour apples into the sugared mixture. Stir well until all the wedges are coated with syrup.
6. Remove apples to greased platter. Sprinkle with sesame seeds.
7. Serve the apples by dipping them into ice water first. This should be done at the table.

May not be prepared in advance. May not be frozen.

Serves 4 to 6

Toffee Sweet Potato   PEKING

We had this dessert in Peking.

3 medium sweet potatoes	½ cup water
4 tablespoons flour	1 cup sugar
2 to 4 cups oil for deep-frying	½ cup sesame seeds, toasted

1. Parboil sweet potatoes 3 minutes. Cool. Peel. Slice ½-inch thick diagonally. Dust with flour thoroughly.
2. Heat oil in wok. Deep-fry potatoes about 2 minutes. Drain. Remove.
3. Boil sugar in water until it is light brown and caramelized. Should form a hard ball when dropped in cold water.
4. Pour potato slices into caramelized sugar. Stir 1 second. Remove.
5. Pour onto a greased plate. Sprinkle with sesame seeds.
6. When ready to eat, dip the potato into ice water to harden the candy coating. Serve hot.

May be prepared in advance through Step 1. May not be frozen.

Serves 4 to 6

Vanilla Ice Cream Flavored with Preserved Red Ginger   ALL REGIONS

Our own creation—an easy dessert.

2 pints vanilla ice cream	2 tablespoons preserved red
8 tablespoons juice from jar	ginger, finely chopped
of preserved red ginger	

1. Thaw ice cream slightly. Stir ginger juice into ice cream until well distributed.
2. Form into balls. Freeze until firm.
3. Remove from freezer. Add chopped ginger on top as garnish. Serve immediately.

May be prepared in advance. May be frozen.

Serves 4 to 6

Walnut Tea   ALL REGIONS

This dessert is usually served at the end of a banquet. The Chinese believe that walnuts are especially good for the brain. They also consider them as a tonic, giving strength to man and beauty to woman.

2 cups walnut halves	**5 tablespoons sweet rice flour**
5 cups water	**5 tablespoons sugar**

1. Blanch walnuts in boiling water 30 seconds. Drain. Remove.
2. Put walnuts and 1 cup water in blender. Blend walnuts very fine.
3. Put rice flour in saucepan. Add remaining water slowly, stirring continually until rice flour is dissolved. Add the walnut mixture and sugar. Bring to boil. Stir constantly. Cover and simmer 15 minutes.
4. Pour in bowls. Serve immediately.

May be prepared in advance. May be frozen.

Serves 4 to 6

Heaven and hell are in this world.

14

Teas

Throughout their long civilization the Chinese have always insisted on having tea as a beverage. The custom started in the Szechwan region centuries ago.

Today tea is still the most popular beverage in China. It is full of vitamin C. It is good for everybody from the noblest to the humblest and they enjoy it equally. The West has coffeehouses. The East has teahouses. Chinese people use them as meeting places for both business and pleasure. Problems can be solved over a cup of tea. Tea has the power to make poets have more poetic feelings and to relax the mind when one is tired. It is incumbent upon a host when a friend calls that he serve tea or he will be considered discourteous. Good teas are expensive and sold by the ounce.

There are three basic kinds of Chinese tea:

1. Green: Unfermented Tea
   Dragon Well—most famous
   Gunpowder—from North China
   Lu An—from Anhwei Province
   Water Nymph—scented with narcissus

2. Oolong: Semifermented Tea
   Jasmine (scented)
   Chrysanthemum (scented)
   Lo Cha—from Formosa
   Oolong—from Formosa

3. Black: Fermented Tea
   Black Dragon—from Kwangtung
   Iron Goddess of Mercy—from Fukien
   Keemun—most famous, from Anhwei
   Lychee Tea (scented)
   Rose Tea with Dried Rosebud (scented)
   Puer—from Yunnan

How to Make Good Tea:

1. Teapots made of glass, china, or earthenware are best. *Never* use a metal pot.
2. Use 1 teaspoon tea (or 1 tea bag) for each cup of water, plus 1 for the pot.
3. Pour boiling water onto tea leaves.
4. Steep from 3 to 5 minutes.
5. After steeping, the tea should be strained off into another heated pot or the tea bags removed.

15

Sauces and Dips

Characteristic of Chinese cooking is the mixture of flavors which are put together in a distinctive fashion. This is only the first step. The proportions of ingredients used and the amount and length of heat and the seasonings applied at each stage are of extreme importance. There are many sauces, including hot, spicy, and sweet sour sauces. Sauces using soy, hoisin, oyster, and bean sauce are prevalent in Chinese dishes.

Chinese Mustard Sauce   ALL REGIONS

½ cup Chinese mustard
   powder
½ cup cold water

1. Stir mustard into water slowly until it becomes a smooth paste.
2. Set aside 15 minutes before using or it will be too bitter.

Note: Use as a dip.

May be prepared in advance. Refrigerate. May not be frozen.

Peppercorn Salt   ALL REGIONS

2 tablespoons Chinese
   peppercorns
¼ cup salt

1. Brown peppercorns and salt in dry frying pan on low heat until fragrance comes out.
2. Place a piece of foil on a flat surface. Pour the mixture onto foil. Fold foil over. Crush with rolling pin. Strain. May be stored indefinitely in a jar on pantry shelf.

Note: Use as a seasoning or as a dip.

May be prepared in advance. May not be frozen.

Sweet Sour Sauce   ALL REGIONS

¼ cup catsup
¼ cup sugar
1 cup water
¼ cup white vinegar
2 heaping tablespoons
   cornstarch, dissolved in 2
   tablespoons water

1 green pepper, cut into
   squares
2 tablespoons canned
   pineapple chunks

1. Combine first 4 ingredients in saucepan. Bring to boil.
2. Thicken with dissolved cornstarch. Stir constantly.
3. Add green pepper and pineapple. Stir.

Note: Use as a dip.

May be prepared in advance. Refrigerate. May be frozen.

Bean Sauce I   ALL REGIONS

1 tablespoon oil
2 tablespoons bean sauce
2 tablespoons sugar

¼ cup water
1 teaspoon sesame seed oil

1. Heat oil in wok. Add bean sauce. Stir on low heat 2 minutes.
2. Add sugar and water. Stir 30 seconds. Add sesame seed oil.
   Stir well.

Note: Use on Chinese Pancakes and steamed buns.

May be prepared in advance, bottled, and refrigerated indefinitely. May not be frozen.

Bean Sauce II   ALL REGIONS

¼ cup hoisin sauce
2 tablespoons water

2 teaspoons sugar
1½ teaspoons sesame seed oil

Combine all ingredients in wok. Stir 1 minute.

Note: Use same as Bean Sauce I.

May be prepared in advance, bottled, and refrigerated indefinitely. May not be frozen.

Oyster Sauce Dip   ALL REGIONS

3 tablespoons oyster sauce
1 teaspoon sesame seed oil

Combine all ingredients. Stir well.

Note: Use as dip.

May be prepared in advance. Refrigerate. May not be frozen.

Dipping Sauce   ALL REGIONS

6 tablespoons red wine   4 tablespoons light soy sauce
   vinegar   4 slices ginger, minced

Combine all ingredients. Stir well.

Note: Use as dip with dumplings, meat, or chicken recipes.

May be prepared in advance. Refrigerate. May not be frozen.

Sesame-Flavored Dip   ALL REGIONS

½ teaspoon sugar
2 tablespoons sesame seed oil
4 tablespoons light soy sauce

Combine all ingredients. Mix well.

Note: Use as a dip with cold meat or vegetables.

May be prepared in advance. Refrigerate. May not be frozen.

Sesame Seed Paste Sauce   ALL REGIONS

2 tablespoons sesame seed
   paste or 2 tablespoons
   peanut butter diluted in 2
   tablespoons water
½ teaspoon salt
2 teaspoons sugar
2 tablespoons light soy sauce

1 tablespoon red wine
   vinegar
2 tablespoons sesame seed
   oil
1 teaspoon pepper oil (recipe
   below)

Mix ingredients into a smooth, thin sauce.

Note: Serve with cooked meat or blanched vegetables (excellent with Mongolian Hot Pot).

May be prepared in advance. Refrigerate. May not be frozen.

Vegetable Dip   ALL REGIONS

2 tablespoons light soy sauce
1 tablespoon sesame seed oil
1 teaspoon pepper oil (recipe
   below)

1 teaspoon sugar
1 tablespoon red wine
   vinegar

Combine all ingredients. Mix well.

Note: Serve with raw vegetables.

May be prepared in advance. Refrigerate. May not be frozen.

Szechwan Pepper Oil   SZECHWAN

1 cup vegetable oil
¼ cup coarsely ground red
   chili peppers
   (approximately 1 ounce)

1. Heat oil in wok until moderately hot. Add chili peppers. Cook 3 to 5 minutes on low heat or until oil becomes red.
2. Cool. Store in covered jar indefinitely in refrigerator.

Note: Use as seasoning or dip.

May be prepared in advance. Refrigerate. May not be frozen.

Dumpling Sauce   ALL REGIONS

2 slices ginger, chopped   1 teaspoon sugar
   fine   ¼ teaspoon salt
1 clove garlic, chopped fine 1 teaspoon pepper oil (recipe
3 tablespoons light soy sauce   on previous page)
1 tablespoon red wine vinegar

Combine all ingredients. Mix well.

Note: Serve with dumplings.

May be prepared in advance. Refrigerate. May not be frozen.

Fruity Fruity Sauce   ALL REGIONS

12 ounces apricot preserves   1 can Koon Chun Plum
12 ounces orange marmalade   Sauce
8 ounces applesauce   2 tablespoons white vinegar
1 8-ounce can pineapple   4 slices ginger, minced
   chunks

Combine all ingredients in blender or food processor and blend
until well mixed.

Note: Use as a dim sum dip.

May be prepared in advance. Refrigerate. May be frozen.

Toasted Sesame Seeds   ALL REGIONS

Sesame seeds

1. Heat dry skillet. Add sesame seeds.
2. Stir until light brown, about 2 to 3 minutes, or roast in 300-
   degree oven 20 minutes.

*May be prepared in advance. May be stored in jar on pantry
shelf. May not be frozen.*

16

Menu Suggestions

No food is really enjoyed unless it is keenly anticipated, discussed, eaten, and then commented upon."

—Lin Yu Tang

Buffet

China has shown more inventiveness in food preparation than any other civilization. When deciding upon a buffet menu, there must be a balance of air, land, and sea. Poultry represents air, pork and beef represent land, and seafood represents the sea. Select a dish from each group. Rice is always included on the buffet table. Be sure the table looks colorful. A large bowl of fresh fruit makes a lovely centerpiece.

The following are sample buffet menus that will serve from 4 to 6.

Hot and Sour Soup with Fish
Sate Beef
Chicken Wings with Onion
Crispy Duck II
Stir-Fry Pork with Broccoli
Squid in Hot Sauce

Spinach and Bean Curd Soup
Chicken with Garlic Sauce
Fried Beef with Green Pepper
Pork with Sweet Rice Cake
Braised Shrimp
Vegetables of Harmony and
   Peace

Yin and Yang Soup
Chicken with Fungus and
   Cucumber
Leek Duck
Beef with Scrambled Eggs
Hunan Lamb
Three-Flavored Scallops with
   Ponzu Vinegar

Chicken Salad with Rice
   Sticks
Crab Meat with Cream of
   Corn Soup
Beef with Onion II
Meatballs with Sweet Sour
   Sauce
Shrimp with Broccoli
Chicken Wings with Leek

Pork and Cucumber Soup
Curry Chicken
Orange or Tangerine Peel
  Beef
Pork with Dried Mushrooms
Chiao's Shrimp
Yard Beans, Ninpoo Style

Seafood Bean Curd Soup
Lemon Chicken II
Beef Stew Szechwan Style
Slippery Shrimp
Steamed Fish with Hot Sauce
Our Special Broccoli

The Formal Dinner

The formal dinner serves 10 to 12 people. The guest of honor should be seated facing south and the host sits opposite. This is the authentic Chinese way. The rice is served separately in individual bowls. For Westerners the dinner may consist of four or five courses and a dessert served sequentially. The table should be attractive and flowers should be placed in the center of the table or in small individual vases at each place setting. Chow-Tse is a family dish that is not generally served at formal dinners by the Chinese; however, Westerners use them as an hors d'oeuvre before a formal dinner. Dry white wine may be served.

Hors d'oeuvres
Vegetable Chow-Tse
Meatballs with Spinach
  Filling

Entree
Soup with Vermicelli and
  Vegetables
Shrimp with Cashew Nuts
Chicken in Taro Root Basket
Beef with Black Bean Chili
  Sauce
Duck with Spinach
Jade Fried Rice

Dessert
Fruits on the Skewer

Hors d'oeuvres
Crab Rangoon
Szechwan Dumplings

Entree
Sour Shrimp Soup
Curry Beef
Pork with Fish Sauce
Boneless Jade Chicken
Ginger Crab
Fried Rice with Raisins and
  Ham

Dessert
Mango Mousse

The Banquet

During the Manchu dynasty, banquets sometimes lasted five days. The chefs were constantly creating new dishes in order to be in favor with the emperors. An average banquet today consists of cold plates, hot soup served at any time during the meal, hot dishes, and entrees. There is a continuous flow of wine. Fruit or sweets are served for dessert.

Cold Plate
Pon Pon Chicken
Garlic Cold Pork

Soup
Green Jade and Red Ruby
   Soup

Hot Dishes
Crystal Shrimp
Chicken with Double
   Mushrooms
Beef Soochow
Three-Colored Fish Slices

Entree
Stuffed Eggplant
West Lake Duck
Amoy Pancakes with Pork
   Filling
Pineapple Fried Rice

Dessert
Toffee Apple

17

Pantry Shelf and Storing Information

Shopping in Chinatown is a gastronomical joy as well as a learning process. It is a vastly different experience for Westerners. One sees mostly Oriental people in the markets. There are new and exciting ingredients to purchase. Sometimes the salespeople, although kind and courteous, do not understand English. If that happens, take your book and point to the Chinese calligraphy in this chapter. Spend the day in Chinatown. Stock up your pantry and stop at a charming restaurant for lunch. You will feel as though you've had a vacation and when you return home you will be inspired to start your Chinese cooking—a great treat for you and your family.

AGAR AGAR. A dried seaweed. Acts like gelatin when put in
洋菜   water. Sold in cellophane packages. Used in salads.
Store on pantry shelf indefinitely.

ANISE SEED. A Chinese spice that resembles a star. It imparts
八角   a delicate, subtle flavor to meat and poultry. Sold
by weight. Store on pantry shelf in tightly covered
jar indefinitely.

ANISE SEED POWDER. Used as a seasoning. Sold in plastic
五香粉   bags. Store on pantry shelf in tightly covered jar
indefinitely.

BAMBOO LEAVES. Dried. Sold in one-pound bundles. Used
粽葉   for Tsoong Tse rice dumplings. Store on pantry
shelf indefinitely.

BAMBOO SHOOTS. Young shoots of bamboo. Sold in cans
冬笋   whole or sliced—best to buy small-size cans. After
opening, refrigerate in covered jar of water. Change
water twice. Will keep about one week.

BARBECUED ROAST PORK. Almost red in color. Sold by
义烧肉   the pound in Chinese delicatessens and meat shops.
Will keep in refrigerator about five days. May be
frozen.

BEAN CURD. 1. Fresh bean curd: Made of pureed soybeans,
鲜豆腐   then formed into cakes. It absorbs the flavor of
other ingredients. Sold in plastic containers in the
refrigerated section. It is also called to-fu. Will keep
in refrigerator about one week.

五香豆腐干

2. Brown bean curd: Also known as baked bean curd or dried pressed bean curd. Well flavored. Sold in plastic bags in the refrigerated section. Will keep in refrigerator about one week. May be frozen.

豆腐衣

3. Dried bean curd sheets: Dried, paper-thin sheets. Sold in packages of 8 ounces and up. Store on pantry shelf for a few months.

白豆腐干

4. White pressed bean curd: Sold in plastic wrap in refrigerated section. Will keep in refrigerator about one week. May be frozen. Also comes shredded.

油豆腐

5. Fried bean curd: Sold in plastic bags, usually six to a package. Used in soup, meat, and vegetable dishes. Will keep in refrigerator one week. May be frozen.

豆腐花

6. Soybean pudding: A very soft, fine bean curd in water. Sold in refrigerated section. Will keep in refrigerator about one week.

BEAN SAUCE. Also known as brown bean sauce or brown bean paste. Made with soybeans, flour, salt, and water. It is salty and pungent. Sold in cans and jars. After opening, refrigerate in a tightly covered jar. Will keep indefinitely.

原晒豉

BIRDS' NESTS. Sold in 1-pound boxes. Store on pantry shelf for a few months.

燕窝

BLACK BEAN SAUCE WITH CHILI. Also known as preserved black beans and chili paste. Made with beans, chili peppers, salt, and soybean oil. Sold in 8-ounce jars. Refrigerate after opening. Will keep indefinitely.

豆
鼓
辣
醬

BLACK BEANS. Fermented. Salty black beans. Used for seasoning. Sold in plastic bags of 4 ounces and up. Store on pantry shelf in tightly covered jar indefinitely.

豆
鼓

BLACK SESAME SEEDS. Sold in plastic bags. Store on pantry shelf in tightly covered jar indefinitely.

黑
芝
蘇

BROWN RICE MEAL. Used as a seasoning. Sold by weight. Store on pantry shelf in tightly covered jar indefinitely.

炒
米
粉

CELLOPHANE NOODLES. Also known as bean thread or vermicelli. Made from mung bean flour. When used in soup, must be presoaked. Not necessary to soak when deep-frying. They will pop up immediately. Sold in plastic bags of two ounces and up. Store on pantry shelf indefinitely.

粉
絲

CHESTNUTS. Dried. Soak overnight before using. May be used as a substitute for fresh chestnuts. Sold in plastic bags. Store on pantry shelf in tightly covered jar indefinitely.

栗
子

CHICKEN STOCK. See Chapter 1 for Helpful Hints. Also see Index for Basic Chicken Stock recipe.

鷄
湯

CHILI OIL. Sold in 8-ounce plastic bottles. Made with ground
辣　　　chili peppers and salad oil. Used as a seasoning.
　　　　May be used as a substitute for Szechwan pepper
油　　　oil. Store on pantry shelf indefinitely.

CHILI PASTE WITH GARLIC. Made with chili peppers, soy-
辣　　　bean oil, and garlic. Used mostly in Szechwan
　　　　dishes. Sold in 8-ounce bottles. Refrigerate after
椒　　　opening. Will keep indefinitely.
醬

CHILI SAUCE. Made with ground chili, onions, lemons, sweet
辣　　　potatoes, and vinegar. Adds spice to dishes. Sold in
　　　　bottles. Refrigerate after opening. Will keep indefi-
椒　　　nitely.
沙
司

CLOUD EARS. Also known as tree ears or fungus. Must be
木　　　soaked in hot water before using. Cook with vegeta-
　　　　bles, chicken, meat, and soup. Sold in plastic bags
耳　　　of 2 ounces and up. Store on pantry shelf in tightly
　　　　covered jar indefinitely.

CRAB APPLE WAFER. Also known as plum wafer. Made of
山　　　crab apples and sugar. Sold in cylindrical packages.
　　　　Store on pantry shelf indefinitely.
楂
片

CURRY PASTE and CURRY POWDER. Used as seasonings.
茄　　　The brands that are made in India are the best.
　　　　Sold in bottles and cans. Store on pantry shelf
厘　　　indefinitely.
揰
蕾
粉

DATES (Chinese). Red in color, dried, the size of marbles. Sold
紅　　　in 4- to 8-ounce plastic bags. Store on pantry shelf
　　　　in tightly covered jar for a few months.
棗

DRIED ORANGE PEEL. A dried spice made from orange
陳   rinds. Used for flavoring meat and poultry. Sold in
       plastic bags. Store on pantry shelf in tightly covered
皮   jar indefinitely.

DRIED SOYBEANS. Yellow in color. Used in many dishes.
黃   Sold in 1-pound plastic bags. Store on pantry shelf
       in tightly covered jar indefinitely.
豆

DUMPLING WRAPPERS. Also known as shao mai wrappers
燒   or round won ton wrappers. Round dough in which
       to place fillings for dim sum and dessert recipes.
買   Sold in 1-pound packages. Will keep in refrigerator
       one week. May be frozen.
皮

EGG ROLL WRAPPERS. Dough in which to place the filling
春   of the egg roll. We use Cantonese square wrappers.
       Usually sold in 2-pound packages. Will keep in
卷   refrigerator about five days. May be frozen.

皮

FAVA BEANS. Dried. Sold in plastic bags. Must be soaked,
蠶   then shelled. Store on pantry shelf indefinitely.
       (Also come fresh during months of May and June.)
豆

FENNEL SEEDS. A dried spice used for flavoring meat and
茴   poultry. Sold in plastic bags. Store on pantry shelf
       in tightly covered jar indefinitely.
香

FISH SAUCE. Made with water, fish extract, and salt. Used as
魚   a seasoning. Sold in bottles. After opening, store in
       refrigerator indefinitely.
露

FIVE-SPICE POWDER. Combination of five spices. Used for 五 香 粉 flavoring. Sold in plastic bags. Store on pantry shelf in tightly covered jar indefinitely.

GINGER ROOT. Fresh. Very important seasoning in Chinese 薑 cooking. There is no substitute for it. Sold by piece or by weight. Peel and put in jar with sherry; cover tightly. Will keep in refrigerator indefinitely.

GINKGO NUTS. Have hard white shells. Sold in 10-ounce cans. 白 果 After opening, refrigerate in covered jar of water. Change water twice. Will keep about one week. May be frozen.

GOLDEN LILIES. Dried and pale in color. Also known as 金 針 golden needles or tiger lilies. Add flavor to meat, fish, poultry, and soup. Sold in plastic bags. Store on pantry shelf in tightly covered jar indefinitely.

HAIR SEAWEED. Very fine, resembles hair. Used with vegeta- 髮 菜 ble dishes. Sold in plastic bags. Store on pantry shelf in tightly covered jar indefinitely.

HAM (Virginia, Smithfield). The nearest tasting to Chinese 火 腿 ham. Very salty. Sold by weight. Wrap in plastic. Will keep in refrigerator for many months. May be frozen. (If not available, use regular ham.)

HOISIN SAUCE. Spicy sauce used in many dishes. Sold in 1- 海 鮮 醬 pound cans or jars. After opening, refrigerate in tightly covered jar. Will keep indefinitely.

LEMON GRASS. A lemon-flavored plant. Sold fresh by the 檸 檬 草 bunch in produce department in Chinatown. Will keep in refrigerator about one week.

LONG-GRAIN RICE FLOUR. A ground flour made from
粘 long-grain rice. Used for making turnip cake and
米 snacks. Sold in 1-pound packages. Store on pantry
粉 shelf. Will keep for a few months.

LOTUS SEEDS. Dried white seeds. Must be cooked. Sold in
蓮 plastic bags. Store on pantry shelf in tightly covered
心 jar indefinitely.

LYCHEE. A tropical fruit. Delicious in sweet sour sauce. Sold
荔 in cans in heavy syrup. After opening, refrigerate in
枝 a tightly covered jar. Will keep several days.

MUNG BEAN SHEETS. Dried. Also known as dried green
粉 paste sheets. Used in salad and vegetable dishes.
皮 Sold in 8-ounce plastic bags. Store on pantry shelf
indefinitely.

MUSHROOMS (Chinese). Dried and black—must be soaked in
冬 boiling water before using. Used in many dishes.
菇 Sold in plastic bags. Store on pantry shelf in tightly
covered jar indefinitely.

MUSTARD (Chinese). Used for dipping when diluted with
芥 water. Sold in powdered form. Store on pantry
末 shelf in tightly covered jar indefinitely.
粉

OILS. See Chapter 1 for use of oil in cooking.
油

OYSTER SAUCE. Thick, flavored sauce made from oyster
蠔 extract. Adds flavor to meat and poultry. Sold in
油 bottles of 8 ounces and up. Store on pantry shelf
for a few months.

PEPPERCORNS. Used to make peppercorn salt (see Index for 四 recipe) and for seasoning. Sold in plastic bags. 川 Store on pantry shelf in tightly covered jar indefi- 花 nitely. 椒

PICKLED MUSTARD GREEN CABBAGE. Also known as 榨 pickled cabbage. Used with any meat or soup. After 葉 opening, refrigerate in a tightly covered jar. Will keep indefinitely. (Pickled snow cabbage may be substituted.)

PICKLED PLUMS. Preserved plums. Used for seasoning meat 酸 and poultry. Sold in jars. After opening, refrigerate 梅 in tightly covered jar. Will keep a few months.

PICKLED SNOW CABBAGE. Preserved salted cabbage. Deli- 雪 cious with pork. Sold in cans (Ma Ling brand). 裡 After opening, refrigerate in tightly covered jar. Will 紅 keep a few months.

PLUM SAUCE. Used as a condiment. Sold in jars or cans. 酸 After opening, refrigerate in tightly covered jar. Will 梅 keep a few months. 將 酋

PONZU VINEGAR. Japanese lemon-flavored vinegar. Sold in 日 bottles in Japanese markets. White vinegar may be 本 used as a substitute. Store on pantry shelf indefi- 白 nitely. 醋

PRESERVED CUCUMBER. Used in cooking many dishes. 將 Sold in cans. After opening, refrigerate in tightly 酋 covered jar. Will keep indefinitely. 瓜

PRESERVED RED GINGER. Sold in jars. Used in sweet and
紅　　　sour dishes for color and flavoring. Delicious as a
薑　　　garnish for chicken salad. Sold in jars. After open-
　　　　ing, refrigerate. Will keep indefinitely.

PRESERVED MIXED VEGETABLES. Used for seasoning,
雜　　　especially in sweet and sour dishes. Mixture of
錦　　　different kinds of sweet vegetables. Sold in cans.
菜　　　After opening, refrigerate in tightly covered jar. Will
絲　　　keep indefinitely.

PRESERVED SZECHWAN VEGETABLE. Used for seasoning.
四川　　Sold in cans. After opening, refrigerate in tightly
榨菜　　covered jar. Will keep indefinitely.

PRESERVED YUNNAN CABBAGE. Used for flavoring meat.
大　雲　Sold in 1-pound plastic bags. After opening, refrig-
頭　南　erate in tightly covered jar. Will keep indefinitely.
菜

QUAIL EGGS. Sold in cans. After opening, refrigerate in
安　　　tightly covered jar with water. Will keep about three
鵪　　　days.
蛋

RED BEAN PASTE. Sold in cans. Used in sweet dishes. After
紅　　　opening, refrigerate in tightly covered jar. Will keep
豆　　　indefinitely.
沙

RED BEANS. Used in pastries and sweet foods. Sold in 1-
紅　　　pound plastic bags. Store on pantry shelf indefi-
豆　　　nitely.

RED PEPPER. Dried. Whole, crushed, or ground. Used for
紅　　　seasoning. Sold in plastic bags. Store on pantry
辣　　　shelf indefinitely.
椒

RED WINE VINEGAR. Used for cooking and as a dip. Sold in
紅　　　bottles. Store on pantry shelf indefinitely.
醋

RICE (Glutinous). Also known as sweet rice. Used for making
糯　　　dumplings, sweet dishes, and poultry stuffing. Store
　　　　on pantry shelf indefinitely.
米

RICE (Red). Dyed raw rice for coloring food. Sold loose by the
紅　　　ounce. Store on pantry shelf indefinitely.
米

RICE (White, Long-grain). Sold in 5-, 10-, and 25-pound bags
白　　　in Chinatown. (Supermarkets sell it in small plastic
粘　　　bags.) Store on pantry shelf indefinitely.
米

RICE (White, Short-grain or Round Grain). Soft rice. May be
白　　　mixed with long-grain rice. Sold in bags (Calrose
　　　　brand). Use for Vegetable Rice with Yam recipe.
圓　　　Store on pantry shelf indefinitely.
米

RICE NOODLE (Chow Fun). Used combined with meats and
沙　　　poultry. Sold in plastic bags in 1-pound packages in
　　　　refrigerated section. Will keep in refrigerator for
河　　　three days. May be frozen.
粉

RICE FLOUR. Ground from rice. Used in sweet dishes and
糯　　　snacks. Store on pantry shelf indefinitely.
米

RICE FLOUR (Sweet). Made from glutinous rice. Used for
米　　　making dumplings and sweet dishes and also as a
　　　　batter. Store on pantry shelf for a few months.
粉

RICE STICKS. Dried (Py Mai Fun). Used in soups and many
排　　　other dishes. Sold in ½-pound packages and up.
米　　　Store on pantry shelf indefinitely.
粉

RICE WINE. Chinese cooking wine. Made from rice. Sold in
酒   bottles. Store in refrigerator. Will keep for a few
釀   months.

SATAY PASTE. Used for flavoring meat. Sold in bottles and
沙   cans. After opening, refrigerate. Will keep a few
爹   months.
撘
酱

SATAY SAUCE. Sold in jars. Used as a seasoning. After
沙   opening, refrigerate. Will keep indefinitely. (Some-
爹   times called Barbecue Satay Sauce.)
沙
司

SAUSAGE (Chinese). Made with liver and pork. Sold in plastic
香   bags in 1-pound packages. Rewrap in plastic. Re-
腸   frigerate for one month. May be frozen.

STAR ANISE SEED. *See* Anise Seed.

SESAME PASTE (SESAME SEED PASTE).   Peanut   butter
芝   can be substituted. Used as seasoning. Sold in jars.
蔴   Will keep a few months in refrigerator.
撘
酱

SESAME SEEDS. Sold in plastic bags of 4 ounces and up.
芝   Store on pantry shelf indefinitely.
蔴

SESAME SEED OIL. See Chapter 1 for use of oils in Chinese
蔴   cooking. Will keep indefinitely in refrigerator.
油

SHANGHAI PANCAKES. Also known as spring roll dough.
春 上   Sold in round plastic bags in refrigerated section.
卷 海   Use in Amoy Pancakes with Pork Filling recipe.
皮   May be frozen.

SHARK'S FIN. Dried. Must soak before using. Sold in ½- to 1-
魚   pound boxes. Store on pantry shelf indefinitely.
翅

SHRIMP (Chinese Dried). Have a sharp flavor. Used in small
蝦 amounts in cooking. Store on pantry shelf in tightly
米 covered jar for many months. May be frozen.

SOY SAUCE (Light and Dark). One of the most important
老 seasonings in Chinese cooking. Sold in bottles from
柚 12 ounces up. Store on pantry shelf indefinitely.
生 Dark soy sauce is heavier in consistency and has a
抽 more pungent flavor.

STRAW MUSHROOMS. Delicious with crab meat. Sold in
草 cans. After opening, refrigerate in tightly covered
菇 jar of water. Change water twice. Will keep several
weeks.

SWEET RICE CAKE. Dried. Sold in plastic bags. Used in meat
白 and vegetable dishes. Store on pantry shelf in
年 plastic or jar indefinitely. May be frozen. (Some-
糕 times available fresh.)

SZECHWAN PEPPER OIL. Also known as hot pepper oil.
四 Spicy homemade oil used a great deal for seasoning
川 Szechwan dishes. Also sold in bottles. Will keep in
辣 refrigerator for a few months. See Index for recipe.
油 Chili oil may be substituted.

TAMARIND CONCENTRATE. Used as a seasoning in Thai
林 泰 dishes. Sold in bottles. Store on pantry shelf indefi-
精 麥 nitely.

TAPIOCA FLOUR. Also known as Tapioca Starch. Sold in
菱 paper packages. Used for dumplings. Store on
粉 pantry shelf indefinitely.

TARO POWDER. Also known as Taro Flakes. Comes in boxes.
粉 芋 Used for dumplings. Store in tightly covered jar on
頭 pantry shelf indefinitely.

TEA. See Chapter 14. Store on pantry shelf indefinitely.

茶

VERMICELLI. *See* Cellophane Noodles.

WATER CHESTNUT POWDER. Also known as Water Chest-
馬   nut Starch. Used for pressed duck and for sweet
蹄   dishes. Sold in boxes. Store in tightly covered jar
粉   on pantry shelf indefinitely.

WATER CHESTNUTS. Used as a vegetable with meats and
馬   poultry. Sold in cans. After opening, refrigerate in
蹄   covered jar of water. Change water twice a week.
     Will keep several weeks.

WATER NOODLES (Chinese Fresh). Noodles made with flour
白   and water. Delicious in soup and stir-fried dishes.
麵   Will keep about five days in refrigerator. May be
     frozen.

WHEAT STARCH (Lee Chung Woo brand).   Sold   in   paper
澄   packages. Used for dumplings. Store on pantry shelf
麵   indefinitely.
粉

WHITE FUNGUS (Moer Fungus). Used in soups. Sold dried in
白   boxes of various sizes. Store in tightly covered jar
木   on pantry shelf indefinitely.
耳

WINE. Used as a seasoning in many dishes. Dry sherry is used
酒   most frequently. Store on pantry shelf indefinitely.

WON TON WRAPPERS. Square dough in which to place won
餛   ton fillings. Sold in 1-pound packages. Will keep in
鈍   refrigerator about one week. May be frozen.
皮

18

Chinese Markets

Should you not have an Oriental food shop in your city, the following is a list that will assist you and facilitate your shopping. Asterisk (*) denotes that mail orders may be placed.

Arizona

Phoenix Produce Company
202 South 3rd Street
Phoenix, AZ 85004

Rolands*
1505 East Van Buren
Phoenix, AZ 85026

California

B & C Market*
711 North Broadway
Los Angeles, CA 90012

Kwan Lee Lung Co.*
801 North Hill Street
Los Angeles, CA 90012

Kwong on Lung Importers*
680 North Spring Street
Los Angeles, CA 90012

Oakland Market
378 8th Street
Oakland, CA 94607

The Chinese Grocer*
209 Post Street
San Francisco, CA 94108
mail order only

Wo Soon Product Company*
1210 Stockton Street
San Francisco, CA 94133

Yee Sing Chong Company
966 North Hill Street
Los Angeles, CA 90012

Illinois

Dong Kee Co.*
2252 South Wentworth
   Avenue
Chicago, IL 60616

Oriental Food Market
7411 North Clark Street
Chicago, IL 60626

Maryland

Maxim's Market
20 East University Boulevard
Silver Spring, MD 20907

Massachusetts

Chong Lung
18 Hudson
Boston, MA 02111

Wing Wing Imported
    Groceries
79 Harrison Avenue
Boston, MA 02111

Michigan

China Merchandise
    Corporation*
31642 John Road
Madison Heights, MI 48071

Chinese Asia Trading
    Company*
734 South Washington Road
Royal Oak, MI 48067

Seoul Oriental Market*
23031 Beach Road
Southfield, MI 48075

New York

K. Tanaka and Company,
    Inc.*
326 Amsterdam Avenue
New York, NY 10023

Wing Fat Company*
103 East Broadway
New York, NY 10013
mail order minimum is $15.00

Ohio

Soya Food Products*
2356 Wyoming Avenue
Cincinnati, OH 45214

Texas

Oriental Import-Export
    Company*
2009 Polk Street
Houston, TX 77003

Washington

Uwajimaya, Inc.*
519 Sixth Avenue, South
Seattle, WA 98104

Washington, D.C.

Chinese Grocery
604 H Street, N.W.
Washington, DC 20001

Mee Wah Lung Company*
608 H Street, N.W.
Washington, DC 20001

Canada

Wing Noodles, Ltd.
1009, rue Côté
Montreal, P.Q. H2Z 1L1
Canada

Wing Tong Trading Co.
137 Dundas Street, West
Toronto, Ontario M5G 1Z3
Canada

Index